why change doesn't work

why change doesn't work

why initiatives go wrong and how to try again —and succeed

harvey robbins and michael finley

Peterson's
Princeton, New Jersey

Visit Peterson's at http://www.petersons.com

Library of Congress Cataloging-in-Publication Data

Robbins, Harvey.
    Why change doesn't work : why initiatives go wrong and how to try again—and succeed / Harvey Robbins and Michael Finley.
      p. cm.
    Includes index.
    ISBN 1-56079-675-8
    1. Organizational change. I. Finley, Michael, 1950– . II. Title.
HD58.8.R62   1996
658.4′06—dc20   96-41282
                                                  CIP

Editorial direction by Carol Hupping
Editing by Nancy Brandwein
Production supervision by Bernadette Boylan
Copyediting by Barbara Sullivan

Proofreading by Joanne Schauffele
Composition by Gary Rozmierski
Creative direction by Linda Huber
Interior design by Cynthia Boone

Printed in the United States of America

10 9 8 7 6 5 4 3 2 1

contents

acknowledgments

It has been our odd fate that the books we write experience the phenomena the books are about.

The first book we collaborated on, *Turf Wars*, fell victim to a bloody turf battle when the press that published it was acquired, and all its editors and marketing staff were let go.

Our next title, *Why Teams Don't Work*, was much more fortunate. It was blessed with the best editing and publishing team we could have hoped for. Our editor was the incomparable founder of Pacesetter Books, Andrea Pedolsky. The publishing team included Martha Kemplin, Carole Cushmore, Bernadette Boylan, Pam Wilkison, Laurie Schlesinger, Lenore Greenberg, Lisa Schrager, and Mel Elberger.

No matter who we were dealing with, whether in editorial, design, or promotion, we were always struck by their professionalism, positivism, and involvement. They were always on our side, which is not as common in the publishing world as one might suppose.

How great a team was it? In March 1996, *Why Teams Don't Work*, in our minds an unassuming addition to the literature of teams, was awarded the *Financial Times*/Booz-Allen & Hamilton Global Business Book Award for best management book published in the Americas in 1995. Two unknown, unconnected guys from Minnesota were picked over thousands of other writers of business books for the honor. We were beyond gratified; try flabbergasted.

So now we write a book about change, and darned if the age of change doesn't envelope us in the process. Peterson's was acquired in late 1995 by International Thomson. It meant new rules, a new team, and new adjustments. Personnel change is always a big adjustment. Our challenge was that Andrea switched in midproject from being our editor to being our agent, as a partner in The Altair Agency. The other challenge was to not expect our new editor to duplicate Andrea, but to look for fresh insights and approaches. That is what we found in Carol Hupping, who stepped in at the eleventh hour with her excellent editing and authorial hand-holding skills. We wish to thank Carol and everyone at Peterson's for their professionalism and esprit de corps over the years, especially publishers Casey and Peter Hegener. We wish to thank Nancy Brandwein for her editorial help as well. Her input occasionally made us wince, but it made the book much better.

Harvey wishes to thank the many people he has consulted with who provided war stories and other ideas for this book, particularly David Rawles, vice president at GTE Directories, and Lynde Sorensen, director of employee development at Toro.

Mike wishes to thank the Masters Forum, a Minnesota executive education group with whom he has worked for several years. Mike writes the training materials for their sessions, which keep him up to speed on emerging management ideas, which in turn inform projects like this book. Thanks to Jim Ericson, Tom Miller, and Katie Boyle of the Masters Forum for their confidence and support.

Thanks also to fellow ink-stained wretches James Thornton and Gerald de Jaager for their editorial help down the stretch. Books have a way of getting a whole lot better during the hours just before deadline, usually because of the generosity and interest of talented friends like Jim and Jerry.

Thanks to our friends on "Ivory Tower," a Minneapolis BBS hosted by the inestimable Topper (Dave Marquette). Our friends there were always generous with their ideas, tips, encouragement, and good humor.

Special acknowledgment is due George Osner and Jeff Shepherd, editor and maintainer, respectively, of the Internet's Serial Quotations Mailing List. Everyday George and other contributors send out a sheet of fascinating quotations fished from the ocean of world literature. If there is a quote in this book without a proper footnote, we probably obtained it from this excellent source.

Finally, to our families, from parents and our spouses all the way down to our little ones and their animals, our deepest thanks for your patience with the changes we put you all through.

introduction

Think about your own job experiences and the changes you have been asked to make in the past few years—TQM, reengineering, restructuring, etc. We're guessing some of these initiatives were modestly successful, a few were total flops, and the rest fell into some vague, plus-minus pile in between. None quite measured up to expectations, though—right?

Ambitious undertakings nearly always result in some degree of disappointment. This fact seems to leave you with three options:

➤ lower your expectations
➤ dig in your feet and stop changing altogether
➤ find better ways to change

You can lower your expectations without our help. As for the end of change, it may sound like a relief to you now, but if it ever happens, you won't like it. So this book is about the last option.

We live in a period of such rapid organizational change that even the bad old days are starting to look good. It's not just happening to companies whose job is change, the innovators like 3M and Motorola and Hewlett-Packard, who somehow come up with a fresh raft of new product ideas every spring. Plain vanilla companies that have offered the same product or service for fifty years are caught in the same buzz saw, because they are expected to continuously renew the processes by which they produce the same-old, same-old.

No organization and no industry are exempt. From funeral homes to filling stations to one-person home businesses to huge multinationals with corporate campuses on four continents, they all feel the pressure to get with the rhythm and march to the drum. Why is this happening? Why this sudden explosion of fads, ideas, trends, and initiatives? We are obsessed with how to do things better, faster, cheaper, more democratically. Benchmarking, continuous improvement, downsizing, mergers and restructurings, reengineering, reinvention, visioning—the list of initiatives is stupefyingly long, and many organizations are pursuing five or six simultaneously.

> **"Time is a river you cannot step into twice."**
>
> *Heraclitus*

People and organizations are torn down the middle about this change. On the one hand, we acknowledge that change is a primary agent in our lives; it enables us to learn, to grow, and to progress toward long-term goals.

On the other hand, there is something in our nature that resists changes imposed upon us, even when we know the ideas are good ones. At some peculiar level, we prefer busy-ness to true business; the "good old ways" to continuous improvement.

We hate change because no matter which of the three classic responses we make to it, it wins. If we don't embrace it, it overtakes us and hurts like hell. If we do try to embrace it, it still knocks us for a loop. If we try to anticipate it, and be ready when it appears—well, it doesn't make any difference, we still wind up on our keesters. Change is pain, even when self-administered.

> **"I am quite tired of the Thames. Flow, flow, flow, always the same."**
>
> *Wm. Douglas, Duke Of Queensbury*

We all know how hard it is to change something in ourselves—a quality, a habit, or some perceived failing. Think how much harder it must be to move an entire group to a new way—sometimes a very large group, scattered far and wide, with many different tastes and wishes.

A single rower can easily alter or impede the group's progress simply by resting on the oars. It's the same in organizations. A few people, with no particular malice in their hearts, can prevent good changes from taking place. It is called resistance, or foot-dragging, and it is the veto privilege even the humblest worker can use.

And there are so many things in need of change. Organizations are anxious to see improvements in a dozen areas at once. Some of these goals are in exquisite tension with one another—one goal can be achieved only at the other's expense:

➤ making our goods or services cheaper while improving their life expectancy and long-term value; cost versus quality

➤ eliciting greater efficiency from people while trying to make the workplace a more attractive place to work; numbers versus people

➤ breaking an organization into smaller, more manageable pieces while seeking to strengthen predictability of the whole; bottom-up versus top-down

It's a riddle. And many times we are tripping over paradoxical problems—early success, high expectations, market rewards.

Change in the last decade became a kind of civil religion for business. We transform, overhaul, reinvent, reenvision, resize, and reengineer. At the same time we don't appear to be achieving anywhere near the success we had hoped to experience. What is going on, and is there any way out of these traps?

We think there is. This book looks into the fabric of both individual human nature and group behavior. Our agenda is to tackle change problems in four steps:

➤ First, we get our bearings, to understand what we are up against and what it takes to move people off square one.

➤ Second, we choose a change approach that is doable within the culture of our organization, combining just the right elements of Push and Pull to advance it in the right direction.

> **May you live in interesting times.**
>
> *Ancient Chinese curse*

➤ Third, we engage individuals on our team or in our organization at the level that works best for each.

➤ Fourth, we examine different kinds of initiatives and address specific problems associated with each.

We are going to show you:

➤ A way of thinking about how people respond to change challenges that will give you greater change leverage in your work, on your team, in your organization.

➤ A way to gauge your organization's and your personal potential for change. You may not become a change master or metaphile overnight. But you can learn to identify where the points of resistance are in your nature and in the personalities and situations of those around you.

➤ A list of a zillion separate change initiatives, the characteristic ways in which each one fails, and ways to avoid failure.

Armed with this knowledge, your odds of surviving life in the blender should improve. The blender won't slow down, but you will get very good at dodging the blades.

When you are done you will understand why resistance in groups and teams occurs and be able to forge a path away from resistance and toward the kind of positive change your organization needs to prosper.

Life in the blender

Perhaps because of the gloomy titles of our books (*Why Teams Don't Work, Turf Wars, Techno-Crazed*), people get the impression that we're negative. Well, we're not. We are "skeptical optimists": we believe good things can and will happen, but these victories will not come easily or automatically. Most will come only after a knock-down-drag-out fight.

We're very much for organizational change. We see it as necessary, desirable, and often quite capable of succeeding. With the wave of global, external change that is continually breaking over us, only a foolish organization would turn its back on the many ways it might improve its efficiency, competitiveness, and morale. The future is a dangerous place, and we are already living in it.

We are interested in any idea that promises a safer ride in the blender global change has plunked us in—the breathless speedup of technology, the collapse of the American standard of living, the globalization of everything. But we are not cheerleaders for change. Indeed, we have experienced enough initiatives and witnessed the disappointment that settles over organizations when they fail that we wince when they are announced. Change hurts.

The pain is flat-out physical in organizations where the response to sluggish productivity has been to downsize and heap the remaining work on the shoulders of half as many people, pummeling them into submission.

In less draconian scenarios, the pain is financial. The learning curves for major change initiatives are steep, and they go on forever,

5

and every hour that a company learns, the meter is running. Tens of billions of dollars are spent annually on consulting and training for change, and many billions more are squandered by companies willing to try anything to catch up to their competitors. When present-day milk production declines because the farmer is spending all of his or her time breeding future cows, imagining future cream, and dreaming of the green grass of a reengineered dairy operation, well, the cows dry up. Only the most sagacious (or befuddled) stockholders reward this kind of crystal-balling. Competitors more interested in beating you today than tomorrow will get their wish.

But the worst pain brought on by change happens between the ears of the people in your organization. Discomfort, anxiety, inconstancy, bloodletting, psychological distress—whatever term you choose, there has never been, nor will there ever be, a change initiative that leaves unscathed the people it purports to benefit.

> **"Any object at rest tends to remain at rest. An object in motion tends to remain in motion. Every action gives rise to an opposite reaction. Force equals mass times acceleration."**
>
> *Sir Isaac Newton*

Consider a paper products company operating in the Upper Midwest. (We base this composite on a couple of companies we are familiar with.) Beginning in 1988, the company put itself through myriad change initiatives against a shifting background of "vision movements." Each change was a raindrop on a tin roof during a cloudburst. Each made its little noise, had its momentary effect, and then drained away.

In a six-year period, the company gradually transformed itself from a place where corrugated paper products were manufactured to a place where meetings were held. We reproduce here the chronology of initiatives at this company (let's call it Fort Mudge Paper). You can dig down through them like an archaeologist discovering Troy, seven layers down. Only when you get there, you'll find the original city squashed flatter than a pancake.

> ➤ **Quality circles.** This effort was initiated in 1988, lashed to an existing quality assurance effort to reduce defects. People at Fort Mudge were excited at the opportunity to offer suggestions. But nothing ever

seemed to get done, and several people who stepped forward to offer criticisms of the system got permanently back-burnered. This was followed by . . .

➤ **TQM (total quality management).** Undaunted by the collapse of quality circles, Fort Mudge sprang big bucks to fly a consultant up from Chicago to show how to get everyone engaged in continuous improvement. Fort Mudge people got to attend classes and learn about fishbone diagrams and statistical process control. Banners were hung and charts displayed. A recognition banquet was scheduled, featuring something chicken-like. The vice president who brought in the consultant was hired away by the consultant, and the program went into a dormant stage. Until . . .

➤ **Reengineering.** The idea was to get away from the seven-signatures way of doing things—simplify, simplify! The union at Fort Mudge hit the ceiling, and why not? The plan changed everyone's relationship to everyone else, and called for the loss of forty people by attrition, and that was just the start. The most tangible result of two years of reengineering was $3 million dollars' worth of new hardware and software, which the staff is still struggling to learn, even as a new consultant starts beating the drum for . . .

> **"The hardest part of reengineering is living through change."**
>
> *Michael Hammer*

➤ **Mission-and-vision.** Management liked this one, because all the top honchos got to go to Lake Tahoe. The organization spent $85,000 on a consultant who helped fashion a values statement for the next millennium. Then they came across the same statement in a competitor's annual report. Verbatim. The anger had just begun to dissipate when a guru somebody's brother-in-law recommended suggested . . .

➤ **Delayering.** The idea was to put managerial talent to work closer to customers. There were only four job descriptions in the entire company: CEO, Customer Service Reps Class 1 and 2, and Night Watchman. The plan met with ferocious resistance from (you guessed it) managerial talent. The plan was hacked to bits, and most of the old job levels were restored as "steps" between the four main categories even as the VP-HR was blinded on the road to Damascus by a vision of . . .

➤ **The learning organization.** This initiative had real appeal. People appreciated the idea that all work was a work in progress. But a few people spoiled everything by pinning a lot of nonproductive time on "learning." Management was not about to be made fools of by fifth-discipline goldbricks, so this program, too, was put on hold. Which was wise, because the senior management team had just been on a mountaineering leadership binge in Aspen, and everyone was hot to trot for . . .

➤ **Teams.** The idea was that people would self-supervise, self-train, self-recognize, and self-evaluate. Management assured workers it was only about quality and never about eliminating middle management. Unfortunately, none of the people who got to stay knew how to manage anything. But that still left a huge gaping hole in the area of . . .

➤ **Customer satisfaction.** The notion that the customer was king had an uphill path to take at the organization. It ran counter to the prevailing opinion, that the customer was an idiot. The company brought in customers for product design focus groups to get their ideas. They didn't have any, unless you count infinite backward compatibility with standards that were already holding the company back. Basically, customers couldn't get you into trouble in the organization's culture; only management could do that. "Customer sat" got sat on. Which spelled an early demise for the company's attempts at . . .

➤ **Empowerment.** The organization called a big meeting and informed people that from that moment on, everyone was encouraged to do whatever was necessary to make customers happy. But "whatever was necessary" had strings attached, and within a couple of weeks those strings were yanked back.

When Fort Mudge management reneged on empowerment, that was the last straw for many workers. In April 1995, they called a wildcat strike out of sheer frustration. Their own parent union did not support them, but they didn't care. They were tired of the electroshock therapy management kept administering, tired of the endless cadres of consultants with their full-wax treatments and spangled bunting, tired of not knowing what their jobs were or who to report to or if they had jobs at all. They struck, the company locked them out, things went downhill, and by August the company had sold off its assets to a competitor for a dime on the dollar.

Too many fads, heaped on top of another, eventually proved too much. In the war for the future, Fort Mudge went over the hill.

It's about change, and the right and wrong ways to undertake it. Fort Mudge tackled change with great energy and desire. But energy and motivation are not enough to carry the day.

In the fast current, some organizations surprise by demonstrating unexpected abilities. The survivors are those organizations that have always struggled to survive. They take nothing for granted and have no illusions about their immunity to trouble. It's the secure, pampered companies that fall hardest and most painfully—IBM, General Motors, Xerox.

People are not natural resisters of change. We have a love/hate relationship to it. We are equal parts yin and yang. We adore change and the stimulation and improvement it can represent; and in the same breath we despise the discomfort and anxiety it imposes on us.

Change is the elixir of life in so many ways. It engages our imagination—sometimes for good, sometimes for ill. People fight change when they feel pain. We must learn to be sympathetic to the reasons people have for failing to move forward; often, they are simply survival responses dictated by past experience. Put simply, we like clear change that is easy to mark off, that has a chance of success, and whose success will make things better. Not surprisingly, we are less enthusiastic about horrible, hopeless ordeals that leave us weaker and unhappier than we were to begin with.

Where we get lost is between these two poles—where we balk unreasonably at challenges that, while they are not slam dunks, have at least some chance of success.

The High Cost of Change Failures

You win some, you lose some. Lest we imagine that a failed change initiative is a victimless crime, however, let us count the victims, and the aftereffects of a false start:

1. **Loss of jobs.** People lose their jobs when change fails to achieve hoped-for results. In the case of many initiatives, lost jobs is the

hoped-for result. Job loss ripples through the organization, through the affected individual and his or her family, then into the community as a whole.

2. **Loss of energy.** Every misstep along the change journey makes the next step more difficult. The most successful change initiatives build in inevitable small successes early to forestall this power-sapping stage. To lose momentum in most cases is to lose the battle.

3. **Loss of trust.** If people were led to believe success was assured before, they will be less likely to believe anything later.

4. **Loss of respect.** See if people look up to their leaders with the same appreciation after they've been led off a cliff.

5. **Higher stress.** You thought things were bad before. Pinning your hopes on a change that fails is like swimming to a life raft and finding out it leaks.

6. **Fragmentation.** Whatever cohesion the team had managed to achieve may begin to come apart, as people drift back to solitary pursuits.

7. **Depression.** There is nothing employed people enjoy less than contemplating unemployment.

8. **Anger.** Where workers once reacted to initiatives by dragging their feet, now they may resort to outright sabotage.

9. **Diminished risk-taking.** A good change initiative lights a flame of creativity under people. If the change is snuffed, so is the light. Some workers are ruined for life—or certainly for as long as they stay with this organization.

10. **Loss of credibility.** People become more skeptical about the employer's claim that they are loyal to employees and that people are their most important resource.

11. **Trouble at home.** Stress in people's personal lives may have contributed to the failure of the change initiative in the first place. Now the stress loops back and makes things even worse at home.

12. **A change in management's attitude.** The stakes are raised when the strike count goes to one and then two. Loyalty to workers may decrease, as management goes into save-the-company mode.

13. **Games.** When the ice is thin, people skate lightly. Do not look for the same directness and disclosure you saw before the change failed.

14. **Less to go around.** All that consulting, training, and reengineering cost big bucks. While the consultants tiptoe away, careful not to let their coins jingle, workers face the prospect of diminished resources.
15. **Craziness.** Flickering inside every man and woman is a lit bomb fuse. Our fuses are all different lengths, but we all go off eventually. Workplace violence claims the lives of 1,400 Americans annually, at a total cost to employers of $42 billion.[2] Not exactly what you hoped for from TQM.

Seven Unchangeable Rules of Change

Mark them well. In 40,000 years, they have not changed one iota:

- People do what they perceive is in their best interest, thinking as rationally as circumstances allow them to think. We call this the law of Push.
- People are not inherently anti-change. Most will, in fact, embrace initiatives provided the change has positive meaning for them. This is the law of Pull.
- People thrive under creative challenge, but wilt under negative stress.
- People are different. No single "elegant solution" will address the entire breadth of these differences.
- People believe what they see. Actions do speak louder than words, and a history of previous deception octuples present suspicion.
- The way to make effective long-term change is to first visualize what you want to accomplish, and then inhabit this vision until it comes true.
- Change is an act of the imagination. Until the imagination is engaged, no important change can occur.

Of Babies and Bathwater

The age of change in organizational thinking—sometimes called New Age management theory—is occurring in part because of the influence of the baby boomer generation. The previous generation flourished in the mass-production economy that grew steadily from the 1920s through the 1960s. It is no Oedipal coincidence that the next generation has done everything it could to trash the success of the generation preceding it.

> **"Plus ça change, plus c'est la même chose."** ("The more things change, the more they stay the same.")
>
> *Alphonse Karr*

Organizations in the 1990s are picking up and trying on new initiatives like a teenager in front of a mirror, uncertain of much, only sure that it does not want to be like its mom and dad. The New Age must be better; it is, after all, new.

It is beyond the scope of this book to analyze all that happened to make the generation that started to come of age in the 1960s so tuned in to one another and so determined to be different from the generation that went before. But you cannot discuss change in our time without addressing the enormous demographic and psychographic blip of our time, and why they (we) can't help trying out every new thing that comes along—and are unable to make many of them stick.

Some of the factors behind the fads:

➤ **Globalization.** Where the older generation made and sold to a single American market, baby boomers make and sell to (and compete against) the whole world.

➤ **Technology.** Baby boomers possess much more intimate information processing technologies, and are thus prone to greater decentralization and individualization.

➤ **Speed.** Baby boomers are impatient because technology has given them that luxury. Previous planned changes, like the moon landing, took years; this generation does not feel it can wait that long. If an idea doesn't take hold and yield quick results, they move on to another idea.

➤ **Education.** Business schools taught only one approach to business in the first half of the century; today there is zero "conventional wisdom," even in the most hidebound academy. Years ago there was no "management theory" section in bookstores; today there is an avalanche of offerings.

➤ **Experience.** People today travel more, read more, pursue continuing education, change jobs more frequently, encounter greater diversity, work across functional lines, and interact with people from other countries, cultures, and industries.

Many change initiatives of the '80s and '90s were inspired by the communal hippie experiments of the '60s. High employee involvement initiatives like TQM and empowerment are analogous to the co-op ethic of no bosses and everyone pitches in. The learning organization concept is reminiscent of the phenomenon of "the perpetual student" of the 1960s, having too much fun in college to venture out into the narrower world of jobs and assigned roles. Diversity, cross-functionality, and "dress-down Fridays" all have their roots in the rebellious mood of the '60s that railed against conformity, squares, button-down collars, and gray flannel suits. "The leader as servant" idea owes more to the I Ching and Che Guevara than to Iwo Jima and Dale Carnegie.

The children of the Age of Aquarius are more abstract, more philosophical, more eclectic, more "big-picture," and more hip than the generation that won World War II. They bring great gifts to the banquet of change they have set for themselves. If there is a gnawing insecurity among this confident generation, it is that they lack the grit and brass-tacks competence of the earlier generation.

The Aquarian school of management must guard against two great hazards. The first is a tendency to trash the past. To the very idealistic, all business ideas predating the first Woodstock are bad, mechanistic, controlling, bureaucratic, plastic, in-the-box, and anal.

> **"Don't just stand there—do something."**
>
> *Anonymous*

The truth is that the conventional wisdom of the industrial age is no less wise in the age of change. Organizations are remarkably like machines, no matter how we "humanize" them. Bureaucracies remain efficient ways to organize complex systems. In-the-box is still the place where most of us dwell, and think, and are happiest. A wise generation would take pains, in tossing out the bathwater from the previous generation, to conduct routine baby checks.

The second hazard is that boomers may fall victim to their own opportunities. People with many choices tend to make many choices and lack the resolve to see any one of them through. If the age of change is a smörgasbord, too many of us have piled our trays too high with desserts. Baby books warn against giving an infant too many choices; so too with adults. We need to focus on a few good ideas and give them a chance to work.

The question that every manager, leader, and team member must ask is whether we are actually in a New Age of management, and if everything has changed, and whether a new philosophy of work can take hold. If so, then the New Age management theories are right on and should be implemented without delay.

On the off-chance that we are in an In-Between age, stepping awkwardly between the Push of Old Age authority and the Pull of New Age optimism, we must guard against two errors simultaneously—too slowly adopting the new and too rapidly off-loading the old.

Some Discarded Babies

The best change ideas out there today are not fads. They are honest, rigorous, and genuine. It is when we become sloppy in our thinking that we make them into fads. When we do that, we start making insipid generalizations. We assign some ideas white hats—these are the ideas that must save us. And we give other ideas, those that had some currency with the previous generation, politically incorrect black hats. Under no circumstances are we to give these ideas an even break. Here are some of these discarded ideas:

➤ **Bureaucracy.** So negative have the connotations of the word "bureaucracy" become that we hardly give a second thought to what the word actually denotes: a system for organizing large bodies of work so that specialized workers attend to specialized tasks. Instead we hear the word, picture waiting in a long line to get our driver's license renewed, and shake our heads. But before computers raised our expectations of quicker turnaround, bureaucracy was an effective way to handle large workloads. Bureaucracy is not antithetical to good service unless it is mismanaged. What people object to about bureaucracy is not its order but its fragmentation—how disconnected, bloated, and unaccountable its parts can be if not watched carefully.

➤ **Command.** No one comes right out and says so, but it is a major no-no in the new world of organizations even to cultivate, much less use, managerial clout. We hear the phrase "command-and-control" and picture Vincent Price as the insane scientist pulling levers and inflicting pain planetwide. New-age leaders, by contrast, are expected to lead solely on the basis of example and outreach. "Do this or you're fired" is an unacceptable throwback to the previous era. On paper, anyway. In reality the boss still casts the tie-breaking vote in any power situation in any organization. Why we don't admit that and figure out some way to deal with it, is an indication of the dreaminess of today's management fashions.

➤ **Complexity.** We picture Einstein standing by a chalkboard riddled with arcane equations, himself the very emblem of a complex universe. And it was Einstein who said, "If you are out to describe the truth, leave elegance to the tailor." The strong preference of baby boomer management theory is away from complexity and toward the concise, elegant solution. It should be a master key that opens all locks, a philosopher's stone that transmutes any element. But if simplicity in human systems were within our reach, why haven't we simply grasped it by now? Sadly, nature is complex and does not yield to a simple scan, and neither do human systems. But that has not hurt the business-book business, has it.

➤ **Hierarchy.** The New Age has made up its mind that the most valid organization is the one that is flattest, in which power derives not from how high on the organizational chart a position appears, but from the quality of leadership demonstrated. In extreme de-hierarchization, no individual holds sway over any other, no one is subordinate to anyone, and no one is better than anyone else. At work here is an ethic of puritanical egalitarianism that recalls some of the tear-down fervor of the Cultural Revolution in China in the 1960s. It also recalls the leveling edicts of marauding conquerors, who decreed that a city that resisted too energetically be razed until not one stone remained atop another. Never mind that nature, the model from which New Age organizations are supposed to take all their cues, is hierarchical to the core—younger learning from older, weaker deferring to stronger, every creature in every phyla knowing its place in the pecking order or food chain and being, if not content, at least resigned.

➤ **Homogeneity.** The passion in recent years has been to yoke people together who have different skills and knowledge. This is done under the rubric of teams, cross-functionality, and diversity. This is all to the good, and it often gets people out of the kind of narrow "silo" thinking that results from working only with people like oneself. Thousands of organizations have broken up functional cadres of accountants, attorneys, information professionals, even clerical and support staff, and sent them out into the midst of new groups, with the idea that they will mesh well in the "real world" and flourish as they regard one another as customers to be satisfied. It often works. Just as often, however, the new challenges—mastering the language of new functions, getting along without the cultural comfort of functional peers—make people very nervous. And for what? For the high cost of relocating, retraining, decentralizing, and reengineering, the visible results are loneliness, anxiety, and diminished productivity. Many valuable people do their best work within their functional tribes.

► **Pragmatism.** The new corporate leader, according to Richard Pascale, a devotee of Japanese management practices, must be less of a "do-er" and more of a "be-er."[3] Other books call on CEOs to emulate classic good guys like Jesus Christ, Lao Tsu, and Abraham Lincoln. Of the three, Lincoln is probably the best model because he was willing to take unpleasant steps to achieve desired goals—precisely the philosophy of Renaissance management guru Niccolò Machiavelli. He appreciated that there was value in secrecy; in shielding his intentions from people until the last moment; in making ambiguous pronouncements that could mean whatever a person wanted to hear; in saying one thing and doing another. Zen business consultants recoil from this, the diametric opposite of "open book management." But who can dispute its power—the flexibility to move this way and that, opportunistically, as the winds of change shift? Most important, this unfashionable expediency acknowledges what the New Age wants to forget: that business is competition, driven by the passion to survive. And even if you manage to retain your purity of heart, you will have problems because your competitors will be less fastidious than you.

► **Blame and accountability.** If you screwed up in the previous era, and got caught, your fate was clear: people jumped all over you, you got at the very least a good dressing-down in the boss's office, your job security diminished, and your pay was docked. Error was punished as if it were sin, and the offender who was discovered was made to bear the guilt for every error they had not found anyone else to blame for. In the new era, we encourage an atmosphere of blamelessness. Finger-pointing and punishment are out, risk-taking and information loops are in. If you screw up, you say so, and explain to other people on the team or in the system what you did, and what can be learned from it. This explanation turns the error into a learning opportunity, and everyone goes on from there, happier and wiser than if the mistake had never been committed.

If only Michael Leeson of Barings Bank had been man enough to admit he had bet $14 billion on risky securities in Singapore, and lost. And if only Barings Bank had learned from the admission and looped that information back into process improvement. Of course, there was no Barings Bank by that time, as Leeson's learning opportunity, alas, had bankrupted the 238-year-old firm. The point is that there must be a balance between terrifying people so that they feel they must sweep their screw-ups under the carpet, and adding failure to the cardinal virtues of faith, hope, and charity. How about "Punishment must not exceed the offense?" Or, "We will strive to learn from mistakes, but not to commit them recklessly or without thought to consequences?"

➤ **Management.** Managers are out and leaders are in. At least, that's the gist of the worst of the recent wave of business books. Management is equated with linear skills, arranging people in boxes and keeping them there. This is opposed to leadership, which is a shamanistic role for people capable of having brilliant visions and casting powerful spells. The prejudice against management is intended to inspire revolt against the factory and the World War II generation of business engineers. What it boils down to, however, is a revolt against competence, for one can't be a "good" leader without first being a good "manager." The opposite, however, is not true. Of course there is a place for managers in the New Age dawning, a point emphatically made in *Fad Surfing in the Boardroom*,[4] a critique of the contemporary rejection of management. The problem organizations are struggling with isn't management per se, but bad management, that which is lacking in conviction or common sense.

➤ **Short-term thinking.** We rail against the American system's attraction to short-term gains, and point fondly toward anecdotes of companies in Japan hewing to a 100-year strategic plan. But the "greed" that drives the American system toward quarterly profits is the same appetite we all have for quick turnaround at the grocery checkout, expeditious processing of our income tax refund, or the satisfaction we get from having the person we are calling pick up the phone, instead of being referred to voicemail. It is illogical that we would like speed in so many areas of modern existence but reject it when it comes to money. But we are loath to forgive short-term thinking, even as we fret about paying our own bills at the end of each month. The New Age has not quite accepted that business is largely about making money so people can feed themselves.

Get the picture? Fashions come and go, and perfectly good ideas are set out at the curb for pickup. Changemakers must give old ideas a fair review regardless of the baggage they have accumulated.

Four Attitudes

There are four attitudes with which an organization can be managed. They run the gamut from maintaining control (Old Age management) and distributing control (New Age management). Four points can be designated to demark four attitudes about control:

➤ **Pummel.** Terror: "Do what I say or you will die." The bad old days. This time-honored method seeks control at any cost and can be used to force either change or non-change. The worker is a slave.

➤ **Push.** Distress: "Do what you must do or the enterprise will die." This is conventional motivation, the deliberate use of fear to galvanize positive action—the burning platform from which people must jump (change) or perish. Push uses force, like Pummel, but it is not brutal force. It encourages people to act by loading them up with negative information. In the hands of some, this is the big lie. The worker is a rat in a Skinner box.

➤ **Pull.** Eustress: "Do what you must do to achieve the future you dream of." Imagination, inspiration. It is less control than a willingness to lead coupled with a willingness to follow. Pull is Push plus empowerment—workers motivate (scare) themselves. The manager is a human being with no power to coerce; the worker is a human being with free will. A kind of fear is involved—*urgency* might be a better word for it. This is the hardest way to achieve change, but the way with the best long-term results.

➤ **Pamper.** Torpor: "Do what you feel like doing." This is the realm of entitlement, the supposedly good new days. Pamper is Pull minus accountability. Zero fear, maximum empowerment, slack performance, scant measurement and evaluation. The worker is a child.

The first two are related, characterized by fear, manipulation, and disrespect for the worker. The second tw are also related, characterized by an acknowledgment of the worker's humanity. The first and last categories are the extremes, but these extremes are not uncommon. Anyone who has been in many different organizations knows that a lot of them operate on these extremes of sadism and permissiveness.

The best hope organizations have for making successful change lies in utilizing a balanced combination of the middle, more temperate two—Push and Pull. Push to get people's attention and start them thinking. Pull to leverage people's knowledge and creativity to put the change over.

Pummel

Before we can understand the moderate positions of Push and Pull, we must confront the extremes surrounding them.

No word is more at home in a discussion of organizational change than fear. The entire history of organizations has been about using fear to get people to do what you want them to. By and large, it has been a smashing success. "Do this or starve"; "Do this or we break your thumbs"; "Do this or suffer the eternal fires of hell" were all compelling motivators: they got us to move. Whether the boss was General Patton or Pope Innocent III, the system worked essentially the same way. The boss knew what was best and held power over you, so you did what the boss wanted, or suffered the consequences.

The history of the world has been one long tale of Pummel. Recall *droit du seigneur*, the right of lords to first choice of their vassals' crops and, in mega-Pummel circumstances, their daughters and wives. Bosses could expose workers to any kind of danger. In the extreme circumstance of slavery, the worker's very life was a commodity to be traded or frittered away. There was not much the boss could demand and not get. This expectation continued until the notions of citizens' and workers' rights began to take hold in the last 200 years.

The fear years were characterized not just by intimidation at the bottom of the heap, but contempt at the top. Russian novelist Fyodor Dostoyevsky illustrated this contempt in a story called "The Grand Inquisitor" that he included in *The Brothers Karamazov*. In the story, Jesus returns during the Middle Ages and preaches a gospel of liberation, only to be arrested and visited in his cell by the ecclesiastic official whose job it is to nip dangerous heresies before they flower.

This authority assails Jesus for making the work of the Church harder. Where the Church guarantees the peace of mind that comes from acknowledging authority, Jesus (a New Ager of the first order) preaches freedom. The inquisitor says that all human beings are drawn to, and can be manipulated by, three great desires:

> "In Italy, for thirty years under the Borgias, they had warfare, terror, murder, bloodshed. They produced Michelangelo, Leonardo da Vinci, and the Renaissance. In Switzerland they had brotherly love, five hundred years of democracy and peace, and what did that produce? The cuckoo clock."
>
> *Orson Welles*

- ➤ for miracle. "Give us an easy solution, a quick fix, and save us from a lot of trouble."
- ➤ for mystery. "Save us from having to think."
- ➤ for authority. "Tell us what to do, and we will unite behind you and destroy whoever does not agree."

These are dark thoughts, but you hear variations on them from time to time in the modern workplace. "We need a strong leader and an ironclad system to protect us from change!" If these thoughts truly depict our deepest human inclinations, then no heresy, no initiative breaking with the truisms of the past, has much chance of success. True human nature is too set in its ways to permit such hopeful experimentation with empowerment, democracy, or shared visions.

The outward sensibility of the age we live in is one of rationality, enterprise, and optimism—very different from the gloomy feudalism Dostoyevsky described. But the mentality called Pummel prevailed until very recent times. We heard it in the remarks of industrial barons as divergent as GM's Charlie Wilson and the USSR's Joseph Stalin. And it is not extinct, not by a long shot. Even in the midst of our cheerful change campaigns, the feudal mind-set is lurking just below the surface. Russia still yearns for another strongman. Simple, brutal solutions are still appealing during hard times.

And many initiatives today are hardly New Age. Downsizing, takeovers and workouts, austere cycle time reduction, outsourcing to sweatshops abroad, and the fast-food model of operational efficiency are all Pummel ideas, seeking to extract benefit for the few by minimizing the humanity of the many. Pummel is alive and well, clad in a new glove. The cog-in-the-works model still works.

Pamper

The democratic age we live in is the first to dally with the idea of easing up on fear. After millennia of mistreatment by tin pots and despots, we decided our humanity entitled us to certain inalienable rights on the job.

The successes of the labor movement at the beginning of this century secured important protections against loss of life and limb and against exploitation and capricious treatment. Quality guru W. Edwards Deming's invocation to "Drive out fear" is the keystone of many of the most idealistic change initiatives, including TQM, empowerment, teams, and the learning organization.

> "Take hope from the heart of man, and you make him a beast of prey."
>
> Ouida (Marie-Louise de La Ramee)

The New Age we are edging toward was prompted in part by the sense among our most prosperous blue-chip organizations that workers deserve better treatment than being whipped like dogs. Out of this notion grew the idea of the humane organization, a place where workers are treated with respect.

The offshoot of this new sensibility has been a new kind of organization. In addition to the traditional terror-based Pummel organization, there is now the nontraditional, leader-as-good-guy, anti-fear Pamper organization.

Many Pamper organizations are old-line industrial companies that achieved great success, then began to loosen up on the reins. In our time, corporate raiders have zeroed in on companies that have gone soft, moved in on them, and kicked all the pets off the sofa. The belly-soft Pillsbury doughboy was put on a strict regimen of calisthenics when the company was acquired by Grand Met PLC in 1988. When Newhouse bought *The New Yorker* in 1985, the literary world was aghast at seeing its gods treated as mere mortals. Pampered journalist Brendan Gill termed the acquisition "the death of kindness."

The sure sign of a Pamper organization: Everyone wants to work in one, and no one wants to invest in one.

Push

Pummel and Pamper are murder for change initiatives, but in different ways. Predictably, Pummel organization employees are a cadre of compliant but disloyal, not especially proactive, workers who are out sick a lot. They do what you tell them, but nothing more.

Almost as predictably, Pamper organization workers are an uninspired cadre of people filing their nails and going through the motions. Like the stereotypical civil servant and union steward, they know they won't be fired, so they don't do the work they are capable of doing.

Our veering between these two extremes is a big reason why change initiatives like TQM and teams come crashing down around us. Either the change doesn't matter to us—we know we'll be OK whether it succeeds or fails—or the initiative is conducted in such a manipulative or dishonest fashion that we can't bring ourselves to comply even with its idealistic requirements.

> "In early times, people did not know their leaders existed. In the next age, they loved them and praised them. In the next they feared them. In the next they despised them. When the rulers lost faith in the Tao, the people lost faith in the rulers."
>
> *Lao Tsu*

And the only way out of the danger zone[5] appears to be by using violence: threatening people with layoffs, conducting surveillance of employees, making an occasional example to the workforce by destroying a worker who has violated the new norms.

Fortunately there is a middle zone, occupied by Push and Pull. They may be likened to two different kinds of doctors.

The first doctor, Push, believes that the disease is the enemy, and is willing to wage war against the body in order to drive out the disease. This doctor has an arsenal of weapons to hurl at the cancer—knives, poisons, death rays.

In the business world, Jack Welch in his early days at General Electric typified this kind of change doctor. When he came to his position in 1980, he deliberately set out to scare the wits out of everyone under his command, to scare those people who were unwilling to change into leaving the organization, and to scare the people willing to remain to new heights of productivity, quality, and shareholder return. He spelled out very plainly to his troops that only those businesses commanding the number one or two position in their markets would be around to enjoy the sunrise. He was given the nickname "Neutron Jack," after the bomb that destroys people but leaves infrastructures intact.

A common metaphor for this kind of leadership is the burning platform. The dying organization is like an offshore oil rig. You want to move the workers to an entirely new rig, at some unseen other location. But how do you get the workers to leave the rig, which at its most basic level is still keeping workers out of the water, employed, insured, dressed, and fed? Why, you set it on fire.

By setting the platform on fire (calling attention to the danger the enterprise is in, perhaps underscoring, hyping, or falsifying it to dramatize the point) you give the workers little choice but to do the thing they thought they dreaded most, jumping into the water, which is deep, cold, and infested with things that bite. The choice is jump or fry. Some people will never jump. Getting them to think imaginatively about change is like petitioning the local crack house to separate its recyclables. But enough will jump to build a new, improved organization around.

> **"The two foes of happiness are boredom and distress."**
>
> *Arthur Schopenhauer*

This is the Push strategy for change. People cooperate because if they don't, they will surely suffer. Push usually has elements of the first category, Pummel. It can be very painful; indeed, it is about pain. But it does not emanate from unchecked power and should stop this side of sadism. At the very least, Push is utilitarian Pummel; it seeks to address the best interests of a wide range of constituencies, from shareholders to workers to customers.

No company is solely a Push company. Even Pamper companies expect some level of performance from their people, with worst offenders paying some kind of price. But it is easy to think of companies that make no bones about their commitment to a Push approach:

➤ Fixed-operations companies like McDonald's that require workers to do precisely as told

➤ Commodity providers like Kroger who compete on price, period

➤ Outsourcers like Nike and Navistar who farm out all manufacturing work

Push by itself is the route most change initiatives take, and it has had its share of successes. It is unabashedly Machiavellian, but do not condemn it out of hand for that reason. Lots of companies really are on fire, and workers do seem to need the wake-up call that a good jolt of fear provides. The trick is to administer the strong medicine of fear in a measured, sensible way. Beware the doctor who cures the disease but loses the patient.

This means "scaring" workers no more than is necessary to achieve the desired response; scaring them more will likely freeze them, like deer in approaching headlights. Most managers find that the secret to eliciting the desired behavior is to tell them the truth, unvarnished, unaudited, and unmassaged, while making sure that workers or team members have some sense of hope.

> **"Fear can be used in a variety of ways as a catalyst of change."**
>
> *Michael Hammer*

Bruce Fulper, founder and CEO of Granite Rock, the Baldrige-winning provider of the consummate commodity product, rock, uses fear to spur workers to inspired heights. How many quarry managers could challenge workers as he has with Granite Rock's short-pay provision? Clearly printed in large type on all its invoices is this offer: "If there is any item on this bill you are not satisfied with, simply deduct that amount and send us the balance."

It is an outrageous guarantee—money back for unsatisfactory slag—and there is not an employee in the 400-person company who doesn't dread the day a short-pay can be traced to a quality failure he or she was responsible for. Fulper calls his a "laurel and thorn" system—a wreath of rewards for associates who contribute to customer satisfaction, the sharp finger of doom for those who think something else is more important.[6]

In the case of the burning platform, workers must have a life preserver or a pathway out of danger. In the case of an organization threatened with downsizing or annihilation, workers need a cogent plan, an achievable schedule, and the training and technology to put the new regimen into effect.

Few managers, however, know how to sustain that sense of manageable crisis for very long, and that is why so many organizations succumb to the "initiative of the month" syndrome—an endless treadmill of change campaigns that no one can stay upright on for very long.

Pull

To succeed on a reliable basis, the emergency-ward doctor, Push, must work in cooperation with a different kind of doctor.

Doctor Pull is not the opposite of Doctor Push but is different in emphasis. Pull focuses not on the disease (what's wrong) but on the body (what strengths may be enlisted in restoring the entire body to good health). This doctor does not claim the title of healer. In Dr. Pull's care, the body heals itself, through its own genius.

In unmotivated people, or people without an appetite for change, Pull will require a little Push (fear) to get going. But Pull moves quickly to step beyond fear to something more positive. Pull works to engage the imagination of patients. It makes them want to survive for reasons all their own. It challenges workers to find the meaning that change holds for them, and for them to make the change driven by desire, by a positive goal as much as by a negative fear.

A good example of a Pull organization is pharmaceutical giant Merck & Company. In 1935 George Merck made what today would be called a vision statement, but back then was it just a man saying what his company stood for: "Medicine is for people. It is not for the profits. The profits follow."[7]

Where Push is conventional, typifying a mixed view of human nature, Pull embodies the best hopes of the New Age, that people are mostly very good and just need a hint of leadership to unleash great waves of creative productivity.

Pummel, of course, holds that people are inherently unreliable; and Pamper, that people are quasi-godlike and cannot fail to make correct choices.

Pull often results in disarray, as different people begin moving at different times and with different degrees of momentum. But Pull has a major advantage over Push: it permanently alters the way workers think of themselves. It has the power to make them metaphiles (changemakers) for life.

With empowerment as its main lever, the Pull movement does for organizations what rational expectations theory did for macroeconomics. That economic theory, developed during the Carter administration and awarded the Nobel Prize in 1993, concedes that people will do what they perceive to be in their best interest. The government may use incentives or scare tactics to bulldoze people toward behaviors it desires—spending more, saving more, etc. But people will bulldoze right back with their own desires and dreams.

Where Push is managed by managers, the Pull change places the fulcrum much closer to workers. The debate is whether Push or Pull requires more "leadership." Yelling at people that they are in grave danger and persuading them to come to their own rescue are two very different approaches to leadership.

> **"If you would persuade, you must appeal to interest rather than intellect."**
>
> *Benjamin Franklin*

Both approaches involve fear, but in different degrees. Evil fear (Pummel) is when management maintains an atmosphere of entirely self-serving terror, and the home team—the people who work for the organization—are treated like the visitors. Useful fear (Push) is when management manipulates workers to achieve results that are deemed to be good for them. Good fear (Pull) is the sense of urgency that workers ignite in themselves to make positive changes. It is the acknowledgment that organizations must compete in order to survive and for the individuals within the organization to prosper.

Pull initiatives show up in surprising places, like the Mirage Hotel in Las Vegas. It was the first "clean" casino there, featuring attractions for the whole family. When Steve Wynn unveiled his plan he met a wall of cultural opposition. But Wynn stuck it out, and his vision prevailed. The results are apparent as soon as one enters Las Vegas today. It is no longer just a place to gamble and drink. It's a fantasy island of Taj Mahals, Camelots, and ancient and modern Memphises. The people working in Las Vegas are not the depressed army of underpaid, illegal maids and janitors one en- counters at many vacation sites—they are uniformed, empowered, trained, and confident that their operations are second to none.

Many management teams think they are instilling the useful, or even the good fear into their workers. But that's not how it comes across to the workers. Something sick happens in the gap between the Horatio Alger story the company founder transmits ("I suffered and prevailed and so can you") and the Edgar Allan Poe tale of terror the workers receive ("He wants us to suffer because he suffered"). They fill in the unknown with negatives.

Change initiatives cannot occur in a work environment overdosed with fright. How can a terrified organization be a learning organization? Why would beleaguered employees share information, as they must in the new organization? How can a team that must run on trust run when there is no trust? What kind of "coach" coaches through brutalization? (When management theorists talk about managers being coaches, they don't mean Woody Hayes.)

Pull is more than a generic "enlightened" attitude. It refers only to the vision offered by the organization and workers' response to that vision. It is most visible in:

➤ High-profile organizations with highly trained employees who are empowered to take risks and show initiative. These are the glamour companies of the business books—the Nordstroms, Motorolas, 3Ms, and Hewlett-Packards. Pull comes naturally to them, because their companies are dotted with natural innovators.

➤ Companies with innovative, change-loving leaders who are not satisfied with the existing contract with workers and work toward something more galvanic. David Kearns at Xerox was such a leader. Bruce Fulper at Granite Rock. Jamie Houghton at Corning. They all had a zest for finding better ways to do things, and the ability to communicate that to people under them.

➤ Companies that have looked into the abyss and formulated cooperative strategies for falling into it.

There are many hero stories of empowered workforces turning companies around, but few can top the achievement of Springfield Remanufacturing Corporation (SRC) as chronicled in *The Great Game of Business* by CEO Jack Stack.[8]

Stack was a college dropout who returned to work a dozen years ago to a broken-down International Harvester diesel engine retrofitting plant. Things were a mess—inefficient, low-quality, and a dispirited, fatalistic blue-collar workforce. Stack wondered if the division was salvageable given the poor morale, lack of training, and dilapidated infrastructure.

But he noticed that workers were expert at memorizing and following sports statistics. He thought, if they can understand the numbers behind baseball (which they knew they cared about), they could surely understand the basics of business (which they also cared about, but didn't know yet).

Stack led a retraining effort that created a startlingly different workforce out of the very same people. Lathe operators who could read a balance sheet, sheet metal workers who appreciated inventory turns and return on investment. Unempowered employees one day, business–literate entrepreneurs the next.

That "open book" retraining, coupled with the most outrageously unbalanced leveraged buyout in corporate history (89 parts debt, 1 part equity), allowed SRC to spin itself out of International Harvester's orbit and into its own remarkable success path: an 18,200 percent stock price increase in eight years, zero layoffs, and sales growth exceeding 30 percent annually.

Give That Man a Fish

   Push: Give a man a fish and no other choices and he will have a fish.

   Pull: Teach a man to fish and he can have a fish any time he wants one.

Pummel: Pollute the water with fear and the fish will all die.

Pamper: Serve him fish with salad and beans in bed until he explodes.

Combining the Four Approaches

A common mistake organizations make is thinking you have to choose one or the other, all Pummel, all Push, all Pull, or all Pamper.

In truth, every organization uses all four all the time, but in an unplanned, herky-jerky, self-contradictory fashion. It is Push one day and

Pull the next. Push with one policy, Pull with another. Little thought is given to consistency. Things happen because that is today's executive whim, or something was written in the employee handbook a long time ago, and is thus hallowed.

Indeed, you can even mix the extremes. Many Pamper organizations shower their yes-people with luxuries, while setting the Pummel dog on whistle-blowers attempting to call attention to the truth. Then you have the quixotic Pummel leader who vacillates between leading by brute force and leading by idealism.

Napoléon Bonaparte and hotelier Leona Helmsley are classic examples of this Pummel vision—people who cracked their dreams open on other people's skulls. Change works best with a balanced approach, in which the concerns of all constituencies are weighed and given rough parity. Napoléon learned that an army that could undergo any privation and fight valiantly in the name of liberty, equality, and fraternity was less enthusiastic fighting in the name of empire. And Helmsley, dubbed "The Queen of Mean" for her harsh treatment of hotel workers, learned that pleasing one constituency with chocolates on the pillow does not erase the bitterness of employment policies that pummel.

> "You can get a lot more done with a kind word and a gun, than with a kind word alone."
>
> *Al Capone*

There is a time and place for all these approaches. Pummel and Pamper work only in the very short term. Pummel is martial law, very useful in times of war. Pamper is pleasant as a short-duration reward, toxic as a long-term lifestyle.

Then we come to the two more useful approaches. Push is reliable in the short to medium term, to pull a flaming airplane out of a nosedive or

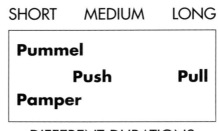

SHORT　MEDIUM　LONG

Pummel		
	Push	**Pull**
Pamper		

DIFFERENT DURATIONS

rally a team to salvage a season. Pull is much more reliable as a long-term change methodology, guiding an organization and its people toward its best values and instincts.

Both approaches can work, but neither is assured of success, and there are many situations when one choice alone just won't do it. When a platform is really burning, it is no time for long-term wool-gathering. When an organization is groping to create a new culture based on learning, cooperating, and trust, any perceived Push will be toxic.

An organization that lies in order to scare people, in order to improve, will eventually be found out, and when it does, it will have eliminated any chance of being taken seriously by its people.

Push by itself is a limited methodology. A Push organization must take care not to push too hard, or work too close to the border of Pummel. When people are more afraid of being found out than anything else, everything else—customer satisfaction, feedback loops, sharing information, team activities—goes right out the door.

The fear of Pummel is purely destructive; the fear of Push also has a destructive aspect, but it must have its heart in the right place. It is Pummel to tell employees to double their output or be let go. It is Push to tell them that if productivity does not improve, jobs cannot be guaranteed.

Purely destructive fear ("Do this or I'll hurt you") works only in a narrow bandwidth of situations. It works where there is zero presumed bond between boss and underling, in which the underling is performing generic tasks that any other person can be readily recruited to do—slavery. The difference between Pummel and Push can be as faint as the difference between a threat and a warning.

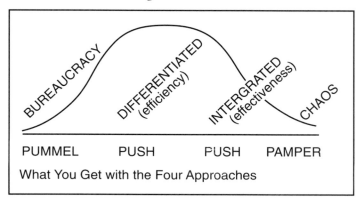

| PUMMEL | PUSH | PUSH | PAMPER |

What You Get with the Four Approaches

Push fades into Pull as brutality fades into acknowledgment of one another as human beings. It is not brutal to spell out the facts of life to colleagues, that your enterprise cannot succeed without them contributing their best efforts, and that the consequences of failure are shiveringly real—people losing their jobs, communities losing their economic engine, families losing their futures.

Healthy fear is nearly an oxymoron. So choose a word that works for you: urgency, intensity, hunger, desire, adaptativeness, determination, competitiveness. They are all the same in the Pull context: the will to live, a preference, when the bodies are stacked and tallied, for not being counted among them.

The secret to successful change is to know when to Push, when to stop Pushing, and when to let workers' own aspirations pull them through change.

A common error is to suppose that a leader must be one or the other: a manipulative despot on the Push side or a benevolent politician on the

PUSH	Reaction	PULL	Reaction
"Improve quality 15 percent or you're fired."	"Uh oh."	"Is there anything in my work that could be arranged more efficiently?"	"Aha!"
"Unless we increase sales this quarter we'll have to shut our doors."	"Uh oh."	"Why don't we link to our customers by e-mail and stay in closer touch that way?"	"Aha!"
"Bumstead, I need to talk to you about your performance."	"Uh oh."	"Mr. Dithers, I have an idea that will earn me that partnership."	"Aha!"
"We have to let twenty people go."	"Uh oh."	"Let me telecommute, and pay me by commission."	"Aha!"

Pull side. The great leaders, like Lincoln and FDR, combined the impulses. Lincoln did not emancipate the slaves until the country was galvanized by the bloodshed of war. FDR could not help European Jews until he had first built a coalition of diverse interests to defeat the Axis powers.

Both men knew when to try one strategy and when to go forward with the other, meticulously building consensus for change. Then, when the people are ready and the goal is within reach, the leader encircles it with the rope of braided ambitions.

The Meaning of Meaning

The Pull approach to change derives in large part from the writings of psychotherapist Viktor Frankl. In 1959, he published a remarkable account of survival, *Man's Search for Meaning*. Because of the insights in this short, readable book, Frankl was hailed by the psychological world as a liberator from the dominance of Sigmund Freud. His ideas center around a "will to meaning" that is as strong or even stronger than Freud's pleasure principle, which depicts people as, essentially, living for their next cheeseburger or sex experience.

It is sweet triumph that Frankl is regarded as a liberator because his pivotal experiences were as a prisoner in three different Nazi camps, including Auschwitz. For the inmates of these camps, there could be no more horrible disruption, no more unthinkable change than to be plucked from a life of normal liberties and choices and set down in a factory whose end product was their own deaths.

What interested Frankl was how prisoners coped with their prospects. Many, treated like animals, became little more than animals, abandoning their sense of self and any vision of the future that had once carried them along. Others, to his astonishment, adapted even to those unadaptable circumstances, by focusing on a future they were determined to experience. That future became their meaning, and that meaning sustained them through their plight.

The final freedom, Frankl concluded, is what is left after every other freedom has been taken away—the freedom "to choose one's attitude in any given set of circumstances, to choose one's own way."[9]

Now page ahead fifty years. Nazism is dead. Ours is in nearly every way a brighter age. The world is not at war. The democratic impulse burns brighter than ever. We have the technology to link soul to soul and to communicate more perfectly than humankind ever dreamed possible. While hate is not extinguished, it has acquired a bad reputation. There is a global consensus that competition is healthy, that diversity is good, that individuals matter, and that systems can be improved.

Yet we live in a world of sullen rage because the promised improvements are not coming easily enough, or quickly enough, or they are not coming at all.

The modern workplace is not a concentration camp, but Frankl's insights are relevant nonetheless.

We change, Frankl says, by envisioning very intensely what we want to happen in the future. Once that picture or vision is clear in our minds, we intuitively take whatever steps are necessary to make the vision reality. The man determined to survive and reunite with his family will take care of himself to guarantee that the dream comes true. The company determined to keep its people employed in the years ahead will stake out new markets, make changes in processes, and lay out strategies and tactics to make it so. The team that wants to make the dreams of all its members come true needs to commit to achieving team goals in order to bring individual goals into focus.

> **"A man is happy so long as he chooses to be happy and nothing can stop him."**
>
> *Alexander Solzhenitsyn*

Once we identify a dream, things become clear. We see where resistance is coming from, why it's happening, what our part is in keeping it alive, and what it takes to mold the organizational imagination to focus more on the positives of change and less on the negatives.

The organizations and the people that will succeed in changing are those that master the art of living in the future and advancing toward it from the past, able to convert the friction of resistance into positive propulsion.

Why Change Fails

Organizations are like minds, and change initiatives are like psychotherapy for these minds. They are especially alike in the reasons they fail: the wrong therapies, too many conflicting therapies, the wrong therapists, or, the most common problem of all, patients who have not made up their minds to get well.

When a change initiative collapses, organizations have to sort through the rubble and reconstruct what went wrong. The reasons for failure vary, from things over which one had control, to things that came out of nowhere to blindside the effort. Some of the most common reasons:

➤ **It is the wrong idea.** A change initiative begins its life, nine times out of ten, in the mind of a manager who knows something is ailing the organization, who then brings in a consultant to prescribe the proper medication. The problem is, consultants are not general practitioners. They usually sell only one product, so inevitably that's the product they will convince your company to implement. It may be a perfectly wonderful product, a tonic to productivity and a tune-up to improved morale. But it's like taking Preparation H for a sore throat: you needed something else.

> "Not much happens without a dream. And for something great to happen, there must be a great dream. Behind every great achievement is a dreamer of great dreams."
>
> *Robert Greenleaf*

➤ **It is the right idea but the wrong time.** Maybe the resource you were expecting to support the change wasn't in place yet. Maybe there weren't enough top-level people behind it yet. Maybe you didn't have time to pick up the pieces from the last change failure or integrate from the last change success. Too often, driven to perform, teams and organizations try to do next week what should take till next year to achieve. Scattering pixie dust over a change initiative and hoping it succeeds is a questionable approach. You cannot do today's initiatives using last year's processes, or a management philosophy that is even more out of date. Pummel can't change to Pull in a day. Success is built in logical stages; this applies even to ambitious stretch campaigns.

➤ **You're doing it for the wrong reason.** Usually, the wrong reason is financial. "We're only in it for the money." Money alone has little meaning for people. Push hopes greed and fear are enough to build a dream around; they never are. An organization driven by short-term monetary goals will not be able to sustain a long-term improvement effort for the simple reason that it does not intend to. There are plenty of other wrong reasons; executive ego or boredom rank high on the list, but not as high as money.

Tufts University HMO knows the importance of having the right reason. It undertook a comprehensive reengineering campaign not because it was hemorrhaging money or losing patients but because its CEO had a vision of providing better low-cost service to members. The organization soon learned that it was suffocating in its own paper flow. Substitution of electronic scans of documents for actual documents relieved weeks of bottlenecks in decision making.[10]

Just because something is a change does not mean it is a good change. A lot of companies, for instance, are dead set on achieving something called reactionary change. This is the kind of change in the Beatles song: "Get back to where you once belonged." Every successful company has a moment in its history when everything clicked—leadership, product design, the personality mix of the key people all helped create a golden era, a sweet spot in time that management would love to return to. So they launch a change

> **"Worshipping the teapot instead of drinking the tea."**
>
> *Wei Wu Wei*

initiative to do that very thing, reinstill a spirit of entrepreneurism, fellow feeling, and working weekends. It is all very touching, but it is the change initiative that fails most certainly and most painfully. Organizations need to learn to let go of their youth, just as individuals do. Change must not be based on sentimentality or a fetish from the past.

➤ **It lacks authenticity.** Not to take away from the merits of reengineering, but isn't it odd that, once ten companies announce they have met some success by overhauling their business processes, another 1,000 follow suit almost immediately?

What is happening is a classic case of me-tooism. Businesses are led to change not because of the inherent merits of the case but because everyone else is doing it. What are the odds that a business undertaking a change in such a faddist fashion will conduct the kind of exhaustive self-examination that successful reengineering (just as an example) requires?

Worse, the sloppy veneer of a me-too initiative does an injustice to the original idea and hastens its demise. The great example of this is illustrated in William Edwards Deming's tirades against organizations implementing cheap versions of TQM, milking the system for a quick-fix advantage, and passing on the long-term philosophical headaches. It's one thing to say quality is job one in your ads; it's another to prove it in your everyday behavior.

➤ **Your reality contradicts your change.** It never fails. A company announces its plans to flatten the workforce. Everyone will be equal, everyone will be a "customer satisfaction agent." But the old perks don't go away. The phantoms don't die. Key managers still get the choice parking spaces, washroom privies, stock options, golden parachutes, and incentive clauses. "Increased pay for increased risk" is quickly forgotten—it was only a ruse to get people to bleed more willingly.

> **"To change and change for the better are two different things."**
>
> *German proverb*

Or the company will make a public commitment to better communication. But the reasons for poor communication aren't addressed. Team members are still boxed off in individual offices, unable to get at one another. Or e-mail is monitored, prohibiting open exchanges. When a company says one thing outwardly and does another thing inwardly, the outcome isn't change but cynicism—the disbelief that things will ever improve.

➤ **You lose perspective.** John Hudiburg was the greatest champion total quality management ever had. When he took over at Florida Power & Light, he set for the company the goal of winning Japan's Deming Prize—something no U.S. company had ever done. He turned the utility company inside out, implementing a rigorous Deming-style statistical process control regimen. And they won. But the story continued. Everyone hated the Demingite system, profits were down, and shareholders were in revolt over what they saw as evangelical grandstanding by Hudiburg, and they replaced him. The company remained committed to quality, but with a more human face and with a clearer eye toward the need to show shareholders a return.

➤ **You have the wrong leader.** When companies are in trouble, a common reaction is to go outside and hire a roughrider to come in, take the reins, and lead the organization to better days. The fallacy here is that any changemaker can work in any organization. A CEO who is at odds with an organizational culture won't achieve spit. Attila was perfect for the Huns, as Francis was for Assisi. Mixing and matching doesn't work.

➤ **Your boss is on a bender.** The worst reason for plunging a company into the boiling oil of change is to alleviate the boredom of senior management. Yet it is clear from the quotes of some CEOs whose organizations are boiling away—and whose employees are getting fried—that they are deriving personal satisfaction from the turmoil. To them it's an adventure, or a military campaign, a break from the routine of monitoring accounts receivable and inventory turns.

Few managers have paid much of a price for going change-crazy. In the eyes of search committees, a manager with his or her finger on the change button usually looks more attractive than a manager willing to let good enough alone. We're talking the managerial equivalent of testosterone here. Better to be thought a proactive disaster than to go down as a mere caretaker. "See that man sleeping under the *Financial Times*? He took care of his company."

> **"What the rule book says will change. In time all ink is disappearing ink."**
>
> *William Warriner*

This is one area where the Japanese business culture has it all over America's. Japan's corporate leaders may be autocratic, but they demonstrate a sense of obligation to the organization and have been known to apologize publicly for strategic misjudgments. Our business culture was forged in the days of the robber barons. We celebrate the corporate exploits of Napalm Ned and Hammerin' Hank and Slashin' Bernie and Butane Bill (the nicknames are changed to protect the innocent), as if they were cartoon figures in a tall tale, and not dictators with life and death power over the thousands that they lead. Change is serious business, too serious to be the plaything of a Napoleonic brat.

> **"The most dangerous thing in the combat zone is an officer with a map."**
>
> *Murphy's Third Military Law*

➤ **People aren't prepared or convinced.** Short-term, this implies training. You didn't bring people in on the idea at the earliest opportunity. They never had a chance to comment or critique or help shape the initiative. Or when you finally did unveil it as a done deal, you made it worse with slipshod or indifferent training.

Long-term, the problem may have lain with an organization's culture. A meaningful change initiative is usually an assault on a culture that is no longer functional, or that is a little sick—an organization where individuals are pitted against one another, or where backhanded tactics are rewarded. When an initiative takes on the power structure of an organization, do not presume it will succeed. Better to presume it won't, and hope you get lucky.

> **"What is now proved was once only imagined."**
>
> *William Blake*

➤ **You get carried away.** Many initiatives fall victim to the sin of excess. Organizations are so enthralled with the idea that they try to see their entire enterprise through that single magic lens. Teams are a good example of an idea that gets carried away with itself. The truth is that most companies operate on a team basis well before it comes up with a teaming plan. The teaming plan is a way to assign people to work together on an ongoing project. But they were doing that before the word "team" swam into senior management's consciousness. People have been teaming very naturally and without a grand scheme for thousands of years. But now comes a comprehensive workforce overhaul that seeks to make a conscious discipline out of an intuitive habit.

To make matters worse, managers become so invested in the initiative that the purpose for the initiative begins to fade from their neocortex, and they slide instead into the habit of setting up teams wherever their gaze alights.

Soon teams of two, three, eight, and ten are performing work that a single person was doing perfectly satisfactorily before. The irony is that the initiative set up to slash through bureaucracy becomes a new point of blockage and slowdown.

➤ **You don't get carried away enough.** You talked the talk of a powerful idea, but you didn't walk the walk with it. You talked quality, but when shipments backed up you ordered products sent out before they were ready. You talked empowerment, but when people didn't guess right, you jerked them back into reality. You talked safety, but when the pressure to launch got to be too much, you ordered the shuttle to lift off.

➤ **Bad luck.** It happens. Contingencies no one planned happened. A natural disaster. A rumor or news report that has everyone obsessing about the wrong thing. A bottle of tainted Tylenol. A tank leak in Bhopal. A death in the corporate family. The collapse of the dollar abroad.

The worst luck is the kind a company brings upon itself. Misunderstandings that no amount of lucid and honest communication can put right, because of the poisonous atmosphere of distrust that has accumulated over the years.

➤ **There is nothing you can do.** Nowhere is it written that a successful change initiative is all that stands between you and long-term survival. Markets change, products die, people flatten flatter than dust. It may help to see that businesses in the U.S. are undergoing all these initiatives because of pressure from other countries. These countries are undergoing a remarkable renaissance of innovation and ingenuity. And they have no consecrated tradition to steer

> "The best laid schemes
> o' mice and men
> Gang aft a-gley;
> And leave us naught
> but grief and pain
> For promised joy."
>
> *Robert Burns*

around to achieve these things. Many organizations here, no matter what they do, haven't a chance against those people. Competing with them is like catching a fly with a spoon. It is their hour.

Why We're Hurting, and What We Must Do

Compared to workplace conditions over the ages, people in organizations today have it pretty good. Pummel is still out there, even in the good old U.S.A. But it has given way to other forms of abuse, from the entitlement woes of Pamper to the many variations of organizational rage that bring each of us home every day desperate for a stiff drink, the TV, or a good cry.

What we want is to be wise so our work will bear the imprint of good judgment at every step—when to hurry up and when to slow down,

Change and Faith

As global change engulfs us, we look for human institutions that won the battle we are fighting, to survive the buffeting waves of change over the long term. There are no old companies. The oldest chartered government worldwide is that of the United States, a young 208 years old.

The oldest extant human institutions are religious in nature. There are religions, churches, and denominations, in the West and in the East, that date back over millennia. These institutions know something about change. Can what they know translate to your organization?

Their success can be explained by their combined use of both Push and Pull techniques. The spiritual impulse underlying most religions is Pull, a sense that there are greater purposes than the self can set forth. The appeal of religion is in the vision; most religions are radical revolutions against existing ideas. They set out to replace an existing culture with something new. As they mature, they tend more toward the Push side, leveraging their authority against unwanted change.

There are two paradoxes in the vitality of religions. The first is the paradox of unanimity. When everyone in a community agrees to and swears by a common vision, to redeem their souls, that organization will be a formidable one. Unanimity is assured by exerting the full authority of revelation, scripture, and the occasional miracle—plus the punishment of exclusion.

You may object that change is anathema to established religions, which brings us to the second paradox—strength through division. Religions are constantly splitting apart, amoeba-style, into sects and subsects with differing emphases and interpretations. The new groups are almost invariably healthier after the rending and pleased with their newfound unanimity—until the next disagreement arises. Thus, Christianity thrives through continuous downsizing.

An important clue may be religion's use of signs and rituals to strengthen connections. A handshake is no sacrament but it is still a powerful physical connection between people working toward a common end. We feel differently about one another when we touch.

Organizations seeking to tighten the sense of inner community would do well to cultivate these rituals—sharing bread, the pat on the back, the moment it takes to break the silence and say "Thank you."

what matters and what *really* matters. An organization comprised of wise individuals will always judge well—but there is no such thing. What we seek instead is to be a wise organization that knows how to create and maintain an environment in which ordinary individuals may, as often as not, choose wisely.

Change fails when workers lose faith in the change leadership has proposed. It succeeds when leaders understand and anticipate trust issues going in to the initiative and honestly address them. Caring leadership must find the right balance and sequence of Push and Pull efforts for the organization or team, given its culture and history. Push to get people's attention, Pull to galvanize their commitment. That is the big picture of successful change.

But it is the little picture of change that causes most leaders to tremble. Success requires more than large-scale organizational redesign. Up close, it requires that attention be paid to the human side of the change challenge. We must learn as much as we can about every individual on our teams, and we must come to understand what combination of Push and Pull will bring out the best in each of them. The micro half is harder than the macro half, more painful and more baffling at every step.

> **"Ability is nothing without opportunity."**
>
> *Napoléon Bonaparte*

The next section will help you understand the process of individualization.

part 2

The people problem

Change means five billion things to five billion people. We ask you to think of there being three kinds of change:

The first is *global change*. It is big change that happens to us no matter what we do. It is everything that is happening all around us: technology, politics, inflation, current events, social change, the environment, stock prices, global competition. It is macro change.

The second is *organizational change*. This encompasses all the revolutionary, interventive change initiatives organizations undertake to cope with the pressures of climatic change: quality, restructuring, new philosophies and methodologies.

The third is *personal change*. It is the little things, the micro changes that assail us on an individual level, and cause continuous stress: aging, the mix of people we work with (good and bad), our personal circumstances, our health, age, job status, finances, our home lives and relationships, what kind of day we're having, etc. Our personal lives are replete with "little murders" that diminish our flexibility to change in our jobs.

Imagine your house is an organization. Think of global change as a threatening lightning storm (a condition affecting everyone). Organizational change is you, climbing a ladder to attach lightning rods (initiatives like teams, TQM, or reengineering). Personal change is a swarm of bees that assails you as an individual (sleep deprivation, overdrawn checking account, etc.) while you climb the ladder.

Imagine three circles overlapping at the center (see next page). The three change spheres are in motion in our lives, sometimes crowding one another out, sometimes wandering away from one another. Human beings partition their lives into "spaces" of things they are willing or unwilling to deal with. We prioritize. We always seem to find space to deal with hunger, crying children, and satisfying the minimum requirements of our jobs, our relationships, and circumstances. This space is our comfort zone.

But as we prioritize some things in, we prioritize others out: unknown people, unfamiliar situations, difficult ideas. Going beyond the required minimum is often too much for us to cope with. We put the unfamiliar or difficult in a special space for things we plan to ignore. We call it the kill zone, the overlap space that shrinks or expands as the circles move in our lives. In the kill zone, resistance is our religion. Moving things from the kill zone to the comfort zone means reversing a decision already made. We do not do this lightly.

The odd, bulging triangle in the middle of the three circles is the kill zone, where change grinds to a halt. To be good at change you need a big change space and a small kill zone. If too many people in your organization have big kill zones, your organizational changes are going to die. Too much change in the other two spheres, in too many people, will stifle the organization's flexibility, its will to change.

> **"Before we can change things we must call them by their real name."**
>
> *Confucius*

Just think of the toll a personal crisis takes on a person's work habits: a painful divorce, a sick child, filing for bankruptcy, living in a high-crime area, hiding a drinking problem. No way will people stressed to the max in their private lives and by the world around them suddenly find an appetite for change where they work.

The importance of creating and maintaining a healthy change space can't be overemphasized. Organizations that have struggled in recent years, like Westinghouse, Sears, and the U.S. Postal Service, have all reported that the difficulty of implementing each new idea becomes greater as it piles onto the failures preceding it.

Every newspaper brings stories of a hapless CEO like International Multifoods' Anthony Luiso, forced to step down in 1996 after seven years of continuous strategic and organizational change. The company was a big

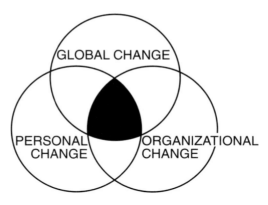

player in the merger and acquisition frenzy of the 1980s. In a relatively short time it tried to change everything about itself, from the kinds of relationships it had with its customers, to the markets it sold to, to its very product lines. Early on, there were signs that some of the changes would take hold. By the end, the company had fallen out of the Fortune 500, probably forever, and Luiso couldn't even get the company coffee machine to work. The company had a kill zone as big as all outdoors.

> "Man has a limited biological capacity for change. When this capacity is overwhelmed, the capacity is in future shock."
>
> *Alvin Toffler*

Organizations that have had better luck, like Marriott and Charles Schwab, succeeded because they took care not to overload people, but to equip them in advance with the information, motivation, imagination, and coping tactics to keep organizational potential from being crowded out by global and personal change. A favorite nostrum of consultants in the last decade is that the way to eat an elephant is one bite at a time.

When the change space fills, that is the end of change. Flexibility flies out the window, and people dig in. No matter how you implore and inspire, people will be dormant, and no change will occur. As they did in the medieval period separating the glory of Rome from the Renaissance, people will turn their backs on new ideas until they find new space for change. Eventually, science and exploration opened up new change space. What your organization needs is a Columbus or Copernicus pointing the way to a new world, or a new paradigm. What you've probably got is Mr. Dithers.

Making space in others for change goes to the heart of leadership. It reminds us that in order to lead we must first know. It is a way of knowing that goes deeper than mere team feeling. Leaders accustomed to distancing themselves from followers and striking meaningful poses will find they have no luck enlarging their organization's change space because they have no knack for knowing people and their change potential. Good leaders know people as individuals; they know what their differences are, their dreams, strengths, weaknesses, and character quirks. They're not best friends—they just know who they are, that they are, and what they need in order to change.

It's not something a CEO can do with all 17,000 employees of a Fortune 500 company. But it is something team leaders can do for team members, and team members can do for one another. You don't have to love everyone, but you must care that they are persons, and have lives apart from clock-in and clock-out. A team is like a family. You get to know people, warts and all, and put up with the bad while coaxing their best out of them.

Many of the New Age management fads that have come down the pike in recent years—empowerment, teams, the learning organization—acknowledge, however hazily, this new level of focus on the individual. But none equips team leaders and managers with the tools to make the breakthrough to people. That's because no bullet-point list of do's and don'ts will turn someone who is not naturally interested in people into someone who is. Up and down the organizational charts of most organizations, the wrong kind of people are in charge—people who are adroit at working the machine, but butterfingers when it comes to people.

Worthy organizational change initiatives fail when the people in the organization are overwhelmed and distracted by other changes, and they lose the mind space to give the change initiative the attention it needs to succeed. A typical manager performs 125 to 150 different activities during a day.[1] New initiatives require that each of those tasks be reexamined for validity and efficiency. How many of us have the mental liberty to do that?

The task of team leaders and managers charged with making a change initiative work is to know and understand the people involved, and to balance each person's change load so that global change and everyday personal change do not steamroll them, leaving them flat and depleted of change power.

When the people side of the process is understood, a lot of change initiatives have a good chance not only of being effectively implemented, but also of achieving the success that is hoped for from them.

This is hard. A change initiative is organizational psychotherapy. It is prone to collapsing in the early stages. It is the hardest kind of change to achieve. Change initiatives are short-term revolutionary strikes, and while all evolution succeeds, most revolutions don't. The forces of entropy and the tendency to drift back into chaos work against the most worthwhile efforts. To make your revolution work, you must face all the uphill battles that every revolution faces—the challenges of maintaining order, establishing legitimacy, getting people to move who have no reason to move for you. The challenge of change is lodged in the human skull.

Change and the Brain

> **"Nothing is permanent except change."**
>
> *Heraclitus*

We begin with the human brain. Believe it or not, we all have one. When an organization hires someone, it is really hiring their brain. Organizations talk about their people being their most valuable resource, but the brain is the real resource. An organization is a barnyard full of strutting, pulsing cerebrums, all different, all incredibly subtle and talented, all desperately in need of group coordination while they pursue their individual goals of life, liberty, and happiness. "Organizations" is a kind description of the chaotic entities organizations are.

The brain controls everything the body does, from lifting boxes to coming up with economy-exploding product innovations. The brain is a skein of 2 to 4 billion neurons—pathways connecting different parts of the brain. Some of these are 12-lane super-autobahns with no speed limits, while others are donkey paths over rocky mountain trails. How and where these paths connect determines our ability to adapt to change and to initiate our own changes.

The three major control centers of the brain are the amygdala, the neocortex, and the prefrontal cortex. To summarize what each does:

➤ The amygdala is called the "old brain," because it also exists in creatures with far less evolved nervous systems than ours. The amygdala governs our emotional reactions to the things we see and hear. Think of it as the Jim Carrey of the brain, holding a stick of dynamite in one hand and a lighted match in the other, with a diabolical gleam in his eye.

➤ The neocortex is part of the "new brain," which exists only in humans and has evolved like Topsy in the span of recordable history, quadrupling in size in the past 50,000 years. The neocortex allows for higher thinking and intellectualizing about what we see and hear. Think of someone very distanced and thoughtful here, like Sandra Day O'Connor. (As you might imagine, the amygdala and neocortex are not especially compatible. In fact they are always at one another's throats. The new brain is forever trying to keep the old brain from beating someone to death with a stick, or committing an emotionally satisfying social gaffe, like calling your boss a stinking maggot. The old brain, for its part, feels contempt for the new brain's inability to get off the dime and do something—anything.)

➤ Finally, the prefrontal cortex is the zebra-shirted referee between the two, blowing whistles and handing out penalty cards (usually in the form of guilt feelings). The prefrontal cortex is the front part of the cortex, right behind the forehead. It acts as a regulator that determines how much time one spends in an emotional reactive state or thoughtful contemplative one.

> "Human inventiveness is overwhelming human adaptiveness. Our ability to judge lags behind our ability to create."
>
> *Robert Ornstein*

The old brain served prehistoric man well. In those days you benefitted from quick, instinctive responses: kill or be killed, react or die, us versus the world. There was neither time nor need for subtler reflection.

As the world evolved and became less perilous, pure survival was less of an issue. Building stable communities became the human norm. While people adapted to this changing environment, their brains grew new appendages, the neocortex and prefrontal cortex. The neocortex, a giant, ornately curling mantle wrapped around the old brain, allowed for more preplanned experience—picnics, planned parenthood, monogamy, war. It allows us to understand and produce language, to think abstractly, to judge, to contemplate, and to plot changes in the way we behave. It is where we think, plan, and commence action. It is where we visualize the future.

Now, here's the kicker. Scientists used to think that there was a one-way road that led from the eyes and ears directly to the neocortex, then on to the amygdala. Thus we would see or hear something, think about it, then add our emotion on top of that thought. All very civilized.

But that isn't how it works. Anyone who's had a three-year-old break something precious, or whose boss has dropped a little bomb on their work priorities, knows that emotions aren't tacked on to intellectual responses as an afterthought. They are right there, nearly instantaneous. One's "better sense" is still taking shape while your "gut reaction" goes ballistic on you.

> **"An enchanted loom where millions of flashing shuttles weave a dissolving pattern, always a meaningful pattern though never an abiding one."**
>
> *Sir Charles Sherrington*

Some recent research into brain pathways seems to bear this out. New studies show a separate set of roads leading from the eyes and ears directly to the old brain. We thought they disappeared when the new brain showed up, but, as luck would have it, they didn't. This helps explain how we can react to something without thinking. While this kind of response can save our lives, it can also get us into tons of trouble. Ever hear, "Gee, I shouldn't have said that"? Or, "Shoot first, ask questions later"?

Despite Spandex, talking cars, and bigger neocortexes, people have not really evolved much in the last 40,000 years. Our brains are still wired the way they were the day Thag first stepped on sharp pebbles and howled. The central observation our brains seem equipped to provide us with is this: something is familiar (good), or unfamiliar (bad).

The bottom line regarding our brains and change is that we react to change first, and think about our reactions later. How long we remain reactionary and emotional is determined to a very large degree by how large and how well paved the roadways are between our prefrontal cortex and neocortex. If the roadways are donkey trails, we react and resist change for a longer time. If they are main highways, we snap out of our instinctual emotional reaction and get on with adapting. If the roadways are damaged by illness or injury, adapting to change may be difficult, if not impossible.

The moral of this information is: If you're going to use a two-by-four to get someone to change, don't hit them in the forehead.

The brain is a formidable piece of flesh, and we understand it only a little. When you consider that the task of conventional management is to get these disparate, brilliant biocomputers to do what we want, when we want, the way we want it, you have some idea of what organizational change initiatives are up against.

Your organization may not benefit in time from the next great leap forward in human evolution, as the neocortex asserts once and for all its dominance over the way people cope with the challenges life throws at us.

But we may learn a few tricks to circumvent the tyranny of fear that our old brains impose on us. Push addresses the brain's passionate fear center, the amygdala, the Jim Carrey in us. Pull makes contact with the brain's more thoughtful reasoning center, the neocortex, the Sandra Day O'Connor in us.

Right Brains and Left Brains

You probably know something about brain hemispheres. Scientists determined back in the

> **"The city is the soul magnified."**
>
> *Plato*

The Damaged Brain

The best evidence of the healthy brain's change capabilities is the behavior of people who have suffered damage to their brains. We all know people who have learning disorders of one sort or another. There are many different kinds of organic brain distress. But a constant among people who have suffered damage, for whatever reason—Alzheimer's, Down's syndrome, head injury, too many drugs, too much sex—is a powerful aversion to change.

They strongly prefer to make each day a repetition of the day before. It is the consistency of their daily routine that gives them a sense of hope of making it through that day. To go home on a different street, to use a different brand of mayonnaise on a sandwich, to carry money in a different set of denominations, throws them for a loop and greatly heightens their anxiety.

1960s that the two halves of the cerebral cortex were not twin hunks of pewter-colored tissue. The left side of the cerebrum is where our logical, analytical, quantitative, and fact-based thinking—our reactive talents— happen. It is the part of us that most instructions are written for, including change initiatives. The right brain, by contrast, is the center for the intuitive, creative, synthesizing, and integrating aspects of our thinking— our proactive talents.

So we are born half poet, half actuary, and we find out early enough that we are better on one side of the equation than on the other. Some of us are hot to change, proactives, while others of us, reactives by nature, balk at it. When those who are strong on one side are asked to be strong on the other side, they usually tie themselves in knots trying to please. It is the rare renaissance-virtuoso type of person who is equally adept on both sides of the melon.

> "Our education system and our society discriminate against one whole half of the brain. The right hemisphere gets only the barest minimum of training, nothing compared to what we do to train the left."
>
> *Roger Perry*

Most organizations in our time have been led not just by left-brain individuals but by left-brain ideas. Scientific management, two-column accounting, the assembly line, and bureaucracy itself are the logical products of logical minds. While people with strong analytical natures have tended to flourish in this era, people drawing on the more associational side of the brain have often felt at sea in the modern organization.

Here is the riddle we must understand: *Visualizing the future is the venue of the right brain. But the task of actually constructing roads toward that vision of the future is the purview of the left.* One hemisphere is not enough. It takes two to tango. An organization must link its talent together, not break them up—that is what organizations are for.

The challenge to the team leader is to try to Pull as many people as possible, as strongly as possible, toward an optimistic view of change, while simultaneously pushing those who are stuck.

Did you ever think the job of management was brain adjustment? They didn't teach that in business school. Yet the manager who overlooks this fact of nature has little chance of making good change stick.

Human Variation

Since the day after the wheel was invented, change initiatives have been instituted to overcome the negative effects of the change initiative that came just before.

The second great change initiative, quality control, was a direct consequence of the first change initiative, Frederick Winslow Taylor's scientific management. By stressing specialization, Taylor helped make possible the kind of mass manufacturing that would lift America to the top of the heap. Quality control was the first line of defense against shoddy production and products that failed to meet specifications.

From the emerging quality control ethic came the call for the elimination of variation in all its guises. This makes perfect sense when describing parts coming off the factory line. It makes less sense when talking about the efforts of the people working on the line. People are different. Taylor knew this, and that is why he elected to circumscribe as much of the variation as possible: This man was a left-to-right widget turner, that man turned widgets right to left, and so on.

But the work world has moved on. Few organizations today can afford the narrow factory job descriptions Taylor recommended. Widgets have become commoditized, and anyone can turn them. The search today is for employees who can do many things. And most workers today want to do other things; they are sick of the monotony of turning, turning, turning.

So the wisdom of the age decreed that widgets should continue to be widgets, as was their custom, but that people should be allowed to be as diverse as they naturally were. All part of the modern trend toward job enhancement.

Most team leaders and managers, however, are now charged with coordinating the goals, roles, and activities of people who differ from one another in more than a score of really significant ways:

sex	family type	character
age	life experience	quality of judgment
culture	work experience	socialness
language	place in birth order	learning style
religion	personality type	sexual identity
politics	personal taste	innie/outie (belly button)

It is fine and dandy to empower all these people to be themselves. But this is diversity squared, cubed, and exponentiated every which way. All these brains in the barnyard in need of corralling—is it plausible to establish any kind of consensus or cooperation among people so different from one another?

> **"Do not do unto others as you would have them do unto you. Their tastes may not be the same."**
>
> *George Bernard Shaw*

You can't eliminate variation in human beings. You can ignore it and hope it will go away or subside. But it won't. You can't ask people to check their individuality at the door. The beauty of Taylorism was simplification—an organization did not have to be all things to suit its workers. But Taylorism failed.

A friend of ours was a disciple of William Edwards Deming, who did more to bring the era of people-as-cogs to a close than anyone. One evening, at a dinner for Dr. Deming, our friend asked him if he could sum up his entire theory of work, production, statistics, variation, systems, knowledge, and control in a single sentence.

Deming did it in two words: "People matter."

Change and Personality

The consultants who sell us change packages never mention an obvious fact: Your workforce is not all made up of the same exact human being, with the same above-average, well-wired brain, and the same set of enthusiastic, change-happy responses.

Comparing this organization or team to your organization or team is like comparing a TV family to your family. Their family follies are all

Change and Gender

The brains of males and females are noticeably different in terms of how the right and left hemispheres of the brain interrelate. The female brain is better at crisscrossing the *corpus collossum*—the space between the two brain halves. The result is that the two genders change in different ways.

The implications of crisscrossing are ominous for men. It suggests that women are natural multitaskers—able to think about more than one objective at a time.

This multitasking ability helps explain why women have historically been ghettoized into pink-collar professions—hospitality, health-care, teaching, telephone work, homemaking. The conclusion is inescapable: our most change-capable people are not being allowed to play their logical role in leading organizational change.

---

amusing, last for 26 minutes, and inevitably lead to a life lesson that changes everyone forever. Your family follies are seldom amusing, and they can go one endlessly, with key members never quite getting whatever it is they are supposed to get.

We are different by countless measures. You can make everyone wear a white shirt and a tie, as Ross Perot did at EDS in the 1960s—and people would still be as different as snowflakes and fingerprints. The odds of you saying the word "X" to your team and having everyone form the same perfect, identical "X" in their minds is, well, not good.

The reason for this was advanced by G. K. Chesterton in a 1920 story called "Surprise."[2] The story is about a puppeteer who wishes his puppets could come to life so that he could know them as individuals. When his wish comes true, he is chagrined to discover that he is not fond of the particular individuals they have become. They are quarrelsome and boastful; they ad-lib; the hero decides to be a villain and vice versa. They're a mess!

People are not puppets. That's the headache managers and teams must live with. We can write scripts for people and concoct wonderful plans that by all "rational" measurement they should fall in with enthusiastically. But we are all different, with formidably free wills, and the best intentions in the world and the most intelligent organizational change initiatives can't alter that fact.

It is not even possible to address everyone at once to tell them what you want. People observe selectively, seeing what they care to see, or not seeing at all. Managers wish we were a flock of birds or a school of fish, shifting without need of visible "leadership," moving intuitively in unison, but we're not. In any organization, any individual can veto any change measure, simply by digging in and opposing it. Or even more simply, by pretending it isn't happening.

Resistance doesn't even have to be a conscious act. We can all vote on an idea and achieve a lovely degree of consensus, and still, when it's time to actually get up and go, not budge from square one. Some stony part of us, deep inside, has prevented the change. What is that part, and what good is it? To get the change started again, the right way, we will need to go inside ourselves, examine why our human nature balks at the challenge of the new, and figure out how to get ourselves unbalked.

You may say, "OK, scientific management is dead, and teams don't go far enough to get at the real reasons change initiatives fail. So how do I learn about the individuals I work with or supervise? Do I invite them all for sleepovers?"

> "You must look into people, as well as at them."
>
> *Lord Chesterfield*

You can get to know everyone on a personal basis, and you will not be sorry you did.

An alternative method is assessment. Psychologists have stepped in to fill the vacuum created by the collapse of scientific management, and through their study of human variation have developed ways to measure and understand various psychological types.

Psychological type is more than a casual phrase. For years psychologists have known something managers need to know much more about: that there are many kinds of people, that our type persists in us throughout our lives, that this diversity can be tested and labeled, and that knowing what type we are relates directly to such down-to-earth business problems as leadership development, team building, and effecting organizational change.

The Importance of Psychological Type

Not long ago we discovered a brand new test that some psychologist in a puckish mood created. It's called the Pig Personality Profile. It's a cute satire on the cult of typology; it's also frighteningly accurate.

The testee is asked to draw a picture of a pig. How you draw it speaks volumes about what kind of person you are and how you interact with the world. How big you drew the ears, how many legs were showing, which direction it was facing—your picture reveals everything there is to know about you. Our favorite indicator is the relationship between the length of the pig's tail and your sex life.[3]

After the laughter and embarrassment die down—the revelations about you are dead-on accurate—you realize that the test works because people have more things in common than they have differences; especially when it comes to the way we view and react to change. Like the signs of the horoscope, each assessment is true enough about us and sympathetic enough about our natures that we sign on to its truths. We are able, therefore, to categorize and predict how people will react to change and what can be done to make change more appealing to all types of pigs—er, people.

To psychologists, a new test is as exciting a discovery as a new galaxy is to astronomers. Tests are capable of providing almost endless illumination about individuals, what makes them tick, and what ticks them off. Using all the tests at our disposal, it is possible to slice and dice your workforce dozens of different ways, and each type of tool has its own uses.

Generally, these tools can be divided into two categories: heavy duty clinical instruments and lighter duty counseling types. The heavy duty tests include the Minnesota Multiphasic Personality Inventory (MMPI), the Thematic Apperception Test (TAT), and the familiar Rorschach inkblot test. The lighter duty tests include the Myers-Briggs Type Inventory and the DiSC profile. These last two are the most widely used in organizations to determine which workers will potentially get along great and which of them might attack each other with machetes.

Building the Personality Matrix

Using elements of both the Myers-Briggs and DiSC tests, we are going to create a model for understanding personality differences in your organization, and specifically, how the mix of personalities facilitates or obstructs the process of change.

Remember the three circles—personal change, global change, and organizational change? Our thesis was that people will not go along with any change in organizational direction or momentum unless and until they get their personal needs met in some way. Imagine a meeting room where workers are getting the lowdown about some proposed change initiative. The leader is blabbing about the new order, and people are doing their best to pay attention. Over each head you may paint a thought balloon, and in each balloon you may write the question, "What's in it for me?" So while all people are different, we all react to change in a circumscribed range of ways.

To find the answer to that question, we must first look at the typical reactions people have to change. We can then use this understanding to develop integrated methods for introducing change with the least destructive impact.

In developing strong teams, understanding and valuing differences is essential. But in adapting to change, understanding and valuing commonalties is the key. We grow by focusing on how we are unique; we progress by focusing on how we are similar.

Let's take a look at the common ways people approach change based on personalities:

To begin with, set aside religion, race, right- or left-handedness, and favorite color as differentiators. There are two axes of human nature, X and Y, that decide our "change personalities." The horizontal X-line is a continuum of action. At the right of the line are people who are naturally proactive. They not only don't shrink from new challenges, they characteristically seek them out and initiate them on their own. They are self-starters, go-getters, proactives, natural lovers of change. They are worth their weight in gold to any enterprise because they do what must be done without being asked.

At the left end of the line are their opposites, people who naturally shy away from new challenges. They are the foot-draggers, excuse-makers, the reactives, or resisters of change. They may be nice people, but they are death to change initiatives.

REACTIVE ⟺ PROACTIVE

What this chart tells us is that organizations have to expend a different amount of energy on individuals occupying different points on the horizontal. People on the proactive end of things don't need to be threatened or bribed—they are ready for change. These people will respond perfectly to a Pull campaign, one that lets people's own inner motivation drive the change process.

People in the middle are capable of being led to change. They are the many individuals who may have a personal reluctance to climbing aboard a change bandwagon, but will do so if it is required of them. The strategy that best energizes them is first to administer a dose of Push ("Less competitiveness leads to fewer employees"), and then to give them the tools, skills, information, and autonomy they need to begin the change journey, which gradually segues into Pull, as their own interests become apparent and acquire power.

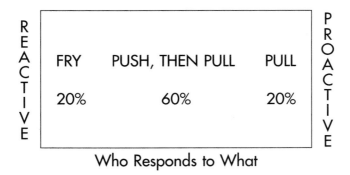

Who Responds to What

People on the far reactive side of things are every team's nightmare. Their change space is wiped out by their kill zone. Some of them have experienced all the change they are capable of handling; their condition is like post-traumatic stress syndrome—like combat veterans or concentration camp victims, they can't handle any more. Some are simply obtuse. These are the people who will end up serving the 80 percent who are willing to move forward. We have labeled them Fry because, if told that the platform is burning, they won't be willing or able to jump into the water.

The vertical Y-line is a continuum of *focus*—the dimension that people care most about. The top end of the line represents a focus on the task at hand. It is where people gravitate who are all business, focused on outcomes, *tasks*, results—the hard-edged, how-to part of work.

At the bottom end are found the people who are focused on processes and *people* issues—the softer, absorptive side of work.

TASKS

PEOPLE

Put the two axes together, tilt it a bit (we'll explain in a second) and you have a box into which we all fit. This is the universe of people who may be on your team, or in your charge. If there are a thousand coordinates in this box, you occupy one of them most of the time. That point describes how you likely think and feel about the circumstances you find yourself in.

Why the tilt? To show that two types of personality are more extreme on the action scale than the other two. Analyticals at the extreme edge are far more reactive and change resistant than Amiables. Expressives at the extreme edge are far more proactive and willing to change than Drivers.

It is easy to see why the four types[4] line up on opposite ends of the action spectrum. We will describe each type, with a thumbnail sketch of extreme cases of each type:

➤ **Drivers** are people who are willing to lead. They do not shrink from commitment—declaring their own or eliciting others'. Strong drivers are natural *metaphiles*, cheerful embracers of the new and untested. Remember the change space diagram, with the three circles representing global, organizational, and personal change, and the kill zone in the middle? A metaphile's change space would have a very limited kill zone—there's little they will not give serious consideration

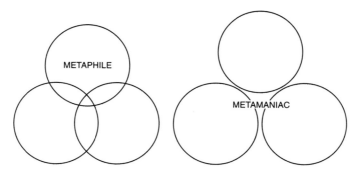

to. Drivers are firmly rooted in the present moment, and they are lovers of action. Their great strength: results. If you want a job discussed, talk to one of the other three types; if you want it *done*, take it to a Driver. They make great leaders because they are natural taskmasters. They aren't the most reflective people in the world, but they make up for that in energy, efficiency, and will-power. Pushed to the brink, Drivers become tyrants.

➤ **Expressives** are people endowed with a hefty amount of imagination, intuition, and creativity. Their natural mode is exploration. At the extreme, they are *metamaniacs,* so enamored of change that they have to be changing to function. The metamaniac can be represented by three nonoverlapping circles; they are so loose they are able to partition their entire lives into discrete, nonconflicting zones. They look at the world in fresh ways, always wondering what the future has in store for them. For inspiration they look forward. They are not the most reliable people, in terms of providing straight answers or objective reporting. They are gloriously sloppy. Their minds keep supplying new facts that they like better than the "real" facts. Pushed to the brink, Expressives can react savagely, by attacking.

➤ **Amiables** are the people everyone else loves to have around. Every nutty go-go Driver needs an Amiable as a spouse, someone who smiles and shrugs and loves and forgives. Amiables tend to be *metaphobes,* people disinclined by nature to enjoy change. A metaphobe's change space would have a noticeably larger kill zone than the metaphile. Their change mode is resistance. Amiables feel great pressure from the three spheres of their life, and it causes them to lock up. Amiables are "people people," expert at relationships, and their orientation is the past, the present, and the future—wherever people have needs and may be hurt. They are nature's diplomats—they know how to consult without ruffling feathers. They may have terrific opinions and extraordinary talents—but they may be more interested in yours. Pushed to the brink, their response may be to cry or cave in.

➤ **Analyticals** are tight, but they are also usually right. These are the perfectionists of the world, dotting every "i" and crossing every "t." They are gatekeepers by nature, barring entry to the unknown until it is proven safe. Their change mode is denial. They may be brilliant doing what they do best, but at the extreme, they are *metamorons,*

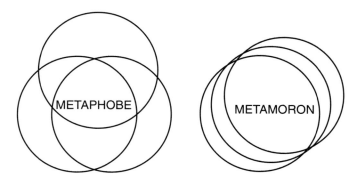

people to whom change is anathema, completely unacceptable. A metamoron's change space would be three circles almost overlapping, creating a huge kill zone, annihilating any new idea that comes within range. Their change space is their kill zone! When it comes to change, Analyticals are the victims of their own clarity. Their facts must be the right facts, and this need for certainty wreaks havoc with the spirit of experimentation. Analyticals are trustworthy because their sense of order prevents them from taking liberties. They occupy the reactive wing because they are incapable of precipitous action. They lose themselves in the task—and lose perspective in the process. They look backward for inspiration. As the saying goes, accountants make poor generals, even in today's JIT army. Pushed to the brink, Analyticals usually duck under the table.

That's what we have to work with. Team leaders and managers need to address individuals on the basis of both their horizontal (Reactive/ Proactive) and vertical (Task/People) predilections. You don't send a metamaniac to remedial quality class, and you don't give a metamoron a pilot program to run.

On the horizontal, the Proactives are constantly pushing for change. They are metaphiles searching for a better way, a different way, continuous improvement. They are the Drivers and Expressives in the DiSC Profiles and the high S's and N's (Sensors and Intuitives) of the Myers-Briggs test. Since these folks are already in continuous flight, they need to be guided by a Pull strategy of compelling vision and purpose.

The Reactives (Analyticals, Amiables, or high T's and F's (Thinkers and Feelers), on the other hand, are constantly resisting change. They are metaphobes searching for ways to cling to the past and to avoid having to generate the energy necessary to change. Since they are looking for ways to remain the same, a Push strategy of fear will get them going. Once on their way bouncing down the hallways, however, a Pull strategy will keep them from hitting too many walls on their trip.

On the vertical, you have your Task (outcome-oriented) People, who see change as a set of outcomes, goals, or steps to be followed to achieve specific results. And you have your People (process-oriented) People, who see change as a process of gaining comfort (moving operating comfort zones) while reducing the negative stress on people.

Assessing Individuals

By now you are curious as to what you are: a reactive or a proactive. Or, worst case, a metamaniac or a metamoron. Here is an informal quiz you

---

Animal Farm

If all this sounds complicated, it is. Think of it as living in a house with four pets, each requiring a different level and kind of attention:

The Driver is the dog that you let out at night, and he roams the countryside on his own. Your task is to make sure he's not out there knocking over garbage cans; apart from that, leave him alone. What he needs more than anything is food and fresh water.

The Expressive is a canary, singing away for all she's worth. That song is a day-brightener for all who hear her; but she may need a drape over her cage at night, or her expressive energy will drain everyone's ability to work. Hold her on your finger and tell her how special she is.

The Analytical is the pet rat, intelligent, purposeful, and thorough in all things. She needs to stack those pellets on the north wall of her tank and keep the area policed. She needs privacy and respect.

The Amiable is the cat who derives meaning just from brushing up against your leg and purring in your lap. He believes he is providing a valuable service just by being there and emitting positive vibes. He needs to be petted and to know he is cherished.

---

can use or adapt to your own organization. It tells you where you align yourself on a scale of ranges describing change potential.

You can test yourself. If you are on a team whose members are really comfortable with one another, you can also score each other's change quotients, and then compare how you score yourself with how they score you.

Most people taking this test are very generous with assessments of themselves; and much less generous assessing others. This is a great way to start a fist-fight, so have a care.

A third way to use the test is to fill it out *as if* you were another person, observing you.

On each line are seven circles, marking your attitude from one end of a continuum to the other. If a 1, 4, or 7 statement sounds too extreme but is close, mark an in-between circle, a 2, 3, 5, or 6.

Answers falling on the left side of the bell curve suggest an inelasticity of personality; answers on the right indicate too much elasticity. The far left is the realm of neurotic control, in which the will perpetually frustrates itself. The far right is the realm of no control—an intense, unfettered region similar to clinical psychosis.

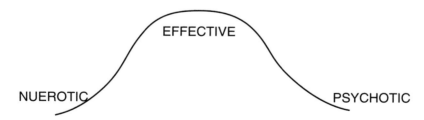

The value of this test is that it begins the necessary process of familiarization. The results are informal, so the point is not to file them away in a confidential cabinet, but to use them as a conversation starter. People should test and score themselves and discuss with their team whether or not they agree with the results. It is not pleasant, even with an off-the-record test like this, to be told you are any kind of maniac, much less a moron. But it is important that people who do have constitutional problems with change acknowledge the fact. It alters their expectations and the team's expectations of them. It may even serve as a Push tool to get them thinking about ways they can do better.

Ideally, you will want yourself and your team to score generally close to the middle. It's not a catastrophe if there is a spread; you can balance out one another's proclivities. It probably is a catastrophe if you are all lumped on one end, or if there is no strong center.

Your Change Personality

REACTIVE ⇔ **PROACTIVE**

✓ FLEXIBILITY

How able are you to change your behavior at will?

| ○ | | ○ | ○ | | ○ | | ○ | ○ | | ○ |
| 1 | | 2 | 3 | | 4 | | 5 | 6 | | 7 |

Unable and unwilling.

Able and willing, if the cause is attractive.

Couldn't stop if I tried.

✓ RECEPTIVITY

How open are you to new ideas?

| ○ | | ○ | ○ | | ○ | | ○ | ○ | | ○ |
| 1 | | 2 | 3 | | 4 | | 5 | 6 | | 7 |

Sphincter-tight. I know what I like, and that's all I want to know.

I enjoy stepping outside the box and hearing a fresh viewpoint.

I live for new ideas. My problem is following through on any of them.

✓ STATUS

How able are you to change right now?

| ○ | | ○ | ○ | | ○ | | ○ | ○ | | ○ |
| 1 | | 2 | 3 | | 4 | | 5 | 6 | | 7 |

Too stressed out in my life as a whole to give a work idea its due.

Looking for an opportunity to try something new in my job.

I'm ready to go, no matter what the idea.

☑ DISTRESS

How might you describe your curent level of negative stress?

O O O O O O O

1   2 3   4   5 6   7

I'm maxed out. My confidence is low and my attention span is for the birds. Kill me.

Copacetic. Things are going well for me at home, and I feel I can handle a new challenge.

Feeling no stress whatsoever—the gears may be stripped.

☑ PATIENCE

How patient are you in the face of change? How comfortable are you with delayed gratification?

O O O O O O O

1   2 3   4   5 6   7

I like results ASAP. I can't go forward unless my results are assured.

I am willing to wait for results if I have reason to think they will be coming.

I can wait forever. I don't care about results.

☑ LOCUS OF CONTROL

Do you focus on yourself or outside yourself?

O O O O O O O

1   2 3   4   5 6   7

I can only be concerned right now about me and my survival.

I feel I have found a good balance between taking care of myself and offering my contributions to others.

I am not important. All that matters is the success and well-being of the group.

☑ MIND SPACE

What is your natural time orientation?

○　　　○　○　　　○　　　○　○　　　○
1　　　2　3　　　4　　　5　6　　　7

Right now, today. I can't think of long-term ramifications or the Big Picture.

I am comfortable with long time frames, but under-stand that goals are achieved in incre-ments.

I don't even think about time. What-ever happens will happen.

☑ DIVERSITY

How do you feel about differentness—the "otherness" of other people's ideas?

○　　　○　○　　　○　　　○　○　　　○
1　　　2　3　　　4　　　5　6　　　7

I have trouble sub-scribing to an idea I know I could never have come up with.

I welcome ideas from people who are different from me.

Unless an idea comes from outside my immediate circle, I'm not inter-ested in it.

Scoring: There are 8 questions and 7 possible points per question; a top score would be 56. You don't want that. Here is the range:

8–10 METAMORON	14–30 METAPHOBE	31–55 METAPHILE	52–56 METAMANIAC
It's no coinci-dence Bob Cratchit worked for Ebenezer Scrooge. Fat for the fryer.	You can change well with the right combina-tion of Push, then Pull.	The change-making ideal. Ideal candidate for a Pull pro-gram.	Way too much of a good thing. Organizational equivalent of idiot savant.

Expanding the Change Space

Return to the metaphor of fixing the lightning rod during a lightning storm while being attacked by bees. The storm was the global change engulfing your organization. The lightning rod was the organizational change implemented to meet the global change head on. The hornets were workers' individual change stressors, distracting them and making the organizational change more difficult.

The more stress your situation piles upon you, the smaller your change space becomes. It is a paradox: instead of getting better at change, the more of it you are asked to do, the worse you get at it. Piled-on change, with no time allotted for reenergizing, causes most people's change potential to diminish: burnout.

Interestingly, this is less true for proactives. The reason is that metaphiles and metamaniacs are so constituted that they do not allow everyday change stress to snowball into intolerable distress.

Now is a good time to point out that it is a good thing we are not all metaphiles, as they can be insensitive and overconfident. But we can all learn a few tricks from them.

As you increase people's stress levels from any of the three sources of stress mentioned earlier, make sure they are able to reenergize their stress tolerance reserves. Use active methods such as focus group discussions to share feelings of anxiety produced by the change. Encourage people to make time for exercise, to follow a diet that helps combat stress, and to adopt relaxation techniques like meditation or catharsis.

> **"There is a word for the absence of stress: death."**
>
> *Hans Selye*

Other stress-reduction ideas:

> ➤ **Be optimistic.** Most metaphiles stay aloft because they are engrossed in a positive, enjoyable way with the change occurring around them. When other people see manure, metaphiles know a pony must be nearby. They survive change in large part because they have pledged allegiance to it.
> ➤ **Be pessimistic,** sort of. *Accepting* may be a better word. In its simplest form, this attitude is simply a shrug. Most change is not fun. But if it is unpleasant and unavoidable, why not adopt a bemused fatalism? "You can't stop progress" is both an American anthem and an American elegy: the natural metaphile makes the best of a substandard situation.
> ➤ **Focus on the trunk.** Change weakens ordinary people because we try to grasp all of its implications at once, which causes our brains to heat up. Like writing a book, it can only be done a chapter at a time. The blind men of Industan could only describe an elephant in terms of the

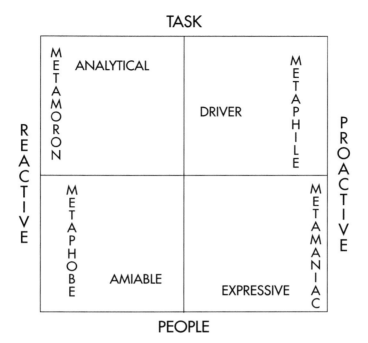

TASK

ANALYTICAL   DRIVER

METAMORON   METAPHILE

REACTIVE   PROACTIVE

METAPHOBE   METAMANIAC

AMIABLE   EXPRESSIVE

PEOPLE

part they were currently touching. Their descriptions were never complete, but at least they were not trampled by the elephant's totality. There is sanity, even in the world of total participation and cross-functionality, in knowing your part and focusing on it.

➤ **Vent.** Create and make frequent use of your support network—any combination of people from among your bosses, coworkers, subordinates, friends, family, and if all else fails, your dog. They are there to talk to and to cry on the shoulder of. The more, the merrier. It is surprising how much stress we can put up with if we just have the occasional opportunity to complain. Bitch about it, then get it behind you. Every parent knows there are two kinds of children: the child who complains about having to take out the trash, but then does it, and the child who utters no word of resistance, but doesn't take the trash out, either.

➤ **Eat well.** If stress is preventing your team from addressing change needs, maybe you need to address your lunch pail first. A common reaction to stress is elevated blood pressure. People under stress often cope by ingesting fatty and salty foods—the very things that drive blood pressure higher.

part 3

Why groups don't work

One reason American organizations have trouble harnessing good old American competitiveness and ingenuity is that another American value gets in the way—freedom. Though we are joiners, we join with ambivalence.

The ultimate freedom each of us has is the freedom of our own attitudes. We decide if we will join, or subscribe, or cooperate, and in what spirit. Most management books depict processes in which people from a broad spectrum of backgrounds cheerfully set aside their native prejudices and preferences and march in lockstep to the heroic leader's drumbeat. We call these books "happy talk." They provide an intriguing metaphor or striking new paradigm people can use to aim for new levels of productivity. But they fail to address the fact that people have their own reasons for doing things. That is the main reason groups falter at their own tasks.

Here are some sub-reasons:

➤ **Groups are anti-holistic.** Group behavior can be a wonder to behold, as when a good team begins to click. More often, however, they are anti-holistic—their whole is considerably less than the sum of their parts. There is a gap in every bit of communication, a falloff in quality at every handoff of work. Every person at every stage in the change process who does not believe in it 100 percent diminishes its chances for success.

You can do the math on this. Say that every person on an assembly team of ten people is 95 percent committed to the program's success. The doubt of each person multiplies the doubt of the next person because each person's work affects every other person's output. The overall confidence of the team is thus not 95 percent, but: 95 percent × 95 percent × 95 percent × 95 percent × 95 percent × 95 percent × 95 percent × 95 percent × 95 percent.

Each weakness adds to the aggregate weakness. By line's end, team confidence is down to about 56 percent, and that is not enough faith to keep the balloon in the air.

➤ **Groups are inherently unpoliceable.** People are free to ignore you, disagree with you, or follow you so far and no further. This is just as true in a free society as it is in a dictatorship. You cannot make a group do anything, least of all think the same way.

➤ **Groups are seldom unanimous.** Within any group, even a committed one, there is a variety of degrees of commitment and understanding.

➤ **Inertia is terrific on both ends of the spectrum—starting and stopping.** Think of individual behavior as a kayak—easy to steer and hard to sink. Think of a group as a fishing boat. (Think of a large organization such as the Exxon Valdez.)

> **"Hell is other people."**
>
> *Jean-Paul Sartre*

➤ **Disappointments are magnified by the social dynamic.** Groups are more prone to gossip, rumor, and innuendo. Negativity lives on in groups when it might have naturally subsided in most individuals.

➤ **Conformity saps diversity.** The very thing teaming sets out to achieve is very often the first thing it eradicates. Jerry Harvey calls this the "Abilene Paradox," in which everyone willingly sets aside his or her druthers in order to accommodate the perceived majority will. Just when you need disagreement, people start to agree.

Of course, we are stuck with groups—an individual is not an organization. But in our eagerness to start moving people around and putting them on teams and coaxing total involvement out of every last one of them, take a moment to remember how daunting the task is.

All those neurons firing at cross-purposes, all those chickens loose in the yard, and you armed with only a clipboard and an org chart.

Assessing the Organization

This is a sample questionnaire to help you gauge your organization's change culture. It's not a fixed instrument, but a model you should adapt using questions more relevant to your specific situation.

Which statement best characterizes conditions and attitudes in your organization?

Answer A, B, C, or D. The scoring is simple: A=Pummel, B=Push, C=Pull, D=Pamper

Use your scores as a conversation starter with your team or group. Don't bother counting up the total score. Focus on individual areas. See if your organization falls consistently into one type, through every question. See who agrees with your assessment and who differs, and ask what can be done to move the scores closer to where you want to be.

The Organizational Profile

I. LEADERSHIP
    A. Leadership expects you to do what you are told.
    B. Leadership does not mind using fear tactics to get desired results.
    C. Leadership provides a vision of possibilities; provides pathways to success, and expects people to use them.
    D. Leadership does not lead; expects people to find their own paths—or find none at all.

II. VALUES
    A. My way or the highway.
    B. Survival through obedience.
    C. Success through adhering to highest ideals (customer satisfaction, highest quality, win/win thinking, equal opportunity, etc.)
    D. Don't make waves.

III. CULTURE
    A. Walls drip with fear.
    B. Emphasis is on measurement; performance evaluation; exhortation.

C. Celebratory; the hum of people working; no special perks at the top, and frequent reinforcement of the troops.

D. Lots of socializing; slack discipline; the customer comes last.

IV. REWARDS

A. Live to work another day.

B. Individual, not team-based rewards; emphasis is on monetary rewards for individuals. Pay is for what you produce.

C. Team rewards as well as individual rewards; there is a mix of monetary, social, symbolic, intellectual and emotional rewards. Pay is for what you know.

D. You are paid well regardless of how you perform. Automatic pay raises; seniority advantages; even tenure.

V. PERFORMANCE FEEDBACK

A. Feedback the instant you screw up.

B. Periodic feedback, often too late to be useful. Feedback is from the top down. Focus is outcome-oriented, on what you do.

C. Feedback is ongoing, informal, and can come from any direction—top-down, bottom-up or sideways. Focus is on process and development; on how you do what you do, and how you might do better.

D. No evaluation, or all evaluation is automatically excellent. The bar is never raised.

VI. COMMUNICATION

A. The thrust of most communication is threatening, angry, manipulative, and stress-inducing. Important information is withheld.

B. The point of most communication is to stimulate high performance. Negative outcomes are emphasized. Management talks, workers listen.

C. The point of most communication is to create and maintain a vision. Positive outcomes are emphasized. All parties are free to talk and listen.

D. All communication is positive, and thus meaningless. The system is infatuated with itself, and the sound of its own voice.

VII. SYSTEMS
   A. People distrust machines. They may even be under surveillance by then. Access is restricted. Security is obsessive.
   B. Noncreative centralized systems, in which the users serve the machines, meeting their demands.
   C. Interactive distributed systems, in which the machines serve the users, meeting their requirements.
   D. People trust machines to the point of worship. The organization is on automatic pilot. So long as the blanks are filled in, everything is OK.

VIII. TEAMWORK
   A. Teamwork is regarded as conspiracy. If there are teams, they are like teams of horses, assigned the task of pulling weight, period.
   B. Team tyranny, in which everyone must be on a team, with the goals of improving efficiency and meeting quotas.

> **"No matter how cynical you get, you can never keep up."**
>
> *Lily Tomlin*

   C. Team equity, in which teams are used only when appropriate, with the ultimate goal of creating a future.
   D. No one is on a team unless they feel like it. Teams are vehicles for socializing.

Change and Unreason

Rational groups of people, presented with the opportunity to improve, will be grateful for the suggestion and take steps to make the improvement. But who is 100 percent rational? Is your neocortex the established master of your amygdala? Doubt it; even the steadiest person indulges in frequent illogic, emotional indulgence, finger-pointing, self-pity, paranoia, denial, and cynicism.

One of the more bravura observations about human behavior in this century was a list of "Ten Common Irrational Ideas" compiled in the 1950s by Albert Ellis and Robert Harper. They weren't talking about organizational change initiatives and why groups balk at the command to jump. Yet their list intuits every feeble, vain response groups throw up to change challenges.

1. **"It is a dire necessity for an adult to be loved and approved by almost everyone for virtually everything he/she does."** Picture a manager or team leader who has a good idea, but who is too insecure to withstand the early stages of introducing the idea and hearing people's objections to it. As soon as the going gets a little rough, the prime mover caves in.

2. **"One should be thoroughly competent, adequate, and achieving, in all possible respects."** A perfectionist team expects to hit high "C" on the very first try, and is unwilling to slog along a failure-strewn path of trial-and-error. This perfectionism protects the team and its leadership from tarnishing their record of uninterrupted success. Imagine anything of value being achieved by people unwilling to experience initial failure and frustration. The error here is thinking the effort is more about the people undertaking it than about the good the effort will accomplish.

3. **"Certain people are bad, wicked, or villainous, and they should be severely blamed and punished for their sins."** What is sweeter than to pin 100 percent of the blame for a failure on someone else, and to focus all eyes not on success but on the subhuman failings of the responsible party? Demonization comes in handy for both management and labor. It is a sign that one's true objective is not improvement but exculpation.

> **"I do not like this word bomb. It is not a bomb; it is a device which is exploding."**
>
> *Jacques Le Blanc*, French ambassador to New Zealand, describing France's nuclear testing

4. **"It is terrible, horrible, and catastrophic when things are not going the way one would like them to go."** Change would not be change if it were predictable. But we rail against the unpredictability of events as if it broke the rules we imagine the world operates by. We move the blame even farther from ourselves by designating these events as "acts of God."

5. **"Human unhappiness is externally caused and people have little or no ability to control their sorrows or rid themselves of their negative feelings."** This is the attitude of the victim, an attitude one holds dearer than success itself. It portrays the individual in an organization as a helpless pawn in a game played by far more

powerful forces. When a change idea is put on the table, it is not a thing to be considered but a thing to be regarded with the darkest sort of suspicion.

6. **"If something is or may be dangerous or fearsome, one should be terribly occupied with and upset about it."** This is the unknown that we automatically fill in with negatives. We are incapable of imagining an uncertain outcome without focusing on the worst-case scenario. In this mindset all change is to be avoided, because all change involves the X-factor, which can only be fatal.

7. **"It is easier to avoid facing many life difficulties and self-responsibilities than to undertake more rewarding forms of self-discipline."** In the classic choice between flight or fight, the easy response is usually flight. People can be sitting around a table discussing an idea, nodding emphatically, and still be in an all-out flight from the idea they are nodding about. To focus on the proposed solution takes courage and commitment—and many of us have exhausted our stores of those things.

> "People only see what they are prepared to see."
>
> *Ralph Waldo Emerson*

8. **"The past is all-important, and because something once strongly affected one's life, it should indefinitely do so."** Taking all our cues from the past is like driving using only the rearview mirror. The past is not all there is, and it is not a map of the future. Overreliance on it robs us of our other resources, our intuition, and creativity.

9. **"People and things should be different from the way they are, and it is catastrophic if perfect solutions to the grim realities of life are not immediately found."** If at first you don't succeed, give up. This attitude is convenient for people who like the idea of change but not the commitment to it. They are forever hopping from initiative to initiative, abandoning each one when it does not yield results the first day. It is the error of externality, always looking for results outside oneself, instead of letting the natural solution bubble up from within.

10. **"Maximum human happiness can be achieved by inertia and inaction or by passively and uncommittedy 'enjoying**

oneself.' "[1] Better not to try than to try. It is the measure of how beaten people are by everyday stress that they believe their best chance is to behave like the mauled camper who acts dead as the bear abuses his bleeding body. Play dead, and maybe the problem will go away. What makes these insights so exasperating is that, while they are irrational, they are not untrue. A great deal of the world's wisdom inheres to the principle of resisting impetuous action. Let sleeping dogs lie. People have been put through too much stress, with too little relief, to sign on glibly to every new crusade that announces itself.

The problem arises when it is time for a legitimate crusade, when joint action is truly required, and as in Aesop's fable of the boy who cried wolf, the people are unable to view this call to arms as different from the previous false alarms.

Rebalancing the Stress Load

There used to be only two schools of thought about increasing groups' acceptance of change: Pummel and Pamper. Pummel's attitude about what workers were feeling was basically: Who cares? Pamper went to the opposite extreme, taking responsibility for everything happening in the individual worker's head.

In recent years a third option, weighted toward Push, has appeared. It involves laying out negative scenarios and options: adapt or you're fired. It feeds into people's naturally negative perspective. The best-known spokesperson for Push in recent years has been Morris Shechtman, once a psychotherapist and now a management consultant. His book *Working Without a Net*, in which he advocates the abandonment of touchie-feelie programs that shield workers from the realities of competition, was cited by Newt Gingrich as one of the must-read texts for the new conservative majority.

The traditional view is that it is not management's job to get inside employees' heads and worry about their anxieties. To anticipate workers' negative feelings amounts to caretaking, one of the more insidious forms of Pamper. Kindness, critics of Pamper like Shechtman say, is not always kind. But being cruel in order to be kind usually winds up being just cruel.

And whether you get inside employees' heads or not, what happens there does affect performance. Reading workers the riot act may quell the riotous. It does not swell the ranks of the ready, willing, and able. What Shechtman calls caretaking is one of the critical jobs of good managers—communicating with workers in ways they can respond to. Putting all the responsibility for communication on the workers, as Shechtman suggests, may seem tough but it is an abdication.

Removing the safety net sends a scary message to people who are trying to help the organization change, but who are not quite there yet. While an anti-caretaking position will flush out your proactives, who are always happy to make a change anyway, it will drive away people caught between the extremes. There are lots of people with good change potential here, and a company that declares war against employee hand-holding is going to lose these people. Remember, there are never enough metaphiles to go around. Your organization needs ordinary people with ordinary change resistance.

The logical next step is to graft a Pull dimension onto the Push position. Make it plain to workers that those who are unwilling to change don't have a future with your organization. They have frying pan written all over them. But provide every possible pathway to allow worthwhile in-betweeners a chance to escape the burning platform.

Change means added stress on people. It drains us of our energy reserves. The more you ask people to change, the more resources you must supply to help balance the stress load.

It's a one-to-one ratio. The third law of physics says that objects seek their lowest level of energy. Translated in terms of people, it means that people seek their highest comfort level, the most security. Psychologist Abraham Maslow explained these needs in his famous "hierarchy of human needs." The first level of need is that of security: food, water, shelter, protection against harm.

Obviously, an employee is not going to be a quick-change artist if he or she is hungry. You may find it politically unappealing to have to feed workers, but at some level that is just what you have to do. If their change space has shrunk to the dot of an "i," you need to expand that space again, so that the person can do what needs doing.

Very important: explain to people that you understand that change is difficult for them. Whatever you have learned about easing the trauma of change, make that knowledge available to people. We suggest that companies adopt a stress-watch program to outline the ways which change-induced distress can swamp a worker and even programs to alleviate the most common kinds of distress.

This is one area where Japanese companies outshine us. There is widespread agreement that working for one of the large zaibatsus in Japan, like Matsushita, Honda, Toyota, and Kao, is tremendously stressful. Failure means disgrace in that culture, and people take it very personally: "I'm sorry I let you all down."

But Japanese companies undertake a variety of efforts to keep stress from tipping over into distress. They place a heavy emphasis on socializing and exercise. Something happens to a team that works up a sweat doing jumping jacks together. Endorphins can paper over a host of misgivings.

Some Japanese companies practice rage management. One factory provides workers with a room where you can beat up a human-shaped dummy with a mask of your manager on it.

If employees at these companies are nursing a grievance, management wants to get it out into the open air. Focus group discussions are another way for people to get their feelings out, which even Shechtman agrees is essential. Satisfaction is never guaranteed—that would be Pamper—but at least there is the relief of getting a problem out of the cramped confines of the worker's stomach lining.

They even borrow a page from ancient Greece. Greece had an annual festival called the Lupercalia. On this day the customary rules were overturned; women were allowed to cheat on their husbands, and slaves were allowed to beat their masters. In Japan, middle managers are invited to socialize with senior management, even to get drunk with them.

Since control and harmony are so important to the Japanese psyche, alcohol works as a kind of chemical crowbar to pry people from their usual propriety, dulling the neocortex and inflaming the amygdala, upshifting aggressive behaviors to lupercalian levels. The literature is full of stories of drunken managers telling their bosses off and living to tell the tale. In the morning, long-term built-up stress has been replaced by short-term hangovers. Propriety is restored, and everyone feels better, after a day or two. The rice wine in this case serves as a Pull pathway. It enables frustrated workers to say what is in their hearts, and thus expands their change space.

You don't have to be Japanese to take a bite out of organizational stress. American companies have pioneered numerous stress reduction programs, from employee exercise workouts, to wellness counseling, company outings and celebrations, softball leagues, and dress-down Fridays. The primary objective of these programs may not always be to reduce group stress, but that is their effect.

Seven Hard Truths

If you are serious about helping your organization increase its tolerance for change, there are seven facts about groups and change that you must understand.

When undergoing change:

> **"Other people are not in this world to live up to your expectations."**
>
> *Fritz Perls*

➤ **Groups feel awkward, ill-at-ease, and self-conscious.** The people best adapted to change are those raised in an ever-changing environment, like army brats who move every three years or so, or research scientists seeking change with every breath. For the rest of us, change is scary, painful, and unwanted.

➤ **Groups will think first about what they must give up.** It's a defense mechanism, the worst-case scenario. People will first think about what they have to lose by being on a team rather than what they have to gain. The job of an effective team leader, then, becomes one of instilling positive expectations to overcome this natural defensive behavior. To get at these lurking doubts, ask and answer this question: "What do I have to lose if this initiative succeeds?"

➤ **Groups will feel alone.** Though they may gossip about impending changes, people in groups will not share their true feelings of change anxiety with other groups members for fear of being seen as uncertain or uncommitted. As a result, little communication occurs at the very moment (during change) when good communication is most critical. When it comes to change, feelings are facts. Now is the moment to have colleagues get their real worries and doubts, not their carping and sniping, out on the table and resolved.

➤ **Groups will demand that you up the dosage.** We've worked with several organizations during major change times—some have been more successful than others. One of the keys to successful change is timing. Companies that dole out change in small doses over long periods of time, hoping to minimize negative impact, are surprised at the sudden dip in morale after about the second or third dose. Until participants can picture in their minds what their tasks and their roles will be when this change is complete, they will probably just nod their heads and not comply. Organizations that have had the best success with change take major steps in short time frames, with the end product carefully described up front. With this information under their belts, people tolerate the short-term pain for the longer-term payoff. The "dribble" or incremental change method only heightens the sense of mistrust of management that many employees already have.

➤ **Groups have different readiness levels for change.** Any time a group of people are asked to change, some members will be excited and ready, and others will appear to have anchors tied to their enthusiasm. One way people

> **"We have met the enemy and it is us."**
>
> *Walt Kelly*

differ from one another is in how fast they can commit to change. The challenge for organizations and teams is to boost the readiness of their least ready members, because these people determine the pace of the group as a whole. Any attempt to push faster will meet with increased resistance that will slow the process down. The personal change inventory in the previous chapter is a good way to identify people who are struggling with change. Taking it also provides a good excuse for getting together and talking about problems they are having, and what it will take to resolve those problems. Use peer pressure to your advantage: move the most change-ready workers along quickly and broadcast their successes. The pressure will bring resisters into line as if a magnet were pulling them.

➤ **Groups will fret that they don't have enough resources.** The first noise you hear from people in change pain is, "We could do it if we only had more resources." Sure, we all would like additional resources—but we usually have not made much use of the resources already at our disposal. Untapped, available, shared, borrowed, stolen, or heretofore unknown resources are usually all groups need to get through a tough change phase. Look around. Use the unused and underused. Make do. Or don't do. One nifty trick, after you've exhausted your search, is to go to the persons blocking the needed resources and ask for their input on alternative resources. Those who block usually know the way around the block, if anyone bothers to ask. They won't volunteer this information, but if asked, they'll usually tell.

➤ **If you take the pressure off, groups will revert to their old behaviors.** Momentum is an amazing and wonderful force. Like a compass, it keeps you going in the same direction. If the direction you're going is the wrong one, however, momentum can kill you. Momentum, like a magnet, will pull you back in the old direction, the old way of doing things. Change is a temporary force that pulls you in a new direction; but it must be applied continuously until the new behaviors become the norm, the new north. If you take the pressure off too early in a change process, the group will revert to the old way of doing business, old relationships, old behaviors, old processes, old habits.

part 4

Making change

The challenge of yoking Push and Pull together, to elicit the strongest change response from the widest range of workers, presents a knot of paradoxes.

It means being the good cop and the bad cop almost simultaneously. It means being open to other people's visions while having a plan of your own. It means being simultaneously Machiavellian (doing whatever works to drag your organization through change) and caring (being genuinely interested in where others are, and incorporating their individual dreams into the larger dream of the organization at large).

We name this nexus of perplexities the "come-as-you-are masquerade party," in which we all arrive disguised as ourselves, each of us a bundle of internal contradictions as amygdala wrestles with neocortex, and our lesser selves get the better of our better selves. From this confusion we are expected to create a new clarity.

How do managers and team leaders unravel this tangle? Let's break change down into its functional parts and apply Push/Pull thinking to each.

Hub and Spoke Planning

We talked about the three kinds of change—personal, organizational, and global. Global change, such as inflation, a new technology, a sudden new demand by customers, or war in the oil fields, is the kind that can't be planned or controlled. All you can do is wear rubbers if it's raining, and stand in the doorway if the house starts to shake.

Organizational change not only can be planned and controlled, it must be. Indeed, if an organizational change is not carefully planned, you are no more managing it than you manage rain or an earthquake.

We plan for change in order to have our say about where we're going and what we're going to become. A plan is not the words of a plan on paper, or the time line for rollout marked on a calendar, but the understanding that exists in the minds of participants. It is the organization's vision of the future reduced to clear, comprehensible action steps describing how to get there and who will do what.

Planning is too complicated for leaders to do by themselves. It requires a team of people from every part of the organization, both at the hub of the organization and out along the spokes—support people, suppliers, customers, distributors, and other secondary parties.

These people do not need to meet as a team—if they did, the group would be bigger than Congress—but hub members will need to meet often and intensively with members out along the spokes. A common mistake managers make is to cook up a plan on their own, usually at a swanky resort, and spring it on workers as a done deal—no improvements invited. Leaders must get workers behind a plan and involve them in it from the very beginning. Not only does this elicit valuable information and practical feedback, but it also starts the change juices flowing in everyone.

Issues to resolve:

➤ **Goals.** Does the entire team agree on what the objective of the change is? It should be easy to state in a few words: faster production, better communication, fewer re-dos, better customer feedback. The goal must fit the larger organizational mission (serving the best danged hamburgers you ever ate) like a glove.

➤ **Strategy.** What Push and Pull engines drive the plan? Have you identified what goes where and when and why? Push is your starter engine—use it to goose people and get their attention. Then provide a pathway to a long-term Pull orientation—a vision of the future that people can buy into, each in his or her own way.

➤ **Behavior.** Change initiatives are all about changing what people do. Whose behavior is targeted by the change? Do they understand what is expected? Are they equipped to adapt? Who is a believer and who still needs to be converted?

➤ **Outcome.** What result do we want from this change in behavior? Is it something that can be measured? Is it something that can be broken down into achievable units?

➤ **Contingencies.** If the plan doesn't work, what then? A backup plan? A prayer service? How do you respond to unexpected events?

➤ **Resources.** Is a major operational overhaul being conducted on a bake-sale budget? Where is the money coming from? Where are the support people coming from? If you run into trouble, who can run interference for you?

➤ **Time line.** If there is no schedule, there is no plan.

➤ **Personnel.** Who's in charge of the plan? Who's planning the plan? Where are these people coming from? Why, if they are valuable people, are they available? That is, why aren't they swamped with prior mission-critical tasks?

➤ **Evaluation.** How will you know when the battle is over and whether it has been won? Finally, if the battle is won, was it worth it? After all that travail, was it in fact a good plan?

> **"We've got to make this stuff we're lost in look as much like home as possible."**
>
> *Overheard at a strategy session*

So when the change is finally formalized and rolled out to people, they are already behind it, from the furthest spoke to the central hub. Sub-teams within the planning team can attend to many of these spoke issues. Keep your hub focused on the overall goal of the change, and the spokes focused on knocking down barriers to the change. Together you can get the wheel rolling.

Introducing Change

Say the word "change" to any randomly selected group, and you will likely get three different types of responses. Some throw up their hands and say, "God, not again." Others say, "Well, it's about time." The third group will simply throw up.

Your team, your organization, includes all three types. The question is, how do you lay out a change regimen that takes into consideration the various ways people will react?

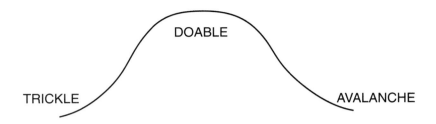

First, you take into consideration people's past experience. Think of a bell curve, with people revolting on either extreme. On one extreme, you've got your avalanche. This is cataclysmic change, major change that must occur in a very short time frame. It's the organizational equivalent of a tornado picking up your neighbor's house and dropping it on your house: much must be done, and quickly. Or a new technology or delivery mechanism has made your product line obsolete overnight, and you've got to reorganize, streamline, and catch up to your competition ASAP.

On the other extreme you've got trickles of change. These are little inoffensive changes that, taken one at a time, would be quite manageable. The problem is that management sends one down about every 2 minutes. If you've been to a bowling alley, think of the changes as having a ganging-up rhythm: for every ball you bowl, three are sent back to you by the ball return. It's too many, too quick. Pretty soon, one ball is going to smunch your finger as you reach for another. After this happens a few times, you just want to sit down and watch.

In the illustration above, the best time to introduce change is at the high point of the curve, between avalanche-scale and trickle-scale change. Then take the change step-by-step:

➤ **Announce** to your team or organization what you want the outcome to look like.
➤ **Lay out the vision** for them, till they begin to see it, too. Engage their imaginations.
➤ **Now designate** an enthusiastic pilot group made up of as many proactives as you can spare to try out the new change.
➤ **Have them play with** and modify the idea as necessary.
➤ **Give them enough time and resources** so they can make the change and show measurable success.
➤ **Then broadcast the heck** out of the success.

Have those who have lived through the change and survived come in to mentor and teach others how they did it. Metaphiles make great teachers because they are natural enthusiasts; they teach in order to further their own understanding. Let them play the role of storytellers and pathfinders.

Then roll the change effort out exponentially. First with two groups, then four. Then eight, then sixteen. Then everyone.

What You Can Do and What You Can't Do

In his book *What You Can Change and What You Can't*,[1] psychologist Martin Seligman lists the most common psychological problems individuals suffer from and the degree to which each problem can be addressed and resolved. Here are items from his list:

PROBLEM	PROGNOSIS
Panic	Curable
Specific Phobias	Almost Curable
Sexual Dysfunctions	Marked Relief
Social Phobia	Moderate Relief
Depression	Moderate Relief
Obsessive Compulsive Disorder	Moderate/Mild Relief
Everyday Anxiety	Mild/Moderate Relief
Overweight	Temporary Change
Post-Traumatic Stress Disorder	Marginal Relief
Sexual Orientation	Probably Unchangeable
Sexual Identity	Unchangeable

What emerges from this list is that problems are changeable in proportion to their difficulty or depth.

Is it possible to create a parallel list of organizational problems that can and cannot be changed? We took a crack at it and came up with one.

Note that these ailments are all internal; they do not include items such as product pricing, market muscle, stock price, or the quality of the competition. The happy news is that the problems receiving the most attention in change initiatives right now—quality, processes, participation—are the most easily remedied. American business is putting its change efforts where it can do the most immediate good.

The other good news is that there are no flat-out "unchangeable" conditions. Nearly every organizational problem has a solution, if one is willing to take extreme measures. The bad news is that most solutions create undesirable side effects, and that most solutions do involve extreme measures.

PROBLEM	PROGNOSIS
Poor Product/ Service Quality	Very Curable. The best thing about the quality movement is that its methodologies—TQM, ISO 9000, zero defects, the Baldrige assessment—have a terrific impact on product/service quality.
Low Productivity	Curable. It is always possible to boost productivity. At the very worst, you simply make people work harder—problem solved.
Slow Cycle Times/ Balky Processes	Somewhat Curable. Just-in-time flow control and process reengineering have succeeded at nearly every company that has implemented them. Success can come at the cost of jobs and morale.
People Reluctant to Change	Moderate Relief. Good people with honest misgivings can be Pushed to better effort. The requirements are leadership people can follow and a core of employees and leaders who are not reluctant.
Obdurate Middle Management	Moderate Relief. Middle management has been made the butt of too many change initiatives. It is no wonder they are suspicious, and they will require more persuasion than anyone else. The most successful middle people will be those who accept the change in "job" from supervising to being a conduit for information, resources, and ideas.

PROBLEM	PROGNOSIS
People Refusing to Change	Moderate Relief. If an organization encounters mass resistance, that is actually more easily addressed than small pockets of resistance. It means the plan is flawed, or has not been communicated well. These people will adapt when Push comes to shove.
Poor Employee Morale	Mild Relief. You can boost morale in the short run by paying people more but no one is doing this. The alternative, an exhaustive assessment of why employees don't like working there, is more than most organizations can handle.
Narrow Vision	Probably Changeable. An organization whose only problem is lack of ambition or foresight can lift itself up out of its trough. But there are not many leaders powerful enough to turn around a large organization that is content with the way things are.
Short-Term Orientation	Probably Unchangeable. There is very little precedent for an organization that has lived for quarterly profit reports to suddenly care about next year, or the year after that. It is like a personality disorder requiring shock treatment to jolt the organization out of its mindset.
Narrow Constituency	Probably Unchangeable. Only dynamite will loosen up an organization that has historically devoted itself to the interests of only one group (shareholders).
Closed Culture	Probably Unchangeable, if the organization is hermetically sealed against new ideas and impulses.
People Unable to Change	Unchangeable, except by removal. In the Push/Pull continuum, file these people under Fry. Not everyone can make the change journey with you.
Obtuse Top Leadership	Unchangeable, except by removal. Even then the problem won't go away, if the culture of the organization, its board and constituents, remains rotten.

Living in the Future

Push is best exemplified by the core message of Niccolò Machiavelli: whatever gets people to do what you need them to do, is good. It generally entails the deliberate application of one kind of stress to distract people from another kind of stress. Creating or naming a "common enemy" is an oft-used Push strategy. Push can be cynical in other ways, as well, as when a leader pits one group against another so that the stronger group will survive. Or it can be benevolent, "cruel to be kind," deliberately hardening workers through arduous work and long hours in the short term to make them more competitive for the long haul. Either way, it hurts. In Push, the leader is a uniter of muscle, and Machiavellian tactics are acceptable.

In Pull, such manipulation is unacceptable. Pull is best exemplified by an insight Viktor Frankl had in the concentration camps of World War II. He noted that people could endure almost any conditions, no matter how deadly, disturbing, or disgusting, if there was reason to hope for the future. But the choice is left to the worker, whether to slog on or to give up. In the Pull approach, the leader may seek to remind the team member of the goal, but the leader has no illusions of being a "motivator." People find encouragement from leaders and incentives; but true motivation comes from within.

> **"Opportunity always knocks at the least opportune moment."**
>
> *Ducharme's Precept*

We call the Pull approach "living in the future" because that is how it works. People look beyond current unpleasantness. Then they look backward to the present and imagine the steps they had to take to get where they wanted to be. It is as if they were already living in the state they are working to create. In their hearts that is exactly what they are doing. In Pull, the leader is a uniter of hearts.

Push and Pull work best together, but there are times when they can be used individually. Push is a burning platform. If your platform is really on fire, Push is the way to go. Leaders use it in wartime, and survival in business can be likened to war. It is rude, and the fine points of etiquette may have to be set aside for the short term. If your platform is merely smoking, however, or if your workforce is already attuned to the danger surrounding them, Pull may be the better option. You have time to teach people about a new kind of organization where things do not routinely burst into flame and to enlist their cooperation in building one.

The conventional wisdom in the change business is that no one changes when the going is good. Like the alcoholic who must first hit bottom and admit to being out of control, an organization is unlikely to admit it is in trouble so long as its defense mechanisms allow it to explain away shortcomings as anomalies or one-time market events.

Fortunately, the conventional wisdom is wrong. It assumes that the change being undertaken will inevitably be seen negatively by workers, and that therefore there must be a more powerful and more negative perception about the status quo. And it overlooks the fact that there have been many good companies, such as Hewlett-Packard, 3M, that have proven themselves capable of innovation and renewal without dramatic swings back and forth into and out of the danger zone.

> **"Next week there can't be any crisis. My schedule is already full."**
>
> *Henry Kissinger*

But the point that a wake-up call (like layoffs, restructuring, or the sacking of senior managers) is sometimes necessary to focus us on change is valid. Leadership is defined in part by the ability to get people to agree both on present dangers (Push) and on a vision of the future (Pull) that will enable them to overcome those dangers.

Some leaders are so talented that they can motivate people to change with only a modestly frightening present (Pull alone). These are the true visionaries.

Some are more talented than that—they can concoct a catastrophic present out of whatever is handy. Sometimes it is necessary to isolate one group to build a coalition, to name a common enemy to compete against. But beware the leader who can lead only by dividing and demonizing. Inflaming the passions of one group against another is galvanic, but it is wrong. It is mind-Pummel of the sort practiced in the ever-shifting alliances of George Orwell's *1984*, in which Oceania was a blood brother one day and a blood enemy the next. Those whom you scapegoat today have a way of grazing on your grave tomorrow. In an age of relatively free information, people quickly learn. "Fool me once. . . ."

Big Change Versus Little Changes

One of the arguments in the change game is whether organizations should take on a whole lot, in hopes of achieving a whole lot, or just a little, on the grounds that something is better than nothing.

Reengineering is one of the "big change" initiatives. It calls for a structural overhaul of the way a business does business. So does Richard Pascale's notion of corporate "reinvention"—changing an organization from the inside out, from its outward behavior to its inner states of "being."[2] Federal Express is a company committed to total overhaul and ongoing all-out revolution to provide the most reliable service at the lowest cost. It doesn't mind installing completely new information systems costing billions every couple of years because information—where is a package? when will it arrive? by what means?—is its lifeblood.

> **"Very few things happen at the right time and the rest do not happen at all. The conscientious historian will correct these defects."**
>
> *Herodotus*

At the other end of the spectrum is the incrementalist philosophy implicit in the continuous improvement movement—the idea that many positive little changes lead to a greatly improved overall performance. United Parcel Service, FedEx's over-the-road rival, embodies this incremental philosophy, always looking to shave a second off a given task—carrying the truck keys in the left hand, for instance, rather than slipping them into a pocket from which they will have to be extracted a minute later.

The big-versus-little argument is remarkably like revolution versus evolution. Is a company better off betting everything on an all-out assault on its future? Or is that too ambitious, and so susceptible to early discouragement that the company will be worse off than when it started? The fashion is to say that complex problems require complex solutions. But initiatives that throw a team into an uproar, that draw people out of their comfort zones and shrink their change space, will result in great resistance.

Meanwhile the revolutionists sniff at incremental change as the trifling of mere "management." Leaders pursue a vision, they say, while managers—you can sense the distaste with which they utter the word "manager"—tinker with the existing system. Michael Hammer will not consider any process improvement to be "reengineering" unless it passes the acid test of being radical. To him, incremental is fine for TQM, but inadequate to the visionary warp change demanded by reengineering.

Which is better? There are two considerations. First, the question is skewed. Your organization doesn't need to decide between big and little. It merely needs to decide what it needs to do. Whether the answer is big or little is immaterial.

Second, both sides are right about something. A grand vision is an inherently better motivator than an incremental way station even if the actual change is an incremental one. Compare the motivating power of:

> "world leadership in the semiconductor industry"
> "zero defects"
> "customer satisfaction absolutely guaranteed"

with these narrow goals:

> "receivables improved from a fifty-one-day cycle to a forty-eight-day cycle"
> "overnight delivery replaced by instantaneous e-mail"
> "turn off lights in storage area when no one is in there"

All "stretch goals" are big visions. An example was British Airways' decision ten years ago to become the airline with the highest quality service and best overall reliability. At the time, BA was a stronghold of Pamper and waste. The airline adopted a Pull philosophy straight out of Viktor Frankl; it imagined itself the industry's top service performer, then took steps to make the vision reality. The goal lifted everyone's eyes out of their lunch bags and toward the horizon.

Organizations predispose themselves to failure by attempting an undertaking so ambitious that success is impossible. Stretch goals can be

> **"The lily is doubling in size every day. In thirty days it will cover the entire pond, killing all creatures living in it. The farmer does not want that to happen, but being busy with other chores, he decides to postpone cutting back the plant until it covers half the pond. The question is, on what day will the lily cover half the pond? The answer is, on the twenty-ninth day—leaving the farmer just one day to save his pond."**
>
> *Old French proverb*

laudable if they are ambitious but doable; or diabolical if their stretch exceeds any human reach.

But stretch goals that are too hard to attain, or that prove too distracting to workers, or that take too long to attain, or that involve too many prior failures can knock the stuffing out of your team, morale-wise. Wang, the creator of dedicated word processors, set development and production goals that were just too much for it. The company overextended and sought bankruptcy protection in the 1990s, reemerging only recently into a world noticeably devoid of dedicated word processors.

Likewise, IBM Rochester won the Baldrige Award in 1990 for its ambitious commitment to teams. Part of the division's metholodogy was to see all organizational processes through team eyes; at one point it counted more than 2,000 separate, formal teams. But the division got so caught up internally in teaming that it took its eyes off the technology scene unfolding outside the company. As the division's cash cow, the AS400 server, began to fade, the division's obsession with teams blinded it to the obvious need for a new flagship product.

> **"People rise to the challenge when it's their challenge."**
>
> *Anonymous*

The word "revolution" will ignite metamaniacs; but it will put everyone else's fires out—dead out. Solution: plan for ambitious, revolutionary changes, but break them into staged, achievable increments.

James Collins describes a psychological experiment showing the power of small changes. Imagine, he says, two sets of houses. With the first set you knock on each door and ask if they would mind putting a two-inch sticker on their porch saying, "I'm for a clean environment." Nearly everyone will agree to this. The other set of houses you ignore until the next round of the experiment, four weeks later. This time you haul giant four-by-eight lawn signs with the same message on them to both sets of houses, and ask if people would mind posting the big signs on their lawns. As you might expect, the households with the stickers will be far more likely to accept the bigger signs than those not given the sticker offer. The little allows them to contemplate the big.

Our view is that big and small can be combined. Dream giant dreams, but make them come true by breaking them into discrete, achievable parts.

Celebrate the little wins as if they were big ones. And avoid breaking tasks into parts so small that they actually make the job harder.

It is said that a mountain disappears more easily if you move it a grain of sand at a time, rather than putting your shoulder to it and trying to move it all at once. But first, try moving it in fistfuls—it's less aggravating.

Crossing the Swamp

A company making an organizationwide change is like a frog crossing a swamp by hopping from one lily pad to the next. We count six leaps that must be made, and they must be made in the sequence we describe. You cannot skip one, or trip over one, and ask for a do-over.

Here are the six critical moments in the change process. Each activity must meld with the activity leading up to it and the activity immediately following it. It is a loping, leaping dynamic, in which rhythm is everything.

> "Make no little plans; they have no magic to stir men's blood and probably will themselves not be realized. Make big plans; aim high in hope and work, remembering that a noble, logical diagram once recorded will not die."
>
> *Daniel Burnham*

1. **Catalyzing. This is the initiating task of leadership:** to bring an abstract idea to concrete fruition. It first appears as a sharp spike, an exclamation point in the sand. Change starts with a single individual, or a single team. They will be its champions throughout the life of the change. Starting with other leaders and drawing both momentum and clarification from them, the idea begins to make its way through the organization.

2. **Encoding. Before people can subscribe to an idea they must understand it.** The task of communicating the need for the change falls to the champions. Heisenberg's Uncertainty Principle can be applied to ideas: the act of taking their measure can alter their meaning. Care must be taken to keep the language alive and in service to the idea. The great danger in the encoding process is that the act of preserving an idea may also embalm it. Engaging the imagination

means going beyond structure and how-to—it requires humor and empathy with the people who will be bringing the idea into the work world.

3. **Imagining. Encoding happens in the leader's mind; imagining happens in the minds of close followers.** The leader's words become a picture. What was not visible before, a picture of the living future, is now swimming into view. People who will be affected by the change are able to imagine it. Understanding prevents surprises. When a critical mass of people see the vision and are willing to be held accountable for it, that is the first sign that the change is succeeding.

4. **Uniting. Once the vision is clear to a few key people, it quickly becomes visible to others.** Like dominoes, most people fall in line under its momentum; some key people may not. Leaders obtain commitment and support both formally and informally, at every level of the organization. Those with dissenting views are met halfway, heard, respected, and responded to. If their views cannot be incorporated into the change, they must decide what their role in the change will be: in or out.

> "Don't be afraid to take a big step when one is indicated. You can't cross a chasm in two small steps."
>
> *David Lloyd George*

5. **Fitting. Leadership throughout the organization is mobilized** to identify aspects of the company that don't mesh with the new vision, rooting out contradictions in systems, structures, and processes. Do your measurements, hiring, training, communications, development, rewards, and other systems advance the idea or weigh it down? While the fitting stage should not be a witch-hunt, neither should any rule or detail be immune to challenge. An organization that absorbs the new without scouring out the old can only be a mess.

6. **Gelling. (Not hardening!) Leadership drives the change down through the organization or the team**, challenging everyone to make it a part of their thinking. Work is monitored to ensure that efforts do not go slack. Achievements are celebrated, and people are rewarded for making the change succeed. What began as vague vision is now institutionalized reality—with all that this term implies about the next wave of organizational change.

Organizational Attitude

Organizational attitude is what organizational culture creates, and it is generally horrible. In a way all change initiatives are about altering this fundamental disposition, about replacing images of impossibility with images of possibility.

Anyone who thinks working in a free country is light years away from working in a totalitarian country should open their ears and really listen to the way people talk. That talk indicates that, while many of our institutions are democratic and participative, most organizations are still run, or are perceived to be run, with all the thoughtfulness of a gulag.

Think about all the places you have worked, all the lunchroom conversations you have ever participated in. Think of the attitude you see where the workers seldom smile: Toys "R" Us, Kmart. Think of places where the organization has been the butt of so many jokes the people seem defensive or defeated: Denny's, USAir, the U.S. Postal Service. What is the constant element? A thread of contempt for an enterprise that is losing battles and hammering its people:

> **"Pick battles big enough to matter, small enough to win."**
>
> *Jonathan Kozol*

- ➤ "We sell it but we don't buy it."
- ➤ "Not invented here—might be good."
- ➤ "Why try, we'll never win."
- ➤ "Quality is our least important product."

Most workers see themselves as so remote from the vision and leadership of their own organizations that the distance has created a strange rift. In this rift, noncompliers think they belong, because they know change doesn't work. The outsider is the leader who cooked up the latest change initiative. He or she hasn't gotten the full, dim picture yet.

The reason is that years of competing against one another, the brutality of restructuring, hypocrisy on topics such as quality and empowerment, and the simple unlikelihood of maintaining a top market position for very long gives most work groups a team inferiority complex. For all the stories we hear about teams and companies that have trained to think of themselves as "winners," "predators," "eagles," and "warriors," most people at most places have the attitude of "who, us?"

A lot of "imagination" goes into this game—bad imagination. It is negative and self-deceiving. The message of workplace gallows humor is that nothing good can come from this place, and nothing good can come from us. The self-insulting is a form of self-protection, carefully veiled. The game goes like this:

➤ "If we say hurtful things about ourselves, it is a charm against someone outside telling us the same thing, or worse, someone above us in the organization who wields actual power."
➤ "If we give a change 50 percent, our failure will be less than if we gave it 100 percent. That would be really depressing."

This adopted inferiority complex might be healthy in a gulag, but in an organization needing to choose between positive and negative, it is toxic. When people are technically free to express themselves and do thoughtful work but slide instead into neurotic habits of indirectness, self-loathing, and going-through-the-motions work, a great betrayal is taking place. Workers are betraying both their own talents and good intentions. And managers who let this continue unchallenged are betraying their workforce and their organizations.

> **"A great wind is blowing that gives you either imagination or a headache."**
>
> *Catherine the Great*

This attitude may seem reasonable in the light of history, but it must be undone for the sake of the future. Rebuilding confidence means teaching cynical teams how to dream again. We need to turn pessimism into optimism, and negative imagination into positive.

Igniting Organizational Imagination

Most people are brilliant at imagining negatives and miserable at imagining positives or giving the future the benefit of the doubt. Our friend the amygdala has negatives on our front stoop before our neocortex gets out of bed.

A few people are naturally adept at imagining positives. They are the metaphiles and, on the extreme end, the metamaniacs among us. If you ever come across a true metamaniac, you have someone like Dostoyevsky's character Prince Mishkin in *The Idiot*, constitutionally unable to think anything but the best of people. Dostoyevsky's title illustrates the downside of a beatific imagination—the rest of the world, hiding behind its shield of pessimism, regards you as a fool, a Pollyanna. In all fairness, that's often what you are.

But there is a middle metaphiliac ground that we can all be led to. It is simply a willingness to keep an open mind. It is an attitude of optimism.

Martin Seligman, author of *Learned Optimism*[3], says that there is much to be gained from cultivating greater innate positivity: better health, diminished stress, greater success on the job and at home. (The only significant downside Seligman found to optimism is that pessimists are usually right!)

If you are ambitious, you may want to think about strategies for increasing your people's ability to imagine positives. This does not mean doffing your critical acumen, donning your rose-colored glasses, and assuming that any proposed initiative will succeed if only you believe, Tinkerbell-style. It does mean striving to overcome your own lazy pessimism and negativity, which in its own way is as far-fetched and as unreliable as knee-jerk optimism.

> **"Always borrow money from pessimists; they don't expect to be paid back."**
>
> *Anonymous*

Here are some techniques for quashing your own pessimistic thinking before it quashes your organization:

➤ **Disagree with your own negative assessments.** Listen to what you say to yourself and the myriad judgments you make every day. "This will never work." "She's lying through her teeth." "What do they think we are, automatons?" "We'll never make that schedule." Most people stumble each day through a hailstorm of self-manufactured negativity. Studies have shown that the average elementary student hears 400 negative comments daily, versus 10 positive ones. Negativity is like the air we breathe; it is everywhere we turn. Naturally we give it credence after a while. You can't change your negative assessments until you first acknowledge that they are a fact of life—and that they are generalizations, lazy, and not a little stupid.

➤ **Replace inferior judgments with better ones.** When you make these awful pronouncements to yourself, dispute them. Get in there and act as traffic cop. Some thoughts need to be refined a bit, made more specific. Some are just not worthy of passing through your brain. It won't be easy, at first. "Well, I suppose it could work, if we had air support." "She might be lying, or I may just be unwilling to hear what she's saying." "That's a tall order. I wonder how close we can come to achieving it." "That's faster than we've ever worked before, but not by much."

➤ **Smash the box.** The customary way of thinking about the world—the paradigm—is that it is like a box people crawl into and find they cannot crawl out of. The box becomes fused to our thought patterns, it is as much a part of us as our memories and habits. In fact, that's exactly what it is. Peter Senge, author of *The Fifth Discipline,*[4] talks about the need to trash the old paradigm or way of doing things (he calls it a mental model) and either retailor it or replace it with a new one. The old saying, "It is easier to tear down than build up," is exactly wrong when applied to our own thinking. We can all imagine a better life, with us successful and sexy and employed; but it is so tough to pry away a paradigm that has imprisoned our thinking for years, and to chase it out of our heads for good. To smash the box, you need the combined power of Push and Pull. Use Push to remind you how vital the change is—it is life versus death—and Pull to think it through and make the exhilaration of success more important to you than the comfort of failure.

➤ **Deck the halls.** One way to overcome negative imagination is to subvert its imagery. If an organization's folk culture holds that nothing good can come from within its walls, take a torque wrench to the culture and show them otherwise. Hold up images of honest effort rewarded in the marketplace. Small improvements that led to greater sales. Thoughtful planning that overturned years of bad habits. Ordinary people coming up with dynamite ideas. Let people know how the marketplace works when it really works. The competitor that enjoys greater market share than you isn't any smarter. It's got the same proportion of lunkheads to rocket scientists as your organization. What it has that you lack is dream and discipline.

➤ **Spell it out.** Organizational imagination means having employees and managers alike visualize what life in the new changed environment will be like. What their new roles will be, new responsibilities, new behavioral expectations, new relationships, new knowledge requirements—specific things that will change for the better.

➤ **Create a time, space, and method for employees to create their own future.** Use what-if scenarios to expand their views from the "now" to the "tomorrow":

> "It is January 2000. Our company has doubled market share in five years without resorting to offshore alliances and without layoffs. Every employee knows what the profit goal of his or her product team is. Money we used to spend on employee turnover is now spent on continuous training. My title has changed from class 1 asssistant administrative officer to customer satisfaction agent. I have an office with a door, and a hook on which to hang my hat."

➤ **Try logotherapy.** This is the survival technique Viktor Frankl observed in concentration camps. He noticed that people who made it through the horrors of Auschwitz and other places went to another place in their minds—to the future. Instead of thinking of specific details, they focused on the important themes of life, the things that had meaning for them. They imagined what the future would be like, better in every way. Employees can do the same thing:

> "It is the future. I will provide for my family. I taught myself how to learn—the most important thing one can learn. I worked regularly for forty years, without burning out. I came to understand our customers and how the system works. While other organizations struggled and failed, ours struggled and prevailed."

With that vision of the future, they plotted the steps they needed to take to make it reality. First rule: keep breathing. Second rule: build a fire to keep the imagination alive.

➤ **Win small battles; pick low fruit.** Look for opportunities to pilot change initiatives in areas where people are willing, able, and enthusiastic to try something new that makes sense for them. As they try out their new behaviors, they are rewarded for approximate successes at first and then, after a while, only for correct behaviors. Once success is achieved, broadcast the results like crazy throughout the organization, as an inspiration not only for those who achieved the success, but as an example for those who are considering the same change but were too hesitant to be first. Before you know it, people you would have classified as foot-draggers before will be sprinting to get in front of the change parade.

➤ **Maintain a sense of humor.** Sometimes this means acquiring one. But it is important to realize that humor is how people cope with insanity. If it helps people survive in the negativity of the gulag, it can be put to work coping with the tensions and doubts of a more positive enterprise. Get people laughing and poking fun and you have, at the very least, made a team of them. Our observation is that change initiatives screw themselves by taking themselves too seriously. If you have a great cartoon or aphorism that nails your initiative to the wall, nail it to the wall. An ounce of Dilbert is worth a ton of Drucker.

The battle to ignite organizational confidence is the most important one your change initiative must fight. Do not think you are going to turn your team into a platoon of gung-ho optimists overnight. They will still be who they are.

> "To improve is to change. To be perfect is to change often."
>
> *Winston Churchill*

The truth is, we have to smash one another's boxes every day, every hour, every minute. The old paradigms never go away. Like ethanol to the alcoholic, the whiff of it is always in the air, enticing and easy. But with a little Push/Pull effort, they can be overcome. Push frightens us away from a destructive course of action; Pull taps us on the shoulder and says, "Hey, there may be a better way."

For reactives in your organization, imagination will be a foreign concept; for the occasional metamaniac, it will be a chore to drag them out of the world of imagination and back into reality. For the majority of employees, the people capable of being coaxed to a position of intermittent metaphilia, the torch of imagination must be relit and fanned fresh every morning. The flame you ignite in them is the vision of future successes that change can bring.

It isn't a game. When things as important as survival, continued employment, and community prosperity are at stake, you are willing to take greater risks. With your livelihood and your kids' future meals on the line, you don't dismiss an idea out of hand. Push gets you moving, then Pull draws you along. You engage the dream as it engages you.

NEGATIVES THEY EXPRESS TO YOU	POSITIVES TO REPLACE THEM WITH
"We're going to lose our jobs."	"You've got a chance to earn your future."
"The change is an excuse to get rid of people."	"The organization wants to become more efficient in the long term, not ruin some people and demoralize the rest in the short term."
"Why don't they just come out and say it's our fault?"	"Management accepts responsibility for ideas that fail. It is unfortunate that your future is hostage to our wisdom, but that drives us to decide as wisely as we can."
"We're better off the way we are."	"Competitors are improving their processes, so we have to improve ours."
"Notice how we never got to vote on this."	"Vote with your enthusiasm, your willingness to try, and your honest effort."
"This place was a drag to work for before and it will still be a drag to work for when this is implemented."	"Tell us how to make it better. If you don't know how to make it better, you might be happier somewhere else."
"This is just another stupid idea."	"If it's stupid, can you make it smarter? Your wisdom is hereby solicited."

NEGATIVES THEY EXPRESS TO YOU	POSITIVES TO REPLACE THEM WITH
"No one told us this was coming."	"We're telling you now. Tell us what you think about the idea itself. We're sorry if we're not communicating well; what should we do to communicate better with you?"
"This thing will do more harm than good."	"If we do not enter into the process with optimism, that prediction is self-fulfilling."
"I'll bet we can cotinue the way we were if we can get through this 'change period.'"	"The way we were is the reason this change is necessary. To survive, the organization must be alert to changes, not hide its head in the sand."
"We're closer to the customer than you are. Why don't you go away and let us do our job."	"There is no 'away' to go to. We are all in this together."

Overcoming Resistance

Though we wish it were not, resistance is a fact of human nature. It is an ancient pattern:

1. Good idea creates aura of hope.
2. Hope inspires some people but causes others anxiety.
3. Anxiety prompts resistance.
4. Resistance trashes good idea.

It doesn't always happen like this. Few lottery winners decline to accept their winnings, to sidestep the changes that wealth brings. If we win a prize, get a promotion, find money, or make a new friend, most of us react positively. It's when we perceive negative consequences to change or continued uncertainty surrounding a change that we resist.

Resistance can come from a number of sources:

➤ **Fear.** People are afraid of failing; of losing (identity, sense of belonging, control, meaning, security, etc.); of the unknown that is out there; of taking the consequences for missteps.
➤ **Low energy.** Unwillingness to commit to the change; laziness. These people see only the short-term Push and miss completely the big picture of long-term Pull.
➤ **Inertia.** We've been doing it the other way for so long and going through the motions is so easy.
➤ **Memory.** People have been challenged before and lied to before. Changemakers must overcome the history of the organization they want to change. People will want to "get even" with you, even though you aren't the party that offended them.
➤ **Percentage.** People want to know what the payoff for them will be. One task of leaders is to clarify the payoff for each individual team member.

> "Educators and futurists can prepare individuals for the future by making the different images of the future more real for them."
>
> *Carl Townsend*

To reduce resistance, try moving the change out of the shadows of negativity and into the light of day. Encourage people to participate as partners in the change, and reward them when they do. Resistance will drop, and willingness and commitment will increase.

Participation can be active, directly involved in asking and answering the questions above. Or it can be passive, simply receiving continuous communication and feedback on the process. For example, bringing problems to the group and soliciting its input to possible solutions tends to overcome many negative expectations of change. Cunningham Hamilton Quilter, the architectural firm that helped design Las Vegas' new Stratosphere, schedules weekly head sessions to do this.

The most important aspect of involvement, however, is getting people oriented toward the future—helping them anticipate and embrace future outcomes. Determine all the stakeholders in any change and try to reach an agreement on "what is a desirable outcome?" Future behaviors must be identified now. How people are to begin practicing them must be laid out, in detail, today.

What will that outcome look, feel, taste, and smell like? Is it OK? The pathways of change toward the future have many twists, turns, and detours. Encouraging people to help drive the change vehicle (determining what maps to use, what off-ramps to take) builds a commitment to the outcome of change. It also allows them to move within their comfort zones—to keep the process moving forward. In other words, it makes the change *their* change.

The Roles of the Changemaker

No change ever succeeded without talented leadership, whether at the top levels of an organization or at the team level. But the definition of leadership varies crazily from place to place. It varies from the dynamic (lead rhyming with deed) to the static (lead with the atomic symbol Pb).

> **"People change through observation, not argument."**
>
> *Will Rogers*

Larry Bossidy, CEO of Allied Signal and coiner of the "burning platform" metaphor, qualifies as the former. Any number of CEOs, who pursue connect-the-dots restructuring strategies, fail like all the others, and are sent packing like all the others, their pockets stuffed with stock options, qualify as the latter.

The key figure in successful organizational change is the changemaker. Changemakers may be CEOs or managers, team leaders or team members. They are individuals who not only champion the idea but also help steward it through the organizational ranks. A changemaker may have little position power. What is essential, however, is power of personality. Not charisma or personal dynamism; the greatest changemakers are often a little dull. We are talking about the powers of commitment, integrity, and consideration that can provide great leverage to even a shaky idea.

The Changemaker as Pathmaker

If your team or organization is living in the present, the changemaker lives a week or a year in the future, relaying descriptions of what lies ahead.

Most important, the changemaker creates a pathway people can follow, to bring them out of the wilderness and into the promised land.

The idea of the pathway is vital because it links the notions of Push and Pull. The leader who announces that the platform is on fire, but does not point to an escape exit, a path leading away from the fire, is not a Push leader. He is just somebody yelling "Fire!"

The pathway is the vision of safety that allows people to endure the distress of the current emergency. On a burning platform it may mean lifeboats, life preservers, helicopters plucking people from the waves. In an organization it means new rewards, policies, and procedures that give hope so that people can continue to commit to the company's prospects; and it means compassionate treatment of those who don't make it through the emergency. The pathway is the positive outcome that all our work is about.

The Changemaker as Integrator

Changemaking requires the use of both your brain halves. Any knack or openness you have for change arises on your right side. But your ability to identify, analyze, critique, and monitor your change occurs on the left side. If you tilt too strongly to one side or the other, you will not be an effective changemaking leader. But finding a balance is tricky. By definition, a left-brain orientation can only analyze what is, what has been safely corralled, defined, and systematized. It takes imagination and a kind of creative recklessness to accept things that are still taking shape, and that may never be subdued to the analyst's satisfaction.

> "If there is another way to skin a cat, I don't want to know about it."
>
> *Steve Kravitz*

But even right-brain people get spooked by the unknown. It is a natural human inclination, upon encountering an unknown entity, to fill in the blanks with negativity. The footsteps you hear behind you on a dark street are never those of a benefactor, until you turn and see someone returning your wallet. The boss's new merit-based compensation plan sounds like pure pain until the particulars are spelled out. The phone call in the middle of the night always means someone has died, until you answer, and it is a man calling about the Irish Sweepstakes.

A changemaker's job is to make change safe for the people it affects. If you wish to be one, but your strengths are one-sided, team up with another, or two others, who can bring balance to the change leadership and help you push it through.

The Changemaker as Negotiator

We use the word "negotiate" to mean different things. We negotiate a river, making our way past the snags and shoals to our destination. And we negotiate deals, cutting away extraneous issues, many of them charged with emotion, to obtain the ends that we desire.

Both senses of the word apply to negotiating change. Change is both an intricate waterway to make one's way through, and a thicket of conflicting wants and tensions that must be resolved to the satisfaction of all parties.

In circumstances where you know you will never have to deal with the other party again, as in a house sale, win/lose negotiation can't be beat.

> **"Never doubt the power of a small group of committed people to change the world. That's about the only way it has ever happened in the past."**
>
> *Margaret Mead*

Yet business gurus pooh-pooh win/lose negotiation as antediluvian. They're right, it's Pummel. And it has no place in intra-organization dealings. A leader who tries to load all the pain of change on one constituency squanders any chance he or she might have of being trusted by that group later, or by any group who witnessed what was done to that group. The essence of successful negotiating between parties who must continue doing business with one another is, therefore, trustworthiness.

A union steward praised British industrialist Sir John Harvey-Jones as a man who, when he makes a promise, never lets you down. "He's the sort of fellow who, when you have a pint with him, you don't have to look to see if he took your shoes off."[5]

Jim Kouzes, author of *Credibility*, tells the story of Patricia Carrigan, who, in her first official act as plant manager at the GM parts plant in Bay City, Michigan, took several days to travel through the plant and introduce herself individually to each worker. It was an unprecedented gesture, and it left many workers open-mouthed. A few remarked that, in the fifteen years that the previous plant manager had held the job, they had never once seen him, much less spoken with him.

Just seeing her come by, say a few words, and smile had a powerful impact on employees. People rally around self-revealing behaviors.

Physical proximity sends several messages: *I acknowledge your existence. I do not think I am too good for you. I am not hiding from you. I do not have eleven and a half heads.*

Said one of Carrigan's front-line workers, "There ain't a phony bone in her body."[6]

A proper change is a negotiated partnership, by which parties within an organization create a deeper relationship by agreeing to be open with one another.

Negotiations are by no means guaranteed success. Bad faith is a fact of life, but it must not be presumed—for that is bad faith itself. Think of the negotiating situation as a balancing act between intelligence (what you already know) and information (what they tell you). The two should grow together and merge into a seamless whole. When the two begin to diverge, something is wrong.

Negotiations don't have to nail down every last contingency. Why not define certain contingencies to the advantage of both sides? Max Bazerman and Margaret Neale suggest that parties negotiating a change lessen the risk by offering rewards and compensations for successes and shortfalls. They call it "making a bet."[7]

> **"What you don't know will always hurt you."**
>
> *First Law of Blissful Ignorance*

If the two sides disagree on the outcome or value of a change proposition, why not word the agreement so that it reflects and rewards those differences? Labor can tell management, if we fail to achieve your productivity goals, we'll give up our raise. Management can come at it from the opposite perspective: achieve the goal, and the bonus is yours. It's not real money until and unless both sides win. I won't mind paying you money if you help me make more money. You won't mind paying me more if I give you greater value than you expect.

The bottom line in change negotiation is to break out of the irrational straitjacket that the two sides create by withholding information. The changemaker takes the lead in disclosing information and laying cards on the table for all to see.

All change is negotiated, and all negotiation is learning.

The Changemaker as Game Player

Organizational politics can be likened to a game in which no party wants to yield any advantage to any other. Too many years of departmentally and functionally divided operations, and too many years of management-labor conflict, have turned most organizations into battle-scarred turf zones. Intra-corporate adversarialism ("The enemy isn't the competition, it's those people in finance/strategic planning/ engineering/quality management.") is too often the order of the day. Tip-toeing through this minefield of bad feeling requires an unlikely combination of delicacy and forthrightness.

First and foremost, if the game in the organization has been interteam feuding, then the game must be changed. If the game was competition within the company, it must be changed to competition against other companies. What was once a hot war between management and workers may be replaced with a true peace, in which both sides work together in harmony, or, more likely, a cold war in which people acknowledge disagreements, but agree with the larger purpose of survival in the marketplace.

> "I meant what I said and I said what I meant.
> An elephant's faithful one hundred percent."
>
> *Horton, via Dr. Seuss*

Game theory trains us to see from the other side's perspective. We all know managers and team leaders who whine that they can't get their employees to see things from the customer's point of view. But have those managers or team leaders tried seeing things from their own workers' or team's point of view?

Game theory is a Push discipline. It can be cynical, and it is unabashedly manipulative. But it can be an invaluable tool in focusing a group on the things it is good at—its best game.

Played well, enemies can become collaborators, and a pattern of years of distrust and demonization can be reversed.

The Changemaker as Confessor

A fashionable role for leaders in American business is that of the organizational messiah. The organizational messiah always has all the answers, and plays to the hilt the role of indispensable know-it-all, without whom the organization would founder. These people are less leaders than statues of leaders: everything is about them. As changemakers they are a walking disease.

True changemakers operate outside themselves, their ego, and their need for recognition. It is in their nature to be interested in the well-being of all parties in a change effort, because without their success, the change has little chance of succeeding.

So their method is essentially Socratic, eliciting information, asking questions, never satisfied with the surface explanation, always going deeper to learn more.

Listening is a Pull discipline. If you are a changemaker, you have faith that people will lend their support if it is in their interest to do so. It is great to go into negotiations with a dossier full of information prepared by your own analysts. The data are usually better, however—more accurate, more reliable, more balanced—if the other party simply tells you what they are.

Changemaking is hard mental work, and there is a temptation to keep the gears turning at all times. Resist the temptation. When the people are talking, listen without worrying about your response. The information in their remarks is valuable and provides many clues, without which the changemaker will not be making much change.

Just listen.

The Changemaker as Salesperson

> "It is not enough to succeed. Others must fail."
>
> *Gore Vidal*

Making a change is like making a sale. The best salespeople understand that success lies not in pushily driving through your selling and personal agendas, as Willy Loman tried to do in Arthur Miller's *Death of a Salesman*, but in demonstrating imagination and empathy—getting outside your agendas long enough to learn what the prospective buyer's agenda is. And tailoring the product to meet that customer agenda to a "T."

The best salesperson is like a tailor, always measuring to see what will fit, unafraid to lay hands in unfamiliar places. The changemaker must treat the organization, or the team, as a customer, to be listened to, understood, fitted, and served. The mistake most often made is to confuse the changemaker's first change solution—his or her "product"—with the final, most satisfactory one, and the task of change as a simple matter of convincing the organization to buy the off-the-rack product. The ideal solution is a cocreation of the changemaker and everyone else in the organization or on the team. The "product" of change must be everyone's; it is always tailor-made.

There are a million opinions on what it takes to be a good salesperson. Some are visions of undefeatable confidence—keep knocking till someone lets you in. Some are invitations to flimflammery—mastering the tricks of persuasion and beating customers over the head with them. But one can imagine a model for honest, proactive conversation that attunes itself to identifying customer needs and meeting them in concert with the customer. That's the kind of salesperson that can effect change, not the Willy Loman kind. Tough but detached. Tough enough to be turned down the first few times and keep coming back. Detached enough that the change idea is never yours alone and is always a work in progress.

Growing Your Own (Changemakers)

In the brutal business of separating human wheat from human chaff, there is a wonderfully usable rule of thumb called the 80/20 law. It states that 80 percent of good things come from 20 percent of your supply pool. Thus 20 percent of customers account for 80 percent of sales; 20 percent of products account for 80 percent of sales; and 20 percent of salespersons account for 80 percent of sales. For all we know, 20 percent of chickens lay 80 percent of eggs.

> **"Attention must be paid."**
>
> Linda, in Death of a Salesman

Now apply the 80/20 law to hiring and organizing. It would be lovely just to hire people who are eager beavers for organizational change—the proactives we have been talking about. Simply identify the 20 percent that can achieve 80 percent of desired results. Use tests, interviews, and references to find the metaphiles, then hire them.

But there's a catch; a handful of catches, actually:

➤ *First*, there are never enough metaphiles to go around. People with proven change talents don't spend a lot of time in the job market; if no one snaps them up, they'll hire themselves and go into business on their own.

➤ *Second*, being in demand, born or trained metaphiles come at a premium. In the era of the new worker, the best workers will cost you. To hire one away from another organization, you will need to strategically place a pot of gold in your doorway. Two pots, maybe.

Three Do-or-Die Rules for Leaders

Mistakes are made in organizations. But there are mistakes that must never be made, as recovery from them is virtually impossible.

1. **Lay off the duplicity.** Leadership can't play internal groups off against one another, telling one group one thing and another group another. People have too much information today to be consistently fooled. They will find out, and you will be out.
2. **Lay off the executive ego.** Senior managements routinely doom change initiatives by investing too much of themselves in them. The idea quickly becomes equated with the individual, complicating the picture for the unpersuaded. It's great when the executive in question is universally admired and revered. But that is seldom the case. Too many leaders see managed change as their legacy, like Stalin's Five-Year Plans. Allow daylight to creep between you and your idea. Any change that is inseparable from the leader who puts it in play has little chance of success.
3. **Lay off the intimidation.** The Push leader activates people by describing the need for immediate change, in the abstract. The Pummel leader goes further than that, motivating by threatening personal retribution. When people live in that kind of fear, they resort to their glands and park their brains at the door.

➤ *Third*, the best way to screen for metaphiles is not to hand out standardized personality tests looking for Expressives and Drivers, or Extrovert/Thinkers. Living live wires have better things to do than fill out multiple-choice tests. Indeed, there is a glaring paradox in using a static form to seek out nonstatic individuals. Compound that error with the kinds of people in charge of hiring in some organizations, and you will almost certainly chase away four metaphiles for every one you lure inside. (Another 80/20 rule!)

➤ *Fourth*, your pressing objective in making a hire is not chameleon tendencies, it's the knowledge and skills to do a certain job—patent attorney, plastics engineer, air traffic controller. Add metaphilia to this basic job requirement and you have really thinned out the herd.

➤ *Fifth*, if every company hires only the top 20 percent of candidates, there will be blood in the streets. What's the difference between discriminating on the basis of one condition beyond people's control (the personality they are born with) and another (skin color, national origin, physical disability, etc.)? Change books don't advise consulting with your corporate lawyer willy-nilly, but on this issue we'll make an exception.

So if your company or team can't effectively screen affordable job candidates for innate positive change attitudes, what can you do?

You can grow your own. Indeed, you have to. You can't send away everyone now working for you. All but a small fraction of them have the potential to move in the direction your organization needs to move, if they are engaged with the right combination of Push and Pull.

You can also commit your organization to a training regimen that unmistakably spells out your change plans, the tools at workers' disposal, and what is expected of newcomers and old-timers alike.

Do not overemphasize existing skills when you hire. In the new world of work, the functional training your high-level applicants have had—a degree in business administration, say, with six years of managerial experience—is no guarantee the candidate will be able to move with your organization's motion.

At the lower levels, people will be showing up at your HR door with nothing like the skills your organization needs. They need to be trained, so why not pick the ones who seem most trainable?

More important than skills is the attitude candidates bring to the work. You must not hire people accustomed to the extreme ends of the change scale—those who have been Pummeled into slavish compliance, or Pampered into a sense of feckless entitlement. You will need people who are susceptible either to the guidance of a Pull approach or the unapologetic manipulation of Push.

When hiring for a change, heed the old injunction to "Hire good people." When we say good, we mean it quite literally. Good people are people with the capacity for responsible ethical conduct. They have the underappreciated quality of considerateness, the willingness to give other people's ideas equal weight as one's own. Empathy is imagination, and imagination precedes change. This capacity is the secret source of team strength.

Unless they are Ted Bundy-type sociopaths, able to fool you with psychotic sincerity, you don't need a personality test to identify who has integrity and who does not. They will have track records, solid references, and they will impress you with their ability to listen to what you are saying, adopt new ways of working, accept higher standards for accountability and communication, and meet you halfway in the change process. They may not be natural-born metaphiles, but they are good enough.

Organizing for Change

The conventional system of organizing workers is no good. This system breaks down each job into a description, a pay scale, and intervals along that scale. It is the heart and soul of the machine approach to human engineering that so many change initiatives seek to change. Yet in organization after organization, everything is subjected to change except this machine.

It takes only a few questions to put this system on the defensive:

➤ If people are expected to do whatever needs to be done, wherever it needs doing, why limit job descriptions to functions? If everyone in a total quality or empowered organization is expected to do everything, what is the point of finely detailed job descriptions?
➤ If people are expected to work on teams and for team rewards, what good is an individual-based job classification and compensation system?
➤ If people are expected to be flexible enough to move quickly to meet customer and technology demands, what system of index cards—and the long-term promises they appear to be making—can keep up with them?

Can a modern organization get by without its job bureaucracy? One alternative model put forward is the free-agency system in baseball. Individuals are paid according to the value they are expected to add, with incentive clauses for individual and team success. Free agency fits in completely with the global market that has developed in recent years. We have seen the demise of cradle-to-grave employment and even of the concept of the job itself, as organizations have moved toward a system of contracts with leased workers, temporaries, and outsource partners.

We all know people who have lost their jobs to downsizing and have been "hired" back the next day as consultants, at higher pay but with no benefits. They have been made free agents, and since they are good at what they do, they will prosper. Some companies farm out whole competencies, even mission-critical ones: Volvo and Chrysler don't even have in-house car designers any more.

But there are problems with the baseball analogy. A happy team cannot have stars whose high salaries are a ceiling quashing new players' aspirations. Individual incentives (pitching 250 innings, making 1,000 sales calls) cannot take precedence over team goals (making the play-offs, customer satisfaction). Though they do have their place: they signal to the individual that the organization wants to know and to meet their needs. This compact is the centerpiece of the New Age organization.

With thoughtful management, an organization can devise a system that organizes around group performance and individual needs, a system that knows what people want from their employment and rewards them in kind.

Motorola invites teams to help define not only what their goals and objectives should be, but also how they will be compensated. A 1991 study[8] of work-group compensation showed that 72 percent are moving away from the conventional system of job classifications and step increases. Some use gainsharing to augment conventional pay; others find ways to reward new skills and knowledge acquired. Some organizations tie rewards to the success of the change initiative itself: Michael Hammer describes one system where employees are paid extra if the reengineering effort they are engaged in meets expectations.[9]

One way to sidestep corporate hiring practices is to move hiring down to business unit levels. Instead of advertising corporatewide for new hires, turn the hiring process over to each business unit or team, as has been done at Eastman Kodak.[10] That's where the people are who will know who will be suitable and who won't. Demassified hiring is a revolutionary move and will rattle corporate cages, but it has worked wherever it has been tried.

First We Kill the Consultants

Consultants can be either the angels or devils of your change initiative. Or even both simultaneously.

They can be invaluable in that they can bring in ideas that a company has been unable to grow in its own soil. They have knowledge about what works and what doesn't that can spare an organization a lot of suffering in the implementation phase. An outsider can bring genetic diversity to an inbred organization, and that's good.

But this very asset can work against an organization's taking ownership of its changes. It's easier to resist an outsider's ideas and easier to demonize them when things hit a rough spot. If your organization is so weak it needs outsiders to decide vital strategic matters, maybe it should just heave itself off the nearest cliff.

Then there is the matter of expense. Consultants often come to organizations during their hour of direst need. The consultant's, that is. How many shekels will you pour into their pockets before they pronounce you healthy enough to carry on without them?

Finally there is the question of originality. How unique is this great new idea, anyway? Though they never acknowledge any intellectual debt to one another, don't the ideas of every change consultant or author seem awfully similar to the ideas of just about every other change consultant or author? Instead they create proprietary systems of organizational theory and sell their ideas as unique. They may do this in the same breath that they advise companies against using proprietary systems of their own.

Next time you want to get a rise out of your consultants, tell them you overheard their staff use the phrase "full wax treatment." Ask what it means.

Communicating for Change

There are monasteries today that maintain a vow of continuous silence to shut out spiritual distractions. These places deliberately insulate themselves from modernity and change. The "businesses" all involve processes that were pretty much optimized ten centuries ago: fruit picking, hot metal book publishing, and brandy making. They have to follow old methods because, unable to communicate the way most people do, it would be impossible for them to adapt to new ones.

The moral of this story: if you are going to spend your life working with people but not talking to them, you can't be in a cutting-edge industry. An all-monk skunkworks won't fly.

You might not think communicating is a difficult topic. All it is is people talking and listening.

On the contrary, everyday communication is fraught with misfires, miscues, and false starts, and communicating for change is not like ordering a sandwich in a restaurant or waving to a friend. Change is dangerous; sandwiches and hellos are not. Though the neocortex may leap at the chance to grow and learn, the amygdala bridles at threatening new information. The team leader who forgets that team members hear information according to their own needs is not team leader very long. Communicating change requires scrupulous honesty, because to be caught in a lie is to end communication. But it also requires artistry and delicacy; artistry to select words that cut straight to the emotional heart of the matter and delicacy so as not to slice through an artery.

Selective Perception

People hear things in radically different ways, all the while nodding as if they were tracking what is being said on radar. And they call the nodding communicating. ("I understand," he lied.)

Communication Philosophies of the Four Attitudes

PUMMEL	PUSH	PULL	PAMPER
"We'll tell you what we think you need to know. If we didn't say it, you didn't need it."	"We'll explain what you have to do to survive."	"Let's stay in touch. If you have a better idea, speak up."	"Any time you want something explained, just ask us and we'll explain it to you."

When people are seeing the same thing in different ways, they start to wonder about one another. "Is he nuts?" "Wow, she is really off in la-la land." "Is it smart for me to lay my cards on the table with someone this unreliable?"

This has probably happened to you. You'll be talking with a colleague about a proposed plan. You'll both be nodding and taking notes. You're thinking, "God, this is good. We're on exactly the same wavelength." The next day, you meet again, compare notes, and realize you're a million miles apart. She's doing one thing, you're doing something very different; she's focusing on an aspect of the proposal you weren't even aware of. How could you both think you were in such agreement and be so far apart?

You each heard different things from the same conversation based upon each person's predetermined focus or priority. Each was listening to their "inner voice," not to what the other person was saying. The conversation founders on the shoals of each side's self-fascination. The conversation is nothing but a dual-monologue.

When communication is this shaky, the trust that links teams and individuals begins to dissolve. To reverse this dissolution, we need to look inside human nature and understand the reasons for confusion.

First of all, we select what we perceive. We have to. If we perceive everything we see, our brains won't have time to categorize it all. So we all have different ways of pre-editing what we are going to think about. It is like note-taking during a lecture. A select few of us can so successfully condense the meaning that a stranger could reconstruct what was said. Some take notes that only they can decipher later. Others think they're taking good notes at the time but can't read their own writing afterward. The best some of us can manage is drawing pictures of Kilroy peeking over a table edge.

> "We trained hard. But it seemed that every time we were beginning to form into teams, we would be reorganized. I was to learn later in life that we tend to meet any new situation by reorganizing. And what a wonderful method it can be for creating the illusion of progress while producing confusion, inefficiency, and demoralization."
>
> *Gaius Petronius Arbiter,*
> *The Satyricon,*
> *first century, AD*

We select what we wish to perceive based on our expectations and our needs. In managing change, we need to know how individuals are perceiving the change idea and present the change to suit each person's perceptions.

A team member who sees the change as positive needs only to be Pulled by the power of the idea. One who interprets the change negatively may need to be jolted by the Push of fear, as a reminder that failure to change is also calamitous.

➤ **Expectations.** If our first impression of someone is negative ("She is a stranger. What is that language she's speaking?"), we will then pick out details that confirm the expectation. ("I hate the dress. And what about that thing in her nose?") We expect certain things to be true and sure enough, we find them. If our first expectation of a change program is that it will be annoying and unrewarding, we will be glad of subsequent information that confirms that dismal outlook. So changemakers have to sense from the get-go what expectations are in the air—dispel the wrong or pessimistic ones, and allow more positive expectations to form ("Who would like to still be here a year from now, making more money?").

How Different Types of Personalities are Likely to Communicate

REACTIVES (and extreme cases)		PROACTIVES (and extreme cases)	
ANALYTICALS (Metamorons)	**AMIABLES (Metaphobes)**	**DRIVERS (Metaphiles)**	**EXPRESSIVES (Metamaniacs)**
Uncomfortable with change but often gifted at critiquing and explaining it.	Naturally skilled in conversation, but not in directing it toward action.	Natural teachers and defenders of change. Not always great listeners.	Terrific emoters and inspirers. Shaky reporters.

➤ **Needs.** Someone who is hungry is more likely to be on the lookout for food than a good detective story. Someone worried about job security is not going to tune in to your lecture on risk-taking. Before they start beating the drum for change, changemakers must sense what people's current and pressing needs are, and take steps to meet or at least acknowledge them and their importance. In an organization in which change thrives, leaders have managed to address existing needs, and then to move the organizational change onto people's need list.

Organization

Information that we edit in our heads must then be arranged in some way so it can be looked at. Human beings have devised two clever methods to do this. One is called *figure-ground*. That is, one set of information becomes the figure we focus on and everything else becomes the ignored background. You can look at the forest, or you can look at the trees, but few of us can see both the forest and the trees at the same time. You may honestly think you are focusing on defect prevention in a presentation you're making to your group, because that was its broad theme, whereas several listeners may focus on the three or four processes you singled out for criticism in the talk, thinking that was what you cared about and the rest was just fluff.

Who is right? It's like asking if a zebra is black with white stripes or vice versa. You may both be right. But the burden is upon each of you to stop before the conversation concludes and you stagger back to your offices to do the wrong thing, and ask each other if you agree on what the main points of the discussion were and what action each person intends to take. And write that action down to prevent "action mutation" later.

The second way we organize information is through closure. Closure is one of the most reflexive behaviors in the human repertoire. We were talking about closure when we talked about the brain and how we tend to fill in blank spots in our understanding with things we already understand. It is the principle that where there's smoke, there's fire. In the case of change challenges, unless we are among the select class of proactives, we paint in the unknown parts negatively, because we have all suffered through some great leap forward that left us with hoofprints on our backs.

Closure isn't necessarily negative; we could as easily paint in an unfinished painting with pastels as shades of gray. But it usually is. So if one group is briefed on a restructuring effort and yours isn't, you imagine the worst—that your continued existence with the organization is a day-to-day thing. Many times we see only a part of what is going on, but will organize it by filling in what is missing. The parts we fill in are as real to us as what we have actually observed. This is why rumors are so easy to start, so powerful once they have started, and so hard to put an end to.

The best way to overcome this reflex is, when you feel the hair on the nape of your neck starting to stick straight out, to stop and check out the facts. Ask the other party flat out what his or her intentions are, what will happen to you, or what else has been left out of the painting.

Workers confronting an ambitious change program have every reason to be distrustful. They know that management knows things that they would desperately like to know as well. So long as the atmosphere is contaminated by this distrust, there is zero chance that change will go forward.

To break the closure deadlock, team leaders and managers must disclose like crazy. Should you blurt out your most important confidence, the maximum concession you are willing to make in return for cooperation? Maybe not; politics is politics. But you can give hints as to what is important to you or what matters most to you: changes in compensation, job stability, access to tools and information. Sharing information communicates the idea that mutual gain is a possibility—that I don't have to make you fail for me to succeed.

Does this mean that the enlightened manager promptly hands over all sensitive information to the other side? No. It does mean that people trying to get change through have to prioritize their concerns. They are not at the table to keep secrets or to gain personal credit for being "tough," but to bring good deals back to their constituency. If sharing information moves the process toward a better deal, it is a sensible strategy.

The best way for changemakers to prevent these kinds of misunderstandings is not to give people half-painted paintings. The old management adage that you give information to people only on a "need-to-know" basis is a throwback to the bygone era; in the age of change people need to know almost everything.

Muddled Interpretation

Selecting and organizing information only accounts for half of our confusion. To understand the other half, we have to look at the goofy ways we interpret things. Our interpretations are affected by any number of factors, such as: the ambiguity of the situation, our attitude, and our orientation.

➤ **Ambiguity.** A favorite banner of ours was on the shop floor of a plastics plant in Rochester, New York. It said simply, "We stand behind our workers." It was a running joke among workers at the extrusion machines. They took it to mean that management was using employees as a human shield to deflect incoming flak. Ambiguity is not the fault of human nature; it's the fault of language and syntax. A given statement can be taken many ways. Changemakers need to stop before telling their favorite stories and ask themselves: "Does this story clarify the picture we're trying to get across, or muddle it even more?"

➤ **Attitude.** How you say something is as important as what you say. If a speaker is exhausted, the message communicated will also communicate exhaustion. Our moods and attitudes are always changing, and the rhythms are not always conducive to clarity. People can tell you are in a mood; it is transparent in the tone of your voice.

Then there is raw emotion, like anger or fear or contempt, which can turn a simple statement inside out. (Say, "You're by far the best person for the job" twice, the first time straight, the second time sarcastically.)

You know what your attitude is when you speak, but others don't. Worse, since attitude is conveyed unconsciously in your tone of voice or facial expression, sometimes you don't even know, and others will see through you. They will see through you when you are distracted, or when you know you are not telling the complete truth, or when you are compelled to make statements you do not personally agree with.

Effective changemakers make no pretense about communication being simple. They acknowledge the emotional pitfalls in any declaration. If you're tired or distracted, acknowledge the fact and apologize for it. If you don't agree with your own words, something is very wrong. The worst thing you can do is give a "happy face" talk when inside you are one big pulsing stomach ulcer.

➤ **Orientation.** When a New York woman and a South Carolina man talk, the result is not always 100 percent agreement and retention.

Culture, personality type, accent, race, geography, politics, philosophy, and education all wreak havoc on our ability to give one another a fair hearing. Imagine how different people from different groups will receive your pep talk about process reengineering if the following seemingly innocent words appear in your remarks: *liberal-minded, sacred cow, salesladies, kosher, plain vanilla, working class, orientation, local yokels, head of household, Christmas season, empty-nesters, crippling, unskilled, point man, upscale, lifestyle, over the hill.*

Every word and phrase has an emotional temperature, and our own temperatures rise and fall, often irrelevantly, with each one. Every moment someone dwells on an irrelevancy is a moment a relevancy falls through the cracks. Anyone thinking that the logical language of business automatically transcends these divisions should lie down and let the blood return to the brain.

Other Considerations

➤ **Process.** People generally do not oppose the content of proposed change—more attention to quality, flow, worker participation, etc. What riles them is the way it is rolled out. The *how* often matters more than the *what*. We all have a crawling dread of a bad process, loaded with miscues, miscommunications, eleventh hour revisions and the like. Effective change demands continuous communication—before, during, and after the change process.

➤ **Anticipation.** Good communication during change requires that you know what people are worried about and address their concerns in advance. Expect questions like:

➤ How do we plan to get from here to there?
➤ What is involved in this change process?
➤ Who will do what, and how will they do it?
➤ What do we have to learn that we don't know now?
➤ When will we start to see results?
➤ How will we be kept informed of progress?
➤ What is expected of me?
➤ Is this change the only change planned, or is it one of many?
➤ Is management committed to this idea or is it a lone ranger pilot?

➤ **Redundant retransmissions.** Saying something one time, one way, won't get through to very many people. Effective change communication acknowledges that different people need to hear things in different ways, and that nearly everyone has to be reminded periodically of what the plan is all about. Use multiple channels of communication to answer and update people so that each individual feels less a victim of, and more an active participant in, the change process. Examples of multiple channels: meetings, memos, Q&A sessions, bulletin boards, employee newsletters, pay envelope stuffers, open discussions, ad hoc committees, informal networks, grapevines, and one-to-one meetings with everyone involved.

➤ **Two-way.** It is an absurdity, but there are companies that have implemented employee involvement programs by decree. "You will be empowered—that is all!" No matter what the initiative, people need the sense that the plan welcomes feedback before, during, and after its implementation. Suggestion boxes work, provided they are emptied daily and every suggestion is personally responded to. Even better are in-person give-and-take sessions with changemakers.

➤ **Predictability.** The more you keep your word, and the closer the future resembles what you said it would be, the better. Change is easier to handle if your team has a clear understanding of what it will look like and feel like beforehand. Unless it is their birthday, no one likes a surprise. Even metaphiles do not like being thrown a steady stream of curveballs and sucker pitches.

Training Versus Learning

Training and learning imply similar things. But they represent diametrically different approaches to solving business problems.

We know what training is. Employers identify shortfalls in what employees know—what ISO 9000 is, what common causes are, what a feedback loop is and how to keep one open. Then they do whatever they have to do to get that information into the employee's head. "Training" is traditional education, symbolized in college coats of arms with the medieval icon of a lamp of knowledge pouring its oil in the passive student's ear.

Language and Change

Sometimes people don't listen to their own words, and the misunderstandings that occur are hilarious, or embarrassing. Michael Hammer delights in recalling the words of Leonid Kravchuk, president of the beleaguered new regime of The Ukraine, in a speech to parliament: "Yesterday we stood poised on the verge of the abyss. Today we take a great step forward!"

Language difficulties also cause problems. John Kennedy's famous saying, "Ich bin ein Berliner," meant "I am a Berliner (a jelly doughnut)" to Germans. He should have dropped the *ein.*

Spelling counts, too. A devastating Dilbert strip recently showed the dimwit boss posting a corporate TQM manifesto. Workers clustered around the bulletin board reading about the company's lofty ambitions. One worker observes, "I thought quality had a U in it."

Though training is a $45-billion industry and a vital item in every organizational budget, it is typically concerned with the humdrum how-to side of organizational affairs—how to do quality, how to do JIT, how to do business process reengineering. Training defines itself as an information delivery system. Whether it is conducted by people in classrooms or on the job, or by machine in the form of videotape or multimedia CD-ROM, it is a static, measurable thing that Pushes employees to the present desired state, as defined by management. It is not a desired thing by itself; it is a means to an end.

Learning is almost the diametric opposite of training. It is not a "business," yet it is everyone's business. Though it makes no one any money, it is the Pull allowing people in an organization to draw near to their cherished objectives. It happens entirely in the learner's head and requires no technology whatsoever. It is by its very nature unmeasurable and undefinable. Learning is an end in itself, not a means to an end.

The two are seldom spoken of together, but they are like the two charged rails of organizational change. One Pushes ("Now hear this!"); one Pulls ("What do you think?"). No organization can leave the station without a determined effort to continually increase its knowledge base.

But the two are often at odds with one another. Training wants to cover the greatest amount of ground in the shortest time, with the fewest interruptions and the highest degree of learner homogeneity. It wants above all to be finished and get paid. Learning, by contrast, knows no clock, respects no formal structure, and occurs in as many ways, and at as many paces, as there are learners.

A lot of lip service has been paid to "the learning organization," a phrase coined by Peter Senge in *The Fifth Discipline*. In the Senge view, the long-term goal of any organization is not making and selling more and more widgets, but managing the knowledge process that allows the company to continuously discover better ways to meet the needs of its widget customers. Some organizations, like global consultancy Booz-Allen & Hamilton, are building it into their structure by creating the new top management position of "chief knowledge officer." The CKO's task: to herd the superintelligent space cats mentioned earlier; to keep knowledge moving between membranes; to manage the company's smarts.

Learning is a component of the philosophy of continuous improvement that holds that one is never done learning, that an organization continually expands its knowledge to create its future. The truly important items in a widget company's inventory are not its widgets, but the knowledge it has about its core competency to provide widget solutions and the malleable intellect of its workers.

All this is a cautionary note reminding us to keep our priorities straight. Focusing on training as an end unto itself is great for the training company, but maybe not so great for your company. All the value for your organization is concentrated at the learning end of the horse, not the training end.

Training is product, and it is what you shop for. Learning is process, the goal of the training. As your organization grapples with its change initiatives, you will want to run reality checks to make sure you are learning, and not just training. Consult a checklist like this one:

➤ **Do you know exactly what knowledge you want to see increased?** Is it generic, like statistical process control or ISO 9000, or specific to your industry, like restaurant service quality management? Do you have that knowledge yourself? Are you competent to evaluate it? How well does the program you are looking at mesh with your needs? Is it efficient—does it overdo or underdo? It can be a great training tool for someone else, but the pits for your group.

➤ **Good training overcomes workers' objections to it.** We've all got bad attitudes, especially when the presumption is that we don't know something. Good training does something from the very outset—uses humor, gets people involved, explains why the training is good for the organization and for the learner—to knock the chip off learners' shoulders.

➤ **Good training should have some kind of human component** beyond the sales pitch of the person who sells it to you. We all need a hand to hold at some stage. It may include facilitation, consultation, installation, customization, tech support, or training of trainers. Even a CD-ROM can embed a level of human interaction (albeit a cold one) to relieve the mechanical flow of information.

➤ **Is the training consonant with your organizational culture?** A Cadillac company won't be happy settling for deliberately cheesy low-end, wham-bam materials. Likewise, an organization noted for its diversity will want that diversity addressed. Training should adjust for the kind of people being trained—even training in a box.

➤ **What will be the outcome of the training?** What proof will you have that the training "took"? Testing is the answer, either formally, with pencil and paper, or informally, by evaluating subsequent behavior. CD-ROMs teaching ISO 9000 or quality techniques are wonderful in that they self-test on the fly. People learning how to cut and paste, for instance, cannot go on to the next lesson until they show that they actually can cut and paste.

➤ **What happens next?** Is the training product a one-shot deal, or will you want to turn to the same source for repeat sessions, or extension products? Is it important to develop a longer-term relationship with the trainer as a sort of strategic partner? Or is it, See you later, facilitator?

Successful training does more than pour information in people's ears. At its best it engages the learner's imagination, triggering a positive change in behavior that Pulls toward greater organizational success. When training does this it crosses the boundary to learning.

Rewarding Change

How can an organization move purposefully toward the future when its people are being paid to live in the past?

We think too narrowly about the whole concept of compensation and reward. We consider only the positive side of the spectrum. If organizations can treat (compensate) their people in a full range of ways ranging from Pummel to Pamper, we can see the full range of rewards and compensations from carrot to stick:

If you think of the whole picture of compensation, rewards, and recognitions, there is much more to play with than year-end bonuses:

TANGIBLES	INTANGIBLES	RECOGNITION
cash	job security	by organization
health and dental	sense of a future	by peers/team
retirement	interesting people	by profession
incentives	interesting work	by public

Consider each of these, and consider their opposites, as well, because organizations reinforce negatively as well as positively. A Pummel company can "reward" you with insult and injury. A Push company can "reward" you with gnawing anxiety. A Pull company can "reward" you with autonomy. A Pamper organization can "reward" you by destroying your reputation and employability.

The most important intangible is job security, the dimension most under attack in the age of downsizing. Can a company guarantee that the world will hold still long enough for it to move people back and forth, from opportunity to opportunity, and never lose one person or one opportunity? That is probably impossible. But workers will fight for a company that tries to hold onto them. When Federal Express dissolved its ZapMail effort, but found a way to retain its 1,300 employees, morale and productivity shot up companywide.

At the same time, job security must not be the only consideration. The market has been exceedingly cruel to Pamper companies in the last decade, and the worst remaining Pummel organizations are the sweatshops and maquiladoras abroad. Far and away, most organizations are locked in a Push mode of compensation, driven by anxiety and individual performance.

Push rewards are often the wrong rewards. In sales, for instance, teams are usually rewarded according to individual sales. So four salespersons may be earning drastically different sums. If you have any regard whatsoever for the principle of teamwork, you have shot it dead by creating a system of haves and have-nots.

This is a difficult point for many managers to get beyond. They are proud of the spirit of competitiveness they have created because they like the numbers the stars put up, and they like the heat they get to apply under people capable of or approaching star status.

But Push rewards do not work long-term. The sense of stress they engender, with no pathways to safety, eats away at winners and laggards alike. The winner is likely to drift over time into feelings of smugness, which can create a Pamper-like cone in which one worker gets special treatment and choice prospects, and the rest of the "team" must fight for scraps. Or into feelings of paranoia, realizing he or she is all that stands between the team's breakthrough success.

> "There is no limit to the amount of good that people can accomplish, if they don't care who gets the credit."
>
> *Anonymous*

You get what you pay for. If you reward people for conspiring against one another, a conspiratorial culture will be the result. If the quick kill is important to your organization, Push rewards will get you through the crisis.

But consider what your true objectives are and what rewards will Pull your organization toward those goals:

➤ sharing, not hoarding information
➤ actively searching for process improvements, not sweeping dirt under the carpet
➤ building market share, not cutting costs
➤ breeding new cows, not milking old ones
➤ an atmosphere that will attract people with potential, not pelt them with garbage

If your rewards are top-heavy, your top performers will not cotton to an overhaul from Push to Pull, and it would be wise not to abandon performance-based rewards entirely. A challenge to management,

The Compensation Game

	PUMMEL	PUSH	PULL	PAMPER
Tangibles	Cash for abuse.	Cash for anxiety.	Cash today plus the possibility of more tomorrow.	Money for nothing.
Security	Life on the tightrope.	The clarity of 9 to 5 commitment. Atmosphere of impending doom.	Substantial anxiety, alleviated by modest hopes.	Illusion of cradle-to-grave security.
Intangibles	Zero positive, maximum negative stimulation.	Moderate satisfaction, maximum anxiety.	Job enrichment is important. Work may be stimulating, people may be challenging.	High degree of boredom.
Recognition	You don't want the kind of recognition Pummel offers.	Recognition not a priority. High performers may be spared some pain.	Individual and team recognition, according to need.	Recognition even when there is nothing to recognize.

however, would be to upgrade your stars from their current status as "indispensable performers" to "player-coaches." There is considerable honor in being called upon to teach, and many (not all) of your stars' talents can be taught. Make it a point of pride: anyone can do, but not everyone can show others how to do.

New Agers long for the day when the word "compensation" is abandoned for something more positive. The old word implies that the organizational vision is not one worth holding—that people must be compensated for the distress of subscribing to it. In the New Age workplace that may or may not be evolving, work becomes an important component of its own reward system:

➤ the satisfaction of engagement and success
➤ the stimulation of working with other talented people
➤ the acknowledgment of people we respect

Of course, that's the same future in which we will ride monorails to the office and swap sandwiches with Nobel Prize winners. It'll be nice.

Till then, work is work, and management's challenge is to find ways to keep people's eyes on the prize and their nose to the stone. Along these lines, cash never goes out of style.

Technology and Change

Is technology itself a change initiative? It can be. It often is. Information technology professionals use the word reengineering as if it were theirs alone. But technology isn't an initiative, no matter how wonderful it may be.

Many organizations sincerely undergo an ambitious regimen of self-improvement. Yet as they set out to implement the regimen, they slide into the habit of seeking change primarily by adopting new technology.

In seeking greater product or service quality, or a more measurable degree of customer satisfaction, or quicker cycle time, or a higher degree of employee involvement, they turn the task over to machines.

Someone will bolt a great customer satisfaction module onto the organization's proprietary software system, or create a process map that clarifies, reengineers and enriches one job for every job it eliminates. In the interest of getting to know each employee on a personal basis, an immense database is created detailing every individual's pet peeves and favorite colors.

Paradoxically, a task with very human goals and that requires very little human guidance is subtly taken over by a machine or a program. And once the machine or program is in place, it becomes the reigning reality. One day—way too late for the realization to do anyone any good—you see that you are working for it, and not vice versa. What was supposed to be a driver of change has become a millstone to a new regime.

Consider the kind of turnkey software system that small professional offices use. The salesperson or consultant will rave about the fabulous new capabilities it will give the firm for billing, marketing, and people management. It will free the group up to do more creative things. Six months after it is plugged in, the system has become The System. Employees would no sooner be creative with it than the Cowardly Lion would snarl at The All Powerful Oz.

Technology curves plateau quickly. They are insidious in their ability to become the system they were supposed to improve. "Sorry, we're down." "Sorry, we can't access that information." "Sorry, you don't have clearance." "Sorry, we're not set up to do that."

Finally, it affects different people in different ways. We see computers as marvelously fair in treating all humans the same: we all sit down, we push the buttons, we obtain results.

But we aren't all the same. Some people take to machines like ducks to water. Other people experience terrific stress as they wrestle with their technophobic intuitions. When people are techno-crazed this way, their ability to cope with new stress—the important stress that comes with actually changing and improving organizational processes—shrinks to nothing.

In a nutshell: You had a good, ambitious change plan. You brought in technology to expedite the plan. But people exhausted their comfort zones adjusting to the machine; they have nothing left to give the original plan. The plan ends up in the kill zone.

Computers don't really "work." They futz. They go through the mechanics associated with work. Real work occurs not in virtual space but in the space between people's ears. People, not computers, must connect your organization's goals with your customers' needs.

Computers are a tool, and only a tool. They are not an initiative. The moment an organization forgets this, ii places in jeopardy the change your organization needs to survive.

A Change Checklist

In the din of battle, it is sometimes useful to whip out a checklist of tactical reminders:

➤ **Are you low on oil?** Oil is attention, the lotion you rub on people to let them know that you see what they are doing and that they are doing OK. The oil that smoothes the progress of a change initiative is recognition, reinforcement, and acknowledgment. You don't have to wait until the battle is won to slap some on—in fact, you had better not wait that long. People are social creatures, and we need encouragement most when we are in the middle of the stress of changing. Public attention to small changes, especially early on, eases the way to achieving big changes long-term.

➤ **Are you ready for the results you asked for?** Sometimes initiatives founder because management is taken by surprise. Unless you have mechanisms for evaluating and implementing them, asking employees for improvement ideas is a hollow gesture. Toyota receives 2 million TQM suggestions a year, and implements 97 percent of them.[11] If you can't support your own initiative, you shouldn't put it forward.

➤ **Did you bring enough cash?** An underfunded change initiative is an endangered change initiative. Short of pawning your organization's birthright, see to it that there is enough money to pay for the training and software the new system will require. You may have to cut deals with other hallowed projects to arrange this, but change is all about money and politics. If you need more, ask for more. History offers few examples of initiatives that were funded without having to go begging first. What's the worst they can say—no?

➤ **How's your follow-up?** The best laid plans of mice and men go down the tube in a jiffy when you are not on top of change processes. The process of follow-up should be viewed not as a policing function, but a coaching one. Many people have habits or concerns that can get in the way of their making changes. This coaching process allows you and them to identify both the personal and work-related barriers to change being experienced and talk about ways to address them. Follow-up can take place either at predetermined times (once a week, month, quarter, etc.), or when people reach predetermined stages in the change process (as when the phones are about to be installed). Let Just-In-Time training be the order of the day, learning what you need to learn at the moment the learning becomes necessary.

➤ **Are you willing to make a down payment of pain?** The high price of change is mistakes. Any organization that heads into new territory planning on a best-case scenario—zero dead and zero wounded—is likely to wind up with the exact opposite. Of course there will be mistakes in planning and communication and execution, and they will hurt like hell. One way to look at it is that today's pain is a down payment on future possibilities. Each one is a valuable lesson. Note: This doesn't mean you should maximize your mistakes in order to learn a lot of lessons quickly.

➤ **Who is with you?** Look around, and count the number of people you know who are solidly behind the idea. You can't do this alone. If you are the leader of a large organization, you will need a loyal cadre of top managers to keep the flame from going out. If you are the leader of a team, you will need an even higher degree of unanimity. A change idea is never assured of success. But there does come a point in the development of an idea when the vision achieves critical mass. When a solid core of people believes in the idea enough to be held accountable to it, victory is at hand.

> "A leader is someone who understands where people are going, and stands in front of them."
>
> *Gandhi*

Rebounding from Failure

Quality-minded companies talk about creating a prevention-oriented organization in which errors are anticipated and avoided. Then they laboriously go over their processes, "mistake-proofing" them.

There is one process that cannot be mistake-proofed, however—change. Change error is hard to prevent because it cannot be anticipated in detail. Setbacks inevitably occur. Every change initiative "fails" at first. We can't think of one, ever, that was such a smashing success right off the bat that no opponent could stand by and say, "See? I told you it wouldn't work."

When you fail, as you will—especially if you squint so you are only looking at the short-term perspective—you must strive to hold onto the psychological ground you won through the Push/Pull struggle. Confidence instilled with great effort can melt away at the first sign of slippage—unless your organization or team is fortified against negativity.

Initiatives like total quality management and employee involvement sometimes succeed for a while, even as we encounter anticipated obstacles, "the usual suspects." It's when we bump up against an unanticipated obstacle, an uncomfortable new truth, something we never counted on, that we lose confidence in our still-fledgling idea. How do you deal with setbacks? We suggest that you embed the idea in advance: there will be setbacks, and they will feel like setbacks. People should know this letdown is coming and that it is inevitable, so when it comes it does not throw them for a loop. If you engineer the right frame of mind, people who have been knocked down can get up off their tushes, dust themselves off, and say, "Hey, that wasn't so bad." And return to the task at hand with no serious diminution of energy.

Fashioning an attitude or culture that promotes learning from past setbacks creates a no-lose environment. Just as companies like Hyundai or Dow Corning or Marriott can reward the discovery of process mistakes and the information feedback they provide, so must they anticipate and learn from change problems.

> **"It was a cross between a screwball and a changeup. It was a screwup."**
>
> *Baseball pitcher Bob Patterson, describing a ninth-inning home-run pitch*

But you must know what business you are in. Are you out to learn how to do things better, even at the cost of embarrassment? Or are you in the business of covering up and finding a fall guy to take the blame? This question sounds more rhetorical than it is. Lots of managers, and thus lots of organizations, are officially in the business of coming up with excuses when things go wrong. Don't you be.

Toro, the yard care company, uses a philosophy of "gritting out" what doesn't work, garnering whatever seems to have potential, jettisoning the rest, and using the new learning to make the next initiative work better. It scans the change scene for new initiatives that, based on its past experiences and learning, would fit comfortably within its culture. It does this to avoid adding to what it calls "the fifth pile"—add-on work that does not fit into the customary "four piles of work" most Toro employees are working on at any one time. The fifth pile is where projects collect that weaken the system instead of strengthening it. By waging war against the fifth pile, Toro's people focus on achievable victories—and neatly sidestep no-win propositions.

By collaborating horizontally throughout the company and sharing past learnings, Toro has been able to gradually integrate changes into its culture. An important tool for Toro has been pilot TQM teams. Instead of rolling TQM out companywide, it does it one team at a time, sharing lessons learned as it goes, so that each new rollout doesn't mean reinventing the wheel.

Incidentally, Toro distinguishes between two classes of change: initiatives and campaigns. The first is aimed at the core values and culture, its strategic initiatives, such as viewing the customer as the driving force behind their products and services. The second type of change initiatives are called campaigns. They are really short-term internal marketing efforts designed to communicate the values required to achieve the strategic initiative. The goal here is to have people learn new behaviors, try them out, and share their results with others. Ultimately, the company hopes to create a pyramid of experiences, each reinforcing the others and strengthening the overall change.

Toro feels it has beaten the change blues by redefining "failure" as opportunity. It's like the Chinese character for "change," which is actually two characters in one: one signifying "danger," the other signifying "opportunity." People are metaphiliac or metaphobic to the degree their organizations let them be. The smart organization sees that when people stumble is no time to Push them back upright with stern warnings. Instead, Pull them to their feet with a reminder of the value of each misstep.

> **"Some mornings it just doesn't seem worth it to gnaw through the leather straps."**
>
> *Emo Phillips*

Push does have a role to play here. Push makes it clear that there can be no backtracking, no return to the way things were. Change efforts may be stymied, but the paths back to the old way of doing business have been bulldozed over. If you are stopped today, you have no choice except to start again tomorrow.

Set your old linear learning paradigms out at the curb for pickup. Now is the time to put zigzag learning into practice. Two steps forward, one step back, every lesson ruefully learned contributing to eventual victory.

Rebounding from Success

Sometimes success creates worse problems than failure. In 1994, GTE Directory Services won the Malcolm Baldrige National Quality Award.

> **"If you haven't struck oil in the first three minutes—stop boring!"**
>
> *George Jessel*

They won it using an eroding customer base as a Push alarm to get people started. Workers responded wonderfully, and everyone in the division was delighted with that outcome. But the award had a sinister downside.

The organization had pushed itself to its limits to bag the Baldrige. While sweet, the victory confused the troops. To many workers, it was like Alexander's army reaching the wilderness and bursting into tears because there were no more worlds to conquer.

Of course, in the continuous improvement world of the Baldrige, there are always worlds to conquer. But with the trophy glistening in the corporate showcase, the incremental improvements that lay ahead were not very interesting to many people. Many sat back on their laurels.

Managers fretted at the difficulty of getting people juiced for the next level of changes. Since they had won the award using stretch goals, they turned to stretch goals again, raising the bar on key quality measurements, and taking aim at still other awards. But people were unable to respond this time. Their change space had shrunk. They needed time to regroup. The division canceled plans to reapply for the Baldrige for 1995.

GTE knows that future advances will be harder than the ones made in the past. By picking the "low-hanging fruit," the company was able to make

---

The Phantom Organization

One thing the happy talk books never tell you is that all organizations do eventually die. They run out of business, the owners die leaving no successors, or the corporate headquarters is struck by a comet.

The good news is that anything that was bad in those organizations also dies. When your organization changes from one kind to another kind, you will not be so lucky. The evil residue of the old will linger on in the new, like the after-image you see when you look away from a bright light. The reason is that the old will survive in the memories of the people, particularly the people who derived benefit and power from the old ways. It will be in their interest to keep the old ways alive in the new entity.

---

tremendous, visible, rapid improvements. Higher up, the advances called for greater effort, but with smaller visible result. What do you do when the bar is raised but it doesn't look raised?

One answer is to move the bar to a different operational sphere—away from zero defects, say, and toward community involvement, or safety, or leadership training. Or maybe give people in the trenches a break, and put management to work on honing the vision thing a wee bit finer.

Just as "failure" plants the seed of doubt, "success" breeds overconfidence. While it's great to win a plaque, people must be made to understand that there is no sunset on success, no imaginary boundary that tells you you've made it.

"Another day, another dollar" is a good philosophy for coping with the stress of striving for ambitious goals. It keeps us loose and reminds us that we are, after all, in the change boat for the journey as much as the destination. It works just as well when you have attained them.

A company that excels at change understands its stop-and-go rhythms. When you hit the wall, whether it is the wall of success or failure, study it well, stay calm, and learn from the experience. You will hit other walls, but you need never hit this one again.

The next section is about hitting the wall, and what it's like from initiative to initiative.

part
5

ChangeLand

In 1994, a *Harvard Business Review* article titled "The Reinvention Roller Coaster" described the characteristic pattern of major change initiatives like reengineering—racing downhill, then grinding anxiously uphill, then streaking downward again.[1]

As though on a roller-coaster ride, organizations attempting big changes find themselves alternately exhilarated and disappointed by the current level of success. There are often moments when people yearn to get off the ride and return to the old way of doing things—as if the old way were still back there, waiting to be returned to.

The roller coaster is a good metaphor. You could create an entire theme park based on different kinds of change initiatives. Call it ChangeLand. Each initiative, after all, hews to one or more guiding "themes"—TQM to improvability, reengineering to reformability, benchmarking to a need to continuously measure what you are doing.

ChangeLand is a sprawling complex. It cannot be experienced all in one day. Some of the events are thrilling. The sudden flush of results from one initiative is like the splashdown of a water ride. When that happens everyone rejoices in the success, little guessing at the time that there may be no second splashdown soon. Other events, like impending downsizing, are like a plummeting elevator ride.

Like tourists, organizations get a little nutty when they first enter ChangeLand, wanting to go on every ride at once. The lines are long, and people soon get tired and crabby. There is just too much to do, and people want to go off in different directions. Expressives want to ride every ride. Drivers wave their arms, trying to direct people toward the next attraction. Analyticals wonder if they are really having fun. Amiables shrug and go along for the ride.

This section is an examination of some of these themes, and which change initiatives they guide, and how they fail to manage the anxieties of the people whose energies they seek to enlist, and where they fail to kindle hope that the future will be better than the present.

Though we point out the characteristic shortcomings of these initiatives, we do not dismiss them out of hand. The ideas behind most of these initiatives, from TQM to reengineering to empowerment, are the most powerful to hit the organizational world in years. And the effort change managers pour into making these initiatives succeed for the organizations and the communities that depend on them command everyone's respect. It should never be a disgrace to try something new, or to undertake to find a better way to do things.

Having said that, it is plain that many of these efforts fail every day, with grave financial and emotional consequences both for the organizations and the people that make them up. Our hope in examining these failures is that by identifying misunderstandings and by pinpointing the moment when a vision fades or an idea loses relevance or gets blown out of proportion, organizations can fail less frequently and succeed the second time around.

Lucky Eleven

In this study, we tried to separate these rides or themes into a lucky eleven. We have arranged them in order from those most likely to have a Push character to those most likely to emphasize Pull:

	RESULTS	MEASUREMENT	REFORM	INTEGRATION	IMPROVEMENT	DIRECTION	CHARACTER	RELATIONSHIP	CULTURE	DEMOCRACY	OTHERNESS	
PUMMEL			PUSH					PULL				PAMPER

If you have difficulty reading sideways, the themes are, from left to right: Results, Measurement, Reform, Integration, Improvement, Direction, Character, Relationship, Culture, Democracy, and Otherness.

Fading the themes from Pummel to Pamper is unscientific. Our thought is to put themes that are clearly linked to conventional business thinking (e.g., benchmarking, statistical process control) on the far left side of the box, and themes that lend themselves to New Age managerial schemes (e.g., empowerment, the learning organization) on the far right.

The division into eleven themes is likewise far from perfect, and people are free to debate whether a given attraction belongs in this theme area or that theme area. The boundaries between themes are fuzzy, and things spill over.

Some initiatives are huge, like total quality management, which is less a single tool than a cabinet bursting with different organizing and measuring tools. Many long books have been written about just that one topic. Other initiatives, like managing by walking around, or One Minute Managing, are like keychain penknives, compact and easy to learn and implement.

Further, the three score initiatives we mention here are just the tip of the iceberg. There are scores more we don't mention. Sometimes this is because the theme does not directly affect people working in the trenches, as is usually the case with strategic initiatives and product and marketing innovations. Sometimes it is because the idea has gotten a little moldy around the edges and no one cares any more, as with matrix management. Or because the idea is so similar to another that there is no compelling reason to discuss both.

Meanwhile, it is a characteristic of nearly all change initiatives that one leads to and overlaps another:

➤ The idea of empowerment is linked to numerous other initiatives: TQM, teams, reengineering, and open-book management.
➤ Customer satisfaction is an element of TQM, but also an item on the Baldrige criteria, and an example of new relationships.
➤ Structural initiatives like flattening, decentralizing, virtual corporations, and strategic partnerships inevitably flow into process improvement, value disciplines, new working relationships, and eventually back to empowerment.
➤ And leadership connects to everything.

Whatever initiatives you think you have underway, chances are you have a dozen other unspoken or implied or overlapping initiatives underway as well. Like the blind men of Industan, we call our reinvention processes by different names, and think of each in a distinct way—a tail, an ear, a trunk. Only at a distance do we see the whole creature in all its peculiar glory.

The Results Theme

Does Nike have any idea that their ad slogan "Just do it" owes an intellectual debt to Karl Marx? It was Marx, around the time of the American Civil War, who conceived of a civic morality in which the end of an endeavor justified whatever means were used to achieve it. Marx inspired a lot more than sports shoes with this observation. He also helped launch some memorable change initiatives.

The theme of results is older than Marx. "Just get me results and don't tell me how," is what tyrants from the beginning of history have told their capos. Senior managers still say it today—indeed, that is what stockholders tell them at annual meetings. It is what organizations tell their suppliers, their distributors, and their employees. It has been a signal to permit bloodletting among the rank and file. It has justified the use of force, coercion, threats, and intimidation.

> **"Just do it."**
>
> *Nike*

Results is a number-driven theme. It covers any change initiative that focuses on achieving a predefined conclusion. We put Results at the far left of our "4-P" chart because it fits very well with the conventional business model of the industrial era. The employee's job is to work so many hours producing so many products, of which so many pass inpection, and so many are sold in so many markets, adding so many dollars to gross revenues.

In our time, the passion for results has acquired new respectability. "Whatever works" is the distillation of the teachings of Machiavelli, and in the short term it works pretty well. To a company undertaking a Push-style initiative, Results are all that matter. Such companies do not usually have the luxury to see beyond the need for quick positive outcomes.

New Age Pull initiatives, on the other hand, deplore the results theme, and they have reason to. Too often, organizations settle for the wrong results. A company can easily show good bottom-line results by selling off its most profitable parts, or letting its most highly paid people go.

The classic case was General Motors in the 1970s. Roger Smith presided over the single most profitable period in GM's history—while ceding 14 percent of its market share to Toyota and Volkswagen. Like Esau, who exchanged his birthright for a mess of pottage, General Motors swapped its future for a fistful of dividends. A shallow plan, aiming at shallow results, can be wildly successful. Garbage in, garbage out.

The Results theme is strongest when the results in question are the right results. That is the thinking behind long-term improvement strategies on the right side of the 4-P box, like continuous improvement and empowerment: Make the system better, and good results will follow as night follows day. Results-oriented initiatives include "excellence," zero defects, and many productivity programs.

But many organizations reject the process-oriented approach. Many of them have plowed millions into process and quality efforts and have never been repaid in the marketplace. No study has ever proven definitively that plain vanilla TQM increases company profitability by focusing attention and resources on quality and processes.[2]

> "Results! Why, man, I have gotten a lot of results. I know several thousand things that won't work."
>
> *Thomas A. Edison*

Results is a Push theme that can slip into Pummel. It makes no effort to engage employees' imaginations. There is not much to be said about Results psychologically, because results-oriented programs aren't interested in human factors.

Excellence

It's hard to argue with excellence as a result. When Tom Peters burst on the scene in 1982 with his surprise bestseller *In Search of Excellence,* it was greeted as the first incisive look at what makes some large organizations better than others. Showing then the eclecticism that has become his trademark, Peters assembled a set of criteria for excellence that still works today, seventy zillion business books later: closeness to the customer, a bias toward action, sticking to knitting, simultaneous looseness and tightness, the ability to manage ambiguity—many of the themes of ChangeLand.

One attraction of "excellence" was that it appeared to be a stationary target. Follow Peters' prescriptions and soon you, too, would be excellent. But industries mutated too quickly in the 1980s for organizations to be excellent for very long. Worse, many organizations and industries defined excellence in horse-race terms, through polls of peer organizations. A college devoted to excellence, for instance, was one that scored high on conventional internal gauges—if the deans of other colleges concurred with its reputation. It was more cozy than revolutionary.

Like winning the Baldrige Award, being labeled excellent raised more questions internally than it answered as a marketing buzzword. If a company was "excellent," where was the motivation to become ten times as great? Within a few years of the book's publication, the dark secret burbling beneath the surface of many of the companies cited as excellent came out—that they were dying of self-satisfaction. IBM was especially taken to task for its culture of Pamper. As a response to the challenge of continuous improvement, excellence ("Relax, we've made it") soon came across as lame.

The companies that led the excellence field in the 1980s and continued to lead a decade later, like textiles giant Milliken, aligned their excellence with brass-tacks disciplines like TQM and the Baldrige criteria. Companies that leaned on a shakier reed, like People's Express, quickly became unexcellent.

Within five years, Peters cheerfully recanted. The opening words of his follow-up book, which did embrace revolution, were: "There are no excellent companies. . . . No company is safe. . . . In 1987 and for the foreseeable future, there is no such thing as a solid, or even substantial, lead over one's competitors. A commanding advantage . . . is good for about 18 months, at best."[3]

The idea of a catch-all descriptor of success survives under different names. As the believability of "excellence" eroded, it has been shored up with fresh synonyms: "world class," "winners," "best practices." But they, too, paled.

Many traditionally excellent companies fell by the wayside due to self-congratulation and Pamper. In the end, excellence was less a vision than a label. What was missing? An ideal that may never be attained, that sticks in people's heads and Pulls them onward, toward a future that means something to them, with or without the applause of the watching world.

Zero Defects

While working for ITT in the 1930s, Philip Crosby developed some keen but simple insights into product failure. In the 1970s, when William Edwards Deming was still an obscure figure in the U.S., Crosby was gaining renown for a very different approach to quality. Crosby never figured out why Deming and the others made quality so difficult. All you need to do, he said, is eliminate defects. Each eliminated defect results in one more product sold and one fewer detoured to the re-do area. If mistakes are costing you money, Crosby said, stop making mistakes. Thus quality pays for itself; it's free.

For years the two men and their respective followers sniped at one another. When Deming rocked the world with his 14 Points, Crosby presented his own set of 14 points. Deming deplored the hip-hip-hooray of exhortation as displaying contempt for workers' intelligence. By contrast, one of Crosby's points specifically called for a Zero Defects Day; the more bunting, the better.

Zero defects is one result-based program that is specific and quality-oriented and that is in its favor. At its most advanced it becomes a burning desire within an organization to be nothing less than perfect, as in Motorola's goal of achieving "Six Sigma" quality—fewer than two or three failures for every million outputs. ISO 9000, the international quality standard, also owes a debt to the zero defects principle.

But there are problems. One is that zero defects finds its most logical application in a mass assembly, manufacturing environment, the industrial sphere in which Crosby originated his theories. Applying Six Sigma thinking to service processes can be awkward: is service with a half-smile instead of a whole one a full defect or a partial one? Second, how do you know that the product you are laboring to minimize mistakes in is the right one? No one wants a defect-free product that is obsolete. The claim that quality is free is debatable. Zero defects focuses considerable organizational resources with no ironclad guarantee of financial reward on the other end.

Demingite TQM insists that quality requires more than just preventing errors. It must be less about butt-covering and more about happiness-making, for everyone. True TQM sees quality as proactive Pull, an offensive strategy—a primary business strategy, in fact. Zero defects at its best is a Pull toward product perfection that may ensure better lives for workers and happier faces on customers. At its least imaginative it becomes industrial anality, a Push strategy of placing numbers ahead of human factors.

Organizations pursuing a zero defects strategy need to be alert to the problems of too obsessive an approach to defect reduction. Implementing complementary humanistic initiatives like empowerment or open-book management can help restore balance.

The Measurement Theme

This Measurement theme belongs next to the Results theme, because what is being measured is results, and both themes are rooted in numbers. We will focus most of our attention on the two great measuring tools in use in organizations today—the Baldrige assessment criteria and ISO 9000 certification. While both are instruments for measuring, what they are measuring is quality performance. Each could have easily appeared in the Improvement theme instead of Measurement, alongside TQM.

Measurement is about the management of numbers to achieve desired improvements in performance. Being numbers-oriented in the 1990s means going against a fashion of humanistic New Age managerial themes.

The last twenty-five years have not been kind to the art and craft of management. First, there has been the trend of extermination of managers—the elimination, by downsizing and creating teams, of the layer of professional managers who for years kept the trains of industry running on time.

Second, there has been relentless antimanager propaganda put out by business gurus, who extol the shamanistic qualities of the politically correct, utterly human leader (who, like the Indian chief in the public service announcement, sheds a tear at the roadside at the sight of litter) versus the mere manager, who has been diminutized and put in his place much as the finance professionals ("number cruncher," "bean counter") have been.

That's a lot of negativity to heap on a single scapegoat, and a contrarian investor knows that the stock price of managerial expertise must rebound soon.

Measurement can be dull and laborious, but it separates doing from guessing and attaining from approximating. It can be boiled down to two questions, How do you know how well you're doing, unless you measure it? And if you do measure it, are your measurements both reliable and valid?

Lots of number-oriented change ideas have come along in recent years. Measures have included fish-bone diagrams, Pareto charts, cause and effect diagrams, check sheets, histograms, scatter diagrams, and control sheets. The most important small-scale ideas have been:

➤ **Statistical process control,** an idea promulgated by Walter Shewhart in the 1930s and advanced by Deming in the 1940s and 1950s, holds that control can be achieved by monitoring and minimizing variation in manufacturing and other processes. The methodology is the linchpin of total quality management.

➤ **Benchmarking,** or competitive comparison, sometimes called "shameless stealing," a regimen for comparing how your organization is doing compared to others inside and outside your industry.

> **"When you cannot measure it, when you cannot express it in numbers, your knowledge is of a meager and unsatisfactory kind."**
>
> *Lord Kelvin*

➤ **Management by Objectives**. First described by Peter Drucker in *The Practice of Management* in 1954,[4] management by objectives was one of the first business fads, and it remains popular today. It is a simple idea: manage with long-term objectives clearly in mind, and state them frequently to keep people aware of them. Each objective should have a deadline; when the deadline comes, the organization assesses to see if the objective was achieved and, if not, why not.

This sounds like a technique that could not possibly steer an organization wrong, but that is what has happened, often. There is, as Tom Peters points out in *Thriving on Chaos*,[5] a tendency for people implementing management by objectives to drop the phrase Peter Drucker originally included: "management by objectives" (Drucker never capitalized or acronymized his idea to "MBO") and self-control." And objectives handed down from on high are strong on Push, but weak on Pull. Having an objective is not enough to engage people to change. For that, a reason must be spelled out, a vision that pulls people toward attaining the objective. Without Pull, MBO is just an exercise in getting people to do things. Management by objective achieves a stronger degree of Pull when objectives are decided by the group, not just by the boss.

Deming thought so little of management by objective that he devoted one of his 14 Points to condemning the practice. The practice works when it is invested in by people working in good will and conscience with one another. Take away the human elements of team commitment and individual accountability, and management by objectives becomes just another chart-driven chore.

All three are proven methodologies for charting improvements in process and production. But measurement is a tricky area. Though the logic of numbers is solid, as with technology, the temptation to have them do one's thinking is also great.

Measurement is best suited to a static playing field. Useful measurements of a game in progress, or whose rules are rapidly mutating, are difficult to design.

The Analytical temperament is responsible for much of the profound thinking that happens in organizations. It provided the mindset undergirding our industrial era, the most dominant commercial era any country has ever enjoyed. But by its nature the Analytical craves a groove, a quiet place and time where options can be weighed carefully and decisions made; not the life-in-a-blender swirl that characterizes most organizations today.

> **"To the blind, all things are sudden."**
>
> *Old proverb*

Use numbers to mark the way, not to lead it.

The Baldrige Award

The Baldrige Award (full title: Malcolm Baldrige National Quality Award) got off to a dubious start in 1987. It was the Reagan administration's answer to the insistence by liberal economists like Robert Reich that the United States required an "industrial policy" comparable to Japan's—a sign to the world that America was officially behind the success of its own businesses.

The Baldrige Award, the closest thing business has to an Oscar or an Emmy, is bestowed on companies that submit to an extensive (and expensive) assessment on a broad array of TQM yardsticks. Each year the names of the assessment criteria change a bit. In 1996 they were:

> Leadership
> Information and Analysis
> Strategic Planning
> Human Resource Development and Management
> Process Management
> Business Results
> Customer Focus and Satisfaction

This measuring framework embraces just about every theme and initiative in this book.

While the award is known publicly for the companies that win it, and subsequently use it in their marketing, its greatest value is as a self-assessment instrument. Thousands of organizations use the criteria as a way to measure how they stack up. The discipline imposed by the assessment is an excellent way to corral all the data that a wide-ranging TQM plan creates. By requiring that these data be put on paper, the assessment helps keep TQM efforts honest.

> **"We aim above the mark to hit the mark."**
>
> *Ralph Waldo Emerson*

By and large, Baldrige has been the object of broad enthusiasm, both in corporate circles and in the business press. But there have been occasional mutterings of displeasure with the way the award process has gone to date.

The biggest problem companies encounter with the Baldrige assessment has to do with how they use it. We believe companies who use it for their own assessment purposes make the best use of it. The criteria are rigorous, thoughtful, and focused.

The other way to use the criteria is as a means to win the actual award. As soon as this becomes your goal, something jarring happens. Because it is public, because it is a government-sponsored project, and because winning brings a bonanza of publicity that can be exploited in marketing, the award competition is a powerful distraction, leading organizations away from the Award's own quality orientation, and into the spotlight of politics and show business.

The award process engenders bitterness that the assessment criteria bypass. These complaints[6] center on four areas:

> **Small companies feel outmuscled by big companies.** Xerox reportedly spent $800,000 cultivating the prize, utilizing 500 employees

in preparing the application. Small companies like Globe Metallurgical won without spending much. Still, the impression persists that the big money companies have an edge.

➤ **The award is held hostage by winners' reputations.** What happens to the award's reputation when one of its high-profile winners appears in the headlines doing something awful?

➤ **The pain's not worth the gain.** USAA Life Insurance Company didn't want to sound like a sore loser, but after making it to the Baldrige finals three times and not winning, they blew a gasket. How could they be good enough to place every year but never good enough to win?

➤ **Winning carries a curse.** Winning entails teaching and touring responsibilities that do not let up after winning. The Wallace Company, which won in 1990, went out of business two years later. Many people blamed its collapse on the distractions of winning.

The Baldrige is too complex a process to do a point-by-point critique of it here. Perhaps the best advice we can offer is to go into the assessment for the right reasons.

If you are a big company, be sure about your motivation for applying. There is a real chance that the Baldrige Award will be torpedoed by the success of its well-heeled winners. While giants like Ford, GM, IBM, and GE vie for top honors, spending millions for the chance to place a Baldrige logo on all their ads, the integrity of the process becomes suspect. If you are truly serious about developing better products and delivering higher levels of customer satisfaction, show us directly.

If you are a small company, use the criteria as if you were competing for the award, fulfilling them the best you can, asking yourselves the tough questions. But when the time comes to send it in with the $1,200 application fee, make out your check to a local charity instead, and get back to pursuing quality and away from massaging data about it.

ISO 9000

If ISO 9000 is so important, why did they give it such a drab name? ISO 9000 stands for International Organization for Standards, 9000 Series. It is a collection of documents, but causes much more pain than most documents. These documents tell organizations what they should do, in a very general way, to bring their operations and processes up to speed with worldwide "best practices."

ISO 9000 does not certify that your products are of high quality but that your company, its processes, and the ways it works with suppliers and customers measure up to current generic quality standards.

What makes ISO 9000 important is that European Community companies have adopted the standards with a vengeance as part of their continuing unification. That means that if U.S. companies want to sell in Europe or to companies in the U.S. that have any kind of European presence, they have to comply with the standards, too.

Does ISO 9000 actually impart an impressive level of quality to the companies that follow it? Not really. The quality tension of ISO 9000 is generally looser than that of the criteria for the Baldrige Award. Achieving ISO 9000 certification won't make you a great company or bring in new business. What it will do is dissuade customers from going elsewhere because you don't have the ISO 9000 seal of approval.

Lots of quality consultants, including Deming, say that ISO 9000, by establishing constant, low, minimum benchmarks for all companies to meet, runs contrary to the spirit of continuous improvement. If quality never stops, why is the ISO 9000 level worth pausing for? In a business milieu requiring WD-40, ISO 9000 is more like Krazy Glue, riveting attention to a level of performance that the non-ISO 9000 world is relentlessly moving beyond on its own.

Since it is an expensive undertaking, the rich get certified sooner and the poor later. Europe leads the way, with the U.S. and Japan following. Behind them come the aggressive countries where certification is subsidized, like Malaysia, and way, way, behind them are the poor countries that haven't got a clue about the politics of certification, like the Philippines, which has scarcely a dozen certified companies, despite an enormous population and a sizable manufacturing installation.

ISO 9000 certification is like the driving exam from hell, where the examiner deducts points without telling you why and without offering constructive feedback on how to pass the test next time. It can be a grueling, frustrating experience made worse by the remoteness of the registering body. Registrars are not always up to snuff on the latest wrinkles in the standard, and instead of conceding the point, they nitpick.

At times it seems that the only people who really care about the standard are the registrars. Sometimes, even they don't seem to care.

The bottom line is that ISO 9000 is a prepackaged change initiative that most companies have no choice but to follow, because it is the price of admission these days to world markets. Companies turning to the certification process may be doing their net sales a favor, but are sending rocket spasms of pain, boredom, and aggravation through the soft tissues of their workforces.

In ISO 9000's favor, it should be pointed out that much of the difficulty is interpretive. It is suggested, for instance, that you document all changes in policies in writing. Most organizations go nuts and create the fattest, most horrible quality procedures book you could shake a caliper at. But the binder is not necessarily necessary. If an "instruction" doesn't make long-term business sense, you are free to rethink your interpretation of it. So some of the pain of ISO 9000 is self-inflicted, the product of connect-the-dots thinking.

Our suggestion: be candid with your people. Do not sell ISO 9000 as a tool for breakthrough quality. Concede the drudgery involved in implementing it. Indeed, have some fun with it, acknowledging that it is a pain but a necessary one. You may just find that ISO 9000 is a bridge management and labor can build toward one another, as they discover something they dislike more than one another.

The Reform Theme

The Reform theme covers a wide range of change initiatives that seek to reshape or resize organizations that feel they have gotten too big and too unmaneuverable to achieve their goals.

Organizations never got big and unwieldy until computers allowed them to manage huge data assets. The development of the mainframe business computer in the 1950s gave existing large companies license to grow to unprecedented sizes. The 1960s were a time of intoxicating expansion, and confidence in management science grew at the same giddy rate. A large corporation was seen as a big circus tent under which many acts might perform simultaneously.

The philosophy that developed was that any skilled manager, armed with enough data muscle, could manage any kind of business, whether it was an investment bank or a hog farm, or both at the same time. This universal management theme has come under attack by New Age organizational theorists. The initiatives this school of thought has advanced to cope with growing complexity have not been very successful in the past twenty years.

Early Reform Ideas

In the 1960s, the idea of corporate conglomerates began to take hold. A *conglomerate* is an umbrella corporation that shelters companies doing several unrelated kinds of business. Some conglomerates were formed by chance; others are carefully assembled to diversify the parent corporation against cyclical shocks. Teledyne, Inc., for example, is a collection of business units running with considerable autonomy, they are geographically scattered, and have little thematically in common. It is the number-one producer of products as unrelated as dental irrigators, swimming pool heaters, and zirconium. Some conglomerates of the 1960s survive, but most, as the failure of diversification became apparent, have broken up into more logical packages.

> "When I hear the word art, I reach for my luger."
>
> *Hermann Goering*

Conglomerates are good for making money, but because of their scattered character they are incapable of sustaining a vision that workers in the different industries can relate to. They can Push but they cannot Pull.

A theoretical cousin of the conglomerate is the *portfolio company*. The portfolio company buys other companies solely on the basis of financial return. If a company in the portfolio fails to meet its annual return minimum (you could peg it as modestly as the going passbook savings rate), it is dropped like a hot potato. Why run a kitty litter plant, the reasoning goes, if you can make the same money buying a bond?

Portfolio companies are imaginary to begin with. Even more imaginary is an enlightened portfolio company. If your stated reason for being is return on investment, what would constitute enlightenment? A portfolio philosophy is to vision what Goering was to art.

The 1970s and 1980s were a period of rapid consolidation and shakeout, dominated by *acquisitions, mergers,* and *corporate takeovers.* The oddly shaped companies, stretched across time zones and cultures, that resulted from these recombinations helped fire the Reform movement, creating new structural concepts to govern these unruly entities.

By the 1990s the burst of acquisition had settled down, and these new ideas have resulted in a zodiac of *new shapes* for organizational architects. It was one thing for investors to swoop down and snap these companies up, but quite another for managers to make the disjointed entities work together.

Corporate *restructurings* were announced on an almost daily basis, many of them caused by the enormous debt loads incurred by acquiring other companies. Restructuring by itself had almost no meaning, except the sense that things were going wrong because of some geometric infelicity on the organizational chart. Inside the organization, it usually meant that someone was being punished for failure, and the punishment was to create a new job title for the next guy to fail under.

Restructuring never implied that the organization itself would change—just the flow of command, widely held by those currently in command to be blemish-free. Too often, restructuring was the Latin form for a familiar concept, *scapegoating*.

Shrinkage

The most familiar reform is reduction in size. The shrinkage subtheme is a sign that management has lost confidence in its ability to grow markets, sell products, and maintain central control.

The shrinkage mentality is summed up by Gary Hamel and C. K. Prahalad as "denominator thinking." If you recall sixth grade math, you will remember a fraction has a top number (the numerator) and a bottom number (the denominator). The numerator is a company's potential for growth, expansion, core competencies, new products, new markets, generativity—profit by doing. Whereas the denominator is various schemes for increasing the bottom line, at least on paper: cost containment, downsizing, flattening, delayering, dehiring.

Numerator companies succeed by doing terrific work and satisfying customers. Denominator companies seek to shrink a company until its current level of profits is higher in relation to reduced costs.

Both numerator and denominator approaches are legitimate. Indeed, all companies pursue both all the time, investing resources where growth potential is apparent, and cutting costs where prospects are more modest. Shrinkage may be attempted by organizations in any mode—Pummel, Pamper, Push, or Pull.

Given the high reliability of shrinkage, it is a wonder that more companies don't simply break themselves up into separate companies and cashier the rest, as AT&T did in 1986 and as Control Data did in 1989. To do so, of course, means surrendering managerial power—an untrod path to executive greatness.

The shrinkage strategies companies have resorted to instead have varied widely from organization to organization. The first sense that smaller was better occurred decades ago at General Motors and Dupont Chemical. In the 1920s these two huge organizations, each in turn under the management of Alfred Sloan, envisioned a greater degree of managerial flexibility by breaking a large organization into divisions. It was a good enough idea to generate a powerful competitive advantage for scores of Fortune 500 companies in the decades that followed. If you didn't decentralize in the 1960s or 1970s, you just weren't trying.

But decentralization failed in its ambition to shrink the actual size of organizations. In fact, by instituting an autonomous management tier within each division, decentralization created the very kind of bureaucratic bloat it was supposed to combat.

The practice suffers, too, from the tendency large corporations have of maintaining control even over autonomous divisions. IBM in the 1980s is a good example of a decentralized company whose decentralization was counterfeit—each division was handcuffed by requirements that product releases be coordinated with other divisions, in order that IBM could get first crack at its own technologies. Net result: a tradition of delays and innovative kludginess that nearly killed "the world's most successful company." IBM was not serious about divisional empowerment until the 1990s.

Because decentralization is more often a dodge from greater efficiencies than a spur to them, and because it is wedded in the minds of most managers to big company empire-building, it has lost much of its currency for today's generation. The saddest commentary is that the effective company ideal modeled by Alfred Sloan in the 1920s in two generations had become the ineffective model we associate with Pamper, entitlement, and being out of touch with customers and markets.

Demassification

The next major shrinkage solution was work group breakup, or *demassification*. Alvin Toffler coined the term in *Future Shock*[7] to describe an unlikely phenomenon—organizations and systems voluntarily reversing their trend from very large to smaller and more manageable. It was the corporate world's version of E. F. Schumacher's "Small is beautiful."

Many organizations attempt a modest degree of demassification as a move toward contained businesses-within-a-business. These would be business units or mini-companies of as many as 500 workers, containing all the functions a business requires, and charged with the mission of making money, but without decision-making autonomy. These groups often foundered because they were a sham; teams were expected to act like businesses without being given power to perform entrepreneurially—Push without a pathway to safety.

A few organizations pursued a radical demassification model, described as a "street of shops" by M. M. Stuckey, in which the business units are even smaller, with a top size of about fifty, and do have a high degree of decision-making autonomy in matters such as purchasing and training. "Street of shops" is like portfolio management in reverse: the work team must figure out ways to produce satisfactory results, or it will be cashed in.[8]

Demassification is Push-intensive, but at least workers have their fates in their own hands. Under such succeed-or-die pressures, "street of shops" groups at Kodak, ABB, Cooper Industries, and Thomas J. Lipton generally performed well. But the net effect of their independent ways was to scare top management. Break General Motors into 5,000 demassified work teams, and good things are bound to happen here and there. On the other hand, it only takes a few horror stories to draw a big company's experimental comfort zone back in.

Flattening

Another general approach to resizing was *delayering*, sometimes called *de-hierarchization*, or *flattening*. These structure-squashing approaches are "burning platforms," but without pathways to safety. The idea of all of them is to collapse the traditional pyramid structure (a CEO on top, management team below, supervisory staff below that, rank and file along

155

the bottom) into something looking more like the head of a garden rake (CEO on top, rank and file one tier below).

The goal of this movement was to direct the maximum amount of organizational muscle toward customer satisfaction. Since management adds no value to customers in this philosophy, there is no point in not minimizing it, and having people at the bottom manage themselves.

But workers generally know full well that "value adding" is not the real point of all this mashing down. Thinning the ranks of middle managers, dumping their salaries, and adding the burden of self-management to an already overloaded staff ("I'm not getting paid to do management's job") is the point of much of it.

Organizations undergoing delayering need to make clear to workers, especially those sent down to the bottom tier, that de-hierarchization doesn't mean the end of the line for them. Most people find hope in the idea of promotion. Removing the hierarchy they hoped to be promoted in dampens that hope. The burden is upon the organization to create new hope, in a new dimension—better pay, higher satisfaction, greater job enrichment. Unless this is done, the delayered organization becomes what its rake-like structure most nearly resembles—a sweatshop.

Downsizing

We come now to the ultimate shrinkage initiative, *downsizing* and its euphemism, *rightsizing*.[9] No change initiative drags with it the attendant bad publicity that downsizing does. This is too bad, since all downsizing is not the same. There are three classes, and only one is the evil thing the popular press depicts:

➤ *Push, or catastrophic downsizing.* This kind of downsizing has been with us since the dawn of time. Think of it as emergency rations. An organization loses a big contract, or it bets everything on a product that fails, or it loses its founder. The result in each case is a desperate effort to trim the company's costs—including its payroll—in order to survive. Analogy: the organization is lost on a raft in the Pacific, and workers must draw straws to see who will eat whom.

➤ *Pull, or visionary downsizing.* Without being in an immediate emergency, the organization sees that down the road, there will be greater chance for companywide success (and overall employment) by cutting away certain existing functions, divisions, product lines, and people. It is impossible to justify such cuts in the eyes of those who will feel the greatest pain, but the cuts are justified by the big picture, and the pain is balanced among constituencies—short-term investors, employees, and even customers. A recent example is AT&T's splitting itself into three separate organizations. True, 12,000 people were laid off—but with a reasonable chance of starting over again, at lower salaries, in the new organizations. Analogy: a surgeon excises moribund tissue to save the patient. It's not anyone's dream to learn they are nothing more to their organization than a polyp or cyst. But today's pain is a prelude to tomorrow's healing.

➤ *Pummel, or evil downsizing*. Downsizing as short-term financial play. One constituency (ownership) feels all the pleasure, while another (workers) feels all the pain. It is the downsizing we see when a company is taken over and sold off when liquidated assets are more valuable than unliquidated assets—the people and processes in place that could yet yield long-term profitability. This sees workers as no more precious or irreplaceable than the gas that is sprayed into an engine to supply power and allowed to dissipate.

It is pointless to urge devotees of the third class of downsizing to adopt more humane attitudes. These people are not interested in soft landings or safety nets. When they put the bite on people, their eyes roll upward like a shark's; it is in their nature to be that way.

We can hope, however, that companies pursuing the other two classes of downsizing give greater consideration to the needs of the people who are cut away from the main. Eye-contact, hugs, and outplacement services—counseling the laid-off on how to stave off depression as they clear the wreckage of their careers from the road—are not enough.

Workers need to know that the company's failure was the fault of management, not themselves. They need to hear it from management's own mouth: "If we had managed better, planned better, trained better, communicated better, this would not have happened. Your loss is our shame."

Workout

Jack Welch stormed to the top of General Electric in 1980 promising a regime of continuous revolution, in which nothing was sacred and no one was safe. His goals were ambitious and culture-wrenching: all GE's businesses had be number one or two in their industries, and GE itself had to grow to be the number one company in market value—the biggest mound on Wall Street. Until that moment, GE was a classic Pamper organization, and he forced it to bend over backwards, to a hard Push.

Some would characterize GE in those days as unrelieved Pummel, with a heavy emphasis on results. Welch borrowed the word workout to describe the lathered-up state of stress the organization is put through to change. He also used the image of a fishbowl to describe the scrutiny managers at every level were exposed to. They had to either produce or vamoose, and there was no hiding from results.

Welch was the ultimate Push manager, treating employees like puppets to be either manipulated or tossed onto the discard pile. He did not blanch at lighting a fire under people and altering their body temperatures. His early reign of terror is the textbook example of a corporate savior pulling every switch and flipping every lever to get results.[10]

Yet Welch remains a cipher, like Quetzalcoatl, the mysterious figure who abolished human sacrifice among the Toltecs, then disappeared and resurfaced among the Maya where he *instituted* human sacrifice. Before the decade ended Welch would reemerge as a self-styled Pull leader, speaking of boundaryless organizations and vision-driven futures. He was like an entirely different person. But why not—if you can change an enormous organization's culture, how hard can it be to change your own?

The Integration Theme

Organizations are by definition complex, made of many parts and many people. Management has been ingenious at creating systems to fit people and processes together. But the more complicated systems get, the more hiding places they create. Integration gives way to fragmentation. After a while it is very difficult to see where things go wrong, where the gleaming complexity is a curtain obscuring all kinds of error and delay.

Thus we have initiatives clustered under the Integration theme, each one addressing in a different way the problems of knitting complexity back together. The best known of these is business process reengineering.

Reengineering

Reengineering is a way of rethinking the way businesses work—green-grass thinking that is unafraid to jettison the tried and true in search of greater efficiencies. The official definition goes like this: *"Business reengineering is the process of fundamentally changing the way work is performed in order to achieve radical performance improvements in speed, cost, quality, market share, and return on investment."* A reengineered definition might describe it simply as "a fresh look."

Reengineering is an open-ended regimen. It invites you to search for an answer ("What's the very best way to run your organization?") when there is no preconceived right answer and no cookie-cutter methodology for finding a right answer. It asks you to imagine, using your best powers of imagination, a quantum leap forward in performance.

Given this open-endedness, it is not surprising that many reengineering efforts are failures. The ideas of reengineering are too often implemented incorrectly, at enormous financial and emotional cost to the organization. Hammer and Champy concede that 70 percent of reengineering efforts fail to achieve any results. There are several reasons for this difficulty—most stem from the organization's unwillingness to go far enough to:

➤ **Ready the wrecking ball**. The first order of repair is often demolition. To build an organization up, we must first tear it down. To solve a problem, we must first erase our wrong answers so that we may begin with "a clean sheet of paper."

➤ **Compress your workforce horizontally.** That is, combine jobs. Reengineered processes move away from the assembly line concept—there is no longer a long chain of individuals, each involved in a single task. Individuals are responsible for processes, such as "customer service," not unitary tasks like "answering phones" or "handling complaints." This consolidation or compression is horizontal in nature—one person now doing the tasks that several did before.

➤ **Compress the workforce vertically.** Compression can be up-and-down as well: workers can take on the tasks of their supervisors, monitoring and managing themselves.

➤ **Enlist technology as partner.** Not technology as automation, simply speeding up the same old tasks, but technology that brings the possible into clearer focus. Hammer, an information technology specialist, devotes an important chapter to the use of computers and telecommunications advances—machines—as the enablers of new visions.

➤ **Discard half-measures**. Too many managers opt for the safe compromise, the hybrid that melds the old with the new. Hammer emphatically rejects the idea of "just fixing things." The main reengineering efforts fail is that they aren't reengineering at all—just quick fixes in drag. What is called for he says, is a new kind of discontinuous thinking that identifies and abandons outdated rules and assumptions.

➤ **Reengineer the right processes.** The most obvious candidates will be those that are clearly in trouble, suffering frequent breakdowns. Beyond these, look for processes in which there are many handoffs, reweighings, rework, and repetition; bloated and costly inventories and protective buffers; a high degree of cross-checking, and a low degree of value-adding; and processes that seem swamped by their own complexity; and the high number of exceptions and "special cases" to be dealt with.

➤ **Clear away clutter.** The modern corporation is a Tinkertoy monstrosity of checks, balances, and reconciliations. All that must be stricken away, and a fresh, clean beginning made amid the rubble. Having work pass through so many hands and lie fallow in so many in-baskets is like watching a pig pass through a snake. Reengineering efforts that fail to straighten out this clutter miss the whole point of reengineering.

As you grapple with the challenge of creating a new machine on the site of the old one, don't forget the human side:

➤ **Before you obliterate, educate.** Obviously, a solution that calls for ten to do the work of twenty or thirty requires a different kind of workforce. It's easy to say "Hire better—hire flexible self-starting generalists with good communication and decision-making skills, judgment, wisdom, maturity, education, and talent." Business and society must become more serious about education.

➤ **Overcome resistance.** Most reengineering efforts fail not because the points of change are poorly designed but because they are poorly

The Burden of Invention

You have to feel a little sorry for Michael Hammer, coauthor of the book that set the reengineering craze in motion, *Reengineering the Corporation*.[11] He is a great success, but is associated in many people's minds with great failure.

Reengineering is the only major change initiative that can be identified with a single person. William Edwards Deming may be "Mr. Quality" to his devotees, but no one attributes all the good or all the bad done in the name of quality to him. Hammer, an exuberant self-promoter, has not been so lucky.

Reengineering has been the biggest change initiative of the 1990s (assuming TQM and teams are seen as creatures of the previous decade). Because Hammer and Champy sold a quarter million copies of the book, they—especially Hammer, who typifies the metamaniac personality type—came to be seen as the owners of the idea. This occurred despite forty other books on business process reengineering by Hammer-Champy wanna-bes and an army of independent consultants, all presenting their own versions of reengineering.

This may explain the defensive tone of his recent work. His three books all include lengthy sections of explanations as to why certain reengineering efforts have gone awry. Even Champy introduced his follow-up book, *Reengineering Management*, with the sentence, "Reengineering is in trouble."

---

communicated. Reengineering should be seen not as a value-neutral proposal but as a war to be fought with propaganda and persistence.

➤ **Allow executive evolution.** The CEO as scorekeeper and punisher/rewarder must give way to one who leads.

➤ **Find a reason to believe.** Workers aren't puppets. You can't put them through a million motions without giving them a reason why. Reengineering rises or falls on the new values and beliefs it engenders. A primary task of management is to communicate these values and beliefs—honestly, clearly, and often.

➤ **Don't try to do too much.** Process redesign requires sharp focus and enormous discipline. Attempting to do it companywide, all at once, is like trying to tackle a dinosaur.

➤ **Or settle for too little.** There is a temptation, when your company is in mid-upheaval, to celebrate too soon and call a few minor improvements a success. Don't succumb—big results require big ambitions. Indeed, Hammer says, incremental improvements can be hazardous to your company's health. Instead of simplifying, they add to the lacework of the organization's existing structure. Most pernicious of all, glorifying "the little things" creates a culture of small think and a company with no valor and no courage.

➤ **Think "case manager."** That's Hammer's concept of the new role of the reengineered worker—a competent, empowered, versatile, informed person who shepherds a problem through to its solution.

The last is the catch-22. Hammer believes that by empowering workers to find their own ways to add value to customers, they will rise to unparalleled levels of compensation. You may spend your entire career as nothing more than a "case manager," but you may earn a salary in the high six figures. Those who excel will rise; those who are average will quickly plateau; and those who are not up to the vision, or lack the skills, will be toast.

> "Reengineering is the new scientific management."
>
> *Tom Peters*

The question is, is this really happening anywhere? Workers at organizations undergoing major change initiatives move heaven and earth to become more customer-conscious, with an eye toward this promised land of higher salaries. From what we've seen, most people, whether they are peak performers or average performers, are making the same pay they made in pre-reengineering days.

Workers are either (a) delivering uncompensated value but keeping their jobs or (b) losing their jobs. For the former group, it's a sped-up world, fraught with tons of accountability (Push) but little perceivable payback (Pull). For the latter group, distinctions between reengineering and downsizing are niggling.

Speedup

Improving cycle time could fall under either the Process or Results themes. It is process reengineering that focuses exclusively on time, and it is the direct descendant of the time-motion studies of the 1920s. Improving cycle time requires that a continuous voice be whispering in your head, "How long does this activity take? Can you find a way to do it quicker?"

Shortening cycle times—how long it takes to develop a product, to test it, to manufacture it, to roll it out to market—can be a major strategic advantage. For certain products and services, such as package delivery or food preparation, short cycle time is synonymous with quality. The reverse is also true: improve quality by eliminating defects, and your cycle can't help but speed up.

But there is a downside to improving cycle times, and Peter Senge nails it:

> "What has concerned me is not the logic but the implementation of the logic. In particular, I believed American corporations, ever in search of the 'quick fix,' would see this as the ultimate bromide. By trying to 'speed up,' we would simply take one more step in a long-term trend of shortening time horizons, discounting the past, and living for the moment."[12]

Overstretched workers are stretched a little more, he said. Managers distracted by crisis after crisis will find even less time for reflection and planning.

Cycle time improvement must be more than just a Chinese fire drill, in which people are made to perform tasks more and more quickly. The Push for measurable improvement must be balanced with the Pull of engaged sympathies: "Faster delivery means greater security."

Companies achieving shorter cycle times through simple fiat—demanding faster results from people without giving them either the means to do so on a sustainable basis or a vision of long-term livability—soon have an organization with its motor racing and its heart about to explode.

Value Disciplines

Value is like looking at quality through a wide-angle lens. Instead of a close-up of a satisfied customer, it shows us the bigger picture of what it may take to put that smile on the customer's face. It broadens the definition of customer satisfaction and allows an organization to see the consequences of all its processes in one neat frame.

The value crusade underway today got a big push from a 1995 book by Michael Treacy and Fred Weirsema, *The Discipline of Market Leaders.*[13] It declared that today's vital companies are those that are attuned to the idea of delivering some kind of value; and that today's moribund companies are those that have lost their way, whose outlook, business traditions, and fixed assets prevent them from delivering "the best deal anywhere."

Future success belongs to organizations that commit to being value leaders in their markets, companies unwilling to settle for parity-level performance.

There are only three strategic approaches, called value disciplines, that result in value leadership.

➤ The first value discipline is *product leadership*. It applies to companies that endeavor to sell products that deliver the best results to customers. Quality hardware and an intense focus on product development are the hallmarks of this kind of company. Examples: Procter & Gamble, Johnson & Johnson, Walt Disney, Intel, Thomas Edison's laboratories in their heyday.

➤ The second value discipline is *operational excellence*. It applies to companies that deliver a combination of high reliability, low price, and hassle-free convenience—Treacy calls this "total cost"—that competitors cannot match. Examples: McDonald's, Price/Costco, Wal-Mart, Dell Computer, and Ford Motor in the days of Henry Ford.

➤ The third value discipline is *customer intimacy*. It applies to companies that offer their customers the best total solution: consultation, individual service, guaranteed products. Price aside, these are companies you cannot lose with. Examples: Nordstrom, Roadway Logistics, Johnson Controls, and IBM in its heyday.

A value leader must commit to being the best in its market at one of these disciplines and to achieving parity performance with the other. Because they are in tension, one cannot commit to excellence in all three. But you have to be best in your class in at least one and "good enough" in the other two.

Reengineering efforts are organized to a large degree around the value concept—moving people away from non-value-adding functions and putting them where they have direct impact on the value proposition.

So organizations caught up in defining what approach they will take to deliver value to customers go through the same headaches as companies gutting their process map.

Companies founder when their strategies don't match up well with the people they have working for them. A company that figures out what its key value discipline is has to rummage through all its processes and policies, rooting out those that are not in alignment with the new regime.

This search-and-destroy mission is not limited to things; it also extends to people. Few employees—a handful of Amiables and Analyticals—are suited to work interchangeably in all three of the value philosophies:

➤ Product leader companies like 3M and Intel employ workers with extraordinarily high levels of knowledge, who are given a correspondingly high degree of autonomy. Workers are like aristocrats; because they are highly self-motivated, the atmosphere is a powerful Pull.

➤ Customer intimacy companies like New York's Plaza Hotel have a Push and Pull orientation, featuring high compensation for individuals who deliver quality to individual customers and intolerance of anything less. Workers function like shopkeepers of quality establishments, proud of their skills and alert to customer needs.

➤ Operationally excellent companies like Taco Bell, which has stopped preparing food and is now just assembling ingredients supplied by vendors, are Push all the way—low wages, low skills, lots of rules. Workers are treated as peasants, who perform best when their work is least distinguishable from the next person's.

When value change initiatives falter, it is often because the existing workforce includes too many people who would enjoy greater success in one of the other two disciplines.

The Improvement Theme

The Improvement theme holds that the challenge of every organization is to keep getting better—forever. The theme has its roots in the ideas of

---

Apocryphal Business Tales

These parables are variations on four overused business anecdotes. We changed them from their inspiring original versions to better reflect everyday reality.

- **The Golden Nugget.** A young associate at an investment bank had been empowered to make decisions that he felt would increase customer satisfaction. One day he sensed that a client's assets could perform better in the futures market, moved $3 million into it, lost the entire amount in less than a week. When the client sued and was awarded the full $3 million, the associate was called to the senior partner's office. "I guess you figure you just spent $3 million educating me, huh?" "Security, this is Mr. Honeywell. Will you get up here on the double?"

- **The Uncooperative Frogs.** Every night in the executive suites of transnational corporations, CEOs are heating up pots of water with frogs inside, to see if it is true that frogs won't escape a slowly heated environment. But as soon as their feet get hot, the frogs jump out.

- **The Prisoner Dilemma.** A jailer gives two sequestered prisoners a choice. If one comes clean, he can go free. If both come clean, you each spend ten years in jail. If neither comes clean, you each spend twenty years in jail. As soon as it is dark, the two prisoners escape.

- **The Heroic Effort.** John, a clerk at a well-known department store, noticed that a customer he had never seen before had accidentally dropped a dollar bill. Before he could return it, the customer had left the area. John consulted the credit slip and determined that she was on vacation from Baraboo, Wisconsin, and that she was booked for a flight home in less than an hour. He debated leaving work, driving to the airport, and if necessary, booking a flight to Baraboo to return the dollar. Then he caught himself and said, "What am I thinking? It's only a dollar."

Frederick Taylor and Frank Gilbreth, who fashioned a new and, for the time, an idealistic internal vision of productivity and specialization in the 1920s.

Quality

In the modern era improvement has meant a focus on boosting quality in products and services. During World War II poor manufacturing quality cost many American lives, and a new generation of engineers and statisticians applied their talents to ensuring reliability in the factory.

Out of this effort grew the idea of inspector-based quality control and, in time, the more preventive, more proactive approaches of quality assurance. It was during the postwar occupation of Japan that William Edwards Deming shared his ideas of industrial quality improvement with leaders of a devastated Japanese industrial base and laid the foundation not just for a revivified Japan, but for a new way of thinking about organizations.

> **"Beijing—Eighteen factory workers were executed today for poor product quality at Chien Bien Refrigerator Factory on the outskirts of the Chinese capital."**
>
> *Wall Street Journal,*
> *October 17, 1989*

This new way was half American and half Japanese. It reached its full flower in the discipline of continuous improvement, or *kaizen*, and its broadest definition in the practice of total quality management, or TQM. But Americans probably first heard about this way of thinking in the context of quality circles.

Quality circles were the breakthrough fad of the 1980s, and they spelled out a pattern that all too many change initiatives would duplicate in the months and years that followed. The idea was that workers would meet formally and propose changes to an organization's quality system. This way people at the shop floor level would have a voice in critiquing and improving the organization.

Quality circles continued to work well in Japan, where a culture of respect compels organizations to hear employees out once they are invited to speak. In the United States, however, there is no such tradition of respect; here, we feel freer to disregard inputs we don't like. Quality circles had no power except the power to propose. Inevitably, a circle would critique something that a higher-up deemed to be beyond reproach—something embarrassing to a manager, or something that cost money, or something that diminished a boss's power—and the circle would be hung out to dry.

Quality circles were a Pull mechanism that, transplanted to the United states, was expected to function in a Push environment. They caught on as a fad, but were unable to survive in the hostile working environment. Of the many thousands of quality circles formed in the early 1980s, it is estimated that 75 percent were extinct within four years.[14]

TQM

When quality returned to the American forefront, it came back roaring. Quality circles had been like bicycles, meek and underpowered. Total quality management came on like an American car, ambitious, wide, with tons of features, chrome, and customability.

> **"If you don't have time to do it right you must have time to do it over."**
>
> *Philip Crosby*

The main things TQM had that quality circles lacked were involvement, empowerment, and feedback. TQM aimed to touch every improvement base. It would look to improve an organization's leadership and its relationships with customers, partners, and suppliers; it would also expect a new attitude about topics never before tied to quality—data management, training, employee involvement. It was called total quality management because its scope spared nothing.

TQM is a mall of change initiatives, a theme-park-within-a-theme-park. It covers more than a dozen revolutionary management themes, including improved worker relations (employee participation), improved communication (feedback loops), improved processes, improved measurement, and above all, a deeper relationship with customers. It is the philosophy undergirding the Baldrige Award.

In application, TQM can be a modest, one-focus-at-a-time program, or it can be a fire-every-gun-at-once overhaul of the entire organization. It succeeds best when its many tentacles are guided by a central principle. Customer satisfaction is the principle most often supplied, but it is possible to fashion a TQM program based on other visions: the drive to innovate, to entertain, to strengthen a cause, to provide long-term employment and profits.

TQM seldom goes 100 percent awry, because there are so many facets of it, several are sure to yield results. But complaints about comprehensive quality improvement programs are common. Usually they arise because of the brand of TQM that is being implemented.

➤ **Too broad**. Attacking everything at once is usually a recipe for exhausted confusion, but that is the approach most companies adopt with TQM. Wise organizations assign pilot teams to make mistakes on a small scale, and roll out the program to other units along with the lessons learned in the pilot stage.

➤ **Too narrow**. Companies that adopt off-the-shelf quality solutions, imitating what they read about another company, or that put all their eggs in the ISO 9000 or Baldrige assessment basket, violate the first law of continuous improvement—open-mindedness to change opportunities. Deming warned that organizations need to craft quality regimens out of their own knowledge and experience—not what we read in a magazine.

➤ **Too rushed**. Doing TQM the way it cries out to be done is like adding a second full-time job to the one you already have. Many companies have implemented a companywide TQM effort only to cut it back later when it proved too distracting and too demoralizing to workers. Florida Power & Light won the Deming Award in 1988 and immediately abbreviated their TQM program to one they could manage.

➤ **Too expensive**. Large corporations have spent tens of millions on TQM measurements, paradoxically without measuring whether the money was well spent. The $64,000 question is still, after twenty years of experience, does higher quality reap higher profits?

➤ **Too bureaucratic**. Quality has been stretched to include every imaginable dimension of product and service success, but it has not been extended to include the corporation itself. Thus many of the companies we associate with highest quality are often bloated Pamper organizations. Quality in products and services is not their problem; quality in operational efficiency is.

If there is a single moment when most quality programs go wrong, it is the moment of deployment, when an organization of some size hands the

---

The Dumbing of Deming

When William Edwards Deming died at age 49 in 1993, he was the most respected figure in the history of organizational thought. But as much as he enjoyed in life telling companies when they were wrong, so would he be dismayed at companies who have simplistically implemented his "14 Points of Management." Deming did not suffer fools gladly, and he abhorred seeing his life of rigorous thinking reduced to a cheat-sheet. There are many stories of him upbraiding quality professionals for taking his 14 Points too literally.[15]

He said that each organization, once it possessed profound knowledge, should come up with its own version of the 14 points. As an exercise in perversity, consider each of his 14 Points, and imagine how each has been routinely misunderstood, imperfectly understood, understood out of context, and downright botched:

1. "Create constancy of purpose toward improvement of product and service."
   ➤ *Adopt a single point of view and close the book on new thinking.*
2. "Adopt the new philosophy."
   ➤ *Trash all that went before and create afresh.*
3. "Cease dependence on inspection to achieve quality."
   ➤ *Stop looking for mistakes.*

(continued on facing page)

TQM package over to its workforce. Leaders who had shepherded the program from its inception to the formulation of fine details have a bad habit of stepping back from the action at this point, perhaps hoping the newly empowered workforce will figure everything out by itself.

That never happens. Leadership is never as necessary as at this moment of handoff. Not only must the champions and sponsors of the quality effort show their support—including the topmost levels of management—but they must hang in there as teachers and coaches, even as the "official" trainers go to work.

Finally, give some thought to differences among workers. The generic two-day quality training course may be appropriate for the heart of

4. "End the practice of awarding business on the basis of price tag."
    ➤ *Form sweetheart unions with key suppliers.*
5. "Improve constantly. "
    ➤ *Focus entirely on improving processes. turning a blind eye to whether what is being improved matters to customers.*
6. "Institute training on the job."
    ➤ *Do only on-the-job training.*
7. "Institute leadership."
    ➤ *Replace managerial acumen with charismatic posturing.*
8. "Drive out fear."
    ➤ *Pamper people.*
9. "Break down barriers between departments."
    ➤ *Weaken functions.*
10. "Eliminate slogans, exhortations, and targets."
    ➤ *Eliminate encouragement and recognition.*
11. "Eliminate quotas. Eliminate management by objective. Eliminate management by numbers, numerical goals."
    ➤ *Eliminate standards. Eliminate objectives. Eliminate arithmetic.*
12. "Remove barriers that rob the hourly worker of his right to pride of workmanship."
    ➤ *Ignore deadlines and cost overruns.*
13. "Institute a vigorous program of education and self-improvement."
    ➤ *Emphasize learning over doing.*
14. "The transformation is everybody's job."[16]
    ➤ *Compulsory drills at dawn.*

the workforce—the people who can be relied on to respond affirmatively to the Push/Pull of a new challenge.

But there will be people at the far end of the scales who will require special attention. The metaphiles will be like rabbits, wanting to get started without delay. If you were smart, you enlisted their help during the pilot stages. These are the people who can fall on their faces and get up laughing—the perfect people to launch a new idea.

At the other end of the scale will be the people who will show the greatest resistance, the metamorons who keep the old system humming, and are likely to balk at the new. These people will need more work, more reassurance, and more time to get with the new regime.

The Direction Theme

The saddest reason for change's failure is that it was the wrong change. It is always disheartening to discover, long after you have stopped shaking, that your organization didn't need electroshock treatment. It was a misread, or a mislead. The Direction theme is about *leadership* and *vision*, the two characteristics pointing organizations in the direction they are going to go galloping off in, giving them that final slap on the hindquarters. We place this theme in the center of the ChangeLand continuum because no change initiative can succeed without both vision and leadership. Organizations aren't like lone scientists, laboring in a lab. They can't "get lucky." They do what they do because someone has an idea and knows how to stand at the levers of Push and Pull to make that idea a reality.

> **"Nine out of ten people who go into a store looking for a self-help book need assistance finding it."**
>
> *Internet graffito*

Leadership

There is so much to say about the new passion for leadership. We included a lengthy chapter in *Why Teams Don't Work* about how leaders come up short. We refer newcomers to the topic to that book. There are no newcomers to the topic, of course, because everyone has thought about leadership and its important role in making change happen. It is the catalyst for nearly all change; without it, even bad change doesn't happen.

The craze surrounding leadership is the most curious development of the Aquarian era of organizational thinking. The traditional meaning of the word summons up manly images of generals on horseback, swords skyward. But the new movement of leadership has gone in almost the opposite direction: toward a vision of the leader as emotionally in tune with others, a nurturer of ideas and aspirations, a sharer of information, a teacher, a helpmeet, a friend.

These descriptives go against the male ideal. The "feminization" of leadership is an idea no one seems to want to take credit for, but that is clearly what it is: a role reaching out to that side of the human personality that traditionally has not been asked, or allowed, to lead. There is tremendous merit in the idea of managers, male and female, allowing the development of this other side. It permits leaders to think of themselves more as motivators, as culture-makers, and providers of pathways out of the macho excesses that have "led" so many organizations to the brink.

That is what is happening in the leadership movement today. The previous generation's leaders were gladiators and whiz-kids, MacArthurs and MacNamaras. New Age leaders, by contrast, are agents of visionary kindness. They are facilitators, map-makers, coaches.

This development fits with the Push/Pull split. Organizations that have tried using traditionally masculine coercion techniques are seeing the wisdom of changing to techniques that bring out the best in individuals, whatever that may be. Stereotypically, it has been the father that wants his son to be just like him, to do what he says. As the son reaches maturity, the father expects the son to become "a man," and be suddenly good at leading, after a lifetime of following. Stereotypically, it is the mother who raises her children, teaches principles, and allows the children to be themselves.

> **"Leadership is nature's way of removing morons from the productive flow."**
>
> *Dogbert, in the cartoon strip Dilbert*

There are other leadership paradoxes. One of the strangest is seeing people lining up and paying money to learn how to become leaders. Another, embedded inside that one, is leadership experts who appear to prefer describing it to providing it.

In recent years we have created a false dichotomy between management, which is held out as bad and mechanistic and cold, and this new thing, leadership, which is in all ways good and transformative and noble. This dichotomy is unfortunate for management, which is still critical to the success of any initiative, and for leadership itself, which is in danger of being apotheosized out of existence and being made too heroic for ordinary business people to do.

Though it is a favorite sport of Americans to hold our leaders up to ridicule, there really is something substantive called leadership and without it, the democratic organization, no matter how empowered its people and no matter how participative its processes, is in deep weeds. We need leaders to keep us on point—to *lead*. And we need them to give us a point or vision to focus on.

Leadership must be real to matter. Recent literature (and ancient literature, going back to Tao) suggests that the modern leader should be a servant to those who follow, and that the leader should forswear privilege and eat with the masses and park far from the front door like everyone else. The new leader should be a counselor, an easer of friction ("facilitator"), a friend.

That kind of presence in an organization must indeed be wonderful, but it sounds more like Mr. Chips than the kinds of bosses most of us have had. Is it likely that busy, important people will have time for everyone? Is it natural for underlings to seek out the counsel of people who have the power of life and death over them? How many of us trust the facilitating skills of someone who is better known for keeping our entrails tied in a permanent knot of stress, worry, and fear?

To put it another way, how many of us have friends who make 60 times more money than we make?

> "An army of sheep led by a lion would defeat an army of lions led by a sheep."
>
> *Arab proverb*

When we turn away from the leadership literature and toward the world of real leadership, the contradictions overwhelm us. For every leader plying Push and Pull to elicit people's best efforts for a common cause, there are a dozen who are obviously only in it for themselves.

In the current scheme of things, the leader is less often a servant than someone who loots a failing company of its diminished resources before parachuting to safety.

The burden of leadership reform should be on leaders. Let them forswear stock purchase plans. Forsake the executive eject button. If earnings come up short, do as Jim Renier did when he was CEO of Honeywell and give some back. Pay back a little more each time your managerial wizardry fails to keep a valuable employee employed.

They may say, that isn't how the market works. CEOs are swapped like baseball cards, the compensation levels quickly reaching sky-high levels that can be 60—even 100—times the average worker salary. You didn't create this crazy system.

If you're a leader, then lead. You don't Pull by words, you Pull by example. So long as leadership maintains its imperial, feudal ways—"Do as I say, not as I do"—efforts to empower, involve, and collaborate ring false.

Mission and Vision

Like chickens and eggs, it can be debated which is more important, leadership or vision. One view is that leadership is enough by itself—that charisma or personal energy, in lieu of an enduring vision, can keep an organization vital. It is a uniquely American idea that a genius leader—a Bill Gates or Walt Disney or Warren Buffett—can take the place of a coherent strategy.

The other view is that leadership is merely a delivery mechanism for vision. The vision itself is what sustains and keeps an unwieldy organization stumbling on through difficulty and discord. The long-term goal is the one thing that everyone knows about and understands, and that can be used to break short-term logjams. It is the trump that can momentarily unite fractured groups and salve open organizational wounds. It is the essence of the Pull part of change—the idea that draws people together to work.

Where organizations go wrong is in assuming that the vision is some precious grail-like object that only the organizational priests are privy to—that it appears in a dream to the executive team, who then hold it up high for the rank and file to ooh and ahh over.

> **"Vision without action is a daydream. Action without vision is a nightmare."**
>
> *Japanese proverb*

To this end, vision-and-mission consultants will often take the management team aside for several consecutive weekends, sequester them at some inspirational high location in the Rockies, Sierra Madres, or Adirondacks—visioning occurs best at altitudes frequented by eagles—and they hold hands, seance-style, until the vision announces itself.

The problem with the priestly approach to vision-and-mission is that the resulting vision is often a lot of garbage. The outcome, instead of being a useful reminder to keep to the change track, is a paragraph held to be so sacred that no one dares change it.

Fairly humming with exalted intentions, most vision or mission statements lead off with: "We are committed to :

➤ "industry leadership. . . ."
➤ "world-class process management. . . ."
➤ "an unsurpassed commitment to customer satisfaction. . . ."

➤ "next-century technology. . . ."
➤ "unshakable integrity in all our dealings. . . ."

This is not communication, but a bouquet of superlatives, a kind of corporate mantra to mutter as the organization tiptoes past the graveyard of change. Since the words have been officially sanctified, the words are what people pay attention to and not the meaning. Of course, since the words are vague and mushy, there is not a lot of attachable meaning anyway.

This is not to say that the mission-and-vision process is useless. Great companies have focused on vision with great success. But they started doing so thirty years before it became the blue plate special at the consulting cafeteria. And they focused not on the vocabulary, grammar, and punctuation of the statement, but on homely, down-to-earth goals:

➤ "We will be first or second in every market we sell to. . . ."
➤ "We will focus our own research on applications, while focusing outside investment on technologies that may not bear fruit for years. . . ."
➤ "We will refuse payment for any job our customers are unhappy with, no matter what the reason. . . ."
➤ "We will promote from within, and train associates in new skills. . . ."

James Collins in *Built to Last* observes that most organizations spend most of their strategic thinking time writing the "vision statement," taking little time beforehand to discuss the topic, and making only a shallow effort afterward to communicate the message down through the ranks and out to the world.

The proportions are all wrong, Collins says. Zero time should be spent on writing down what the core values and core purposes are. "Wordsmithing" is a pointless exercise if the meaning underlying the statement is fluff, or if it will never be put to the test of reality. What portion of time should be spent on fixing the system so the values cannot be ignored? Try 80 percent.[17]

A proper vision may make mention of market penetration or improved cycle times, but its roots go deeper. They extend all the way down to the first questions a business must ask: Why are we doing this? What is the point of all this toil? What's it all about?

Is it just money? Making money, purely, solely, and totally, is the legitimate vision for results-driven investment vessels like Buffett's Berkshire Hathaway. Such companies have no operations; they are purely financial entities, and their shareholder constituency far outweighs their other constituencies—the handful of employees such companies employ, the communities in which they do business. It could be argued that they do not really do "business," because they are never "busy."

Most companies, however, are rooted in the more concrete world of making products and performing services, and their visions must answer a philosophical question: Do we want to make a difference in the lives of the constituencies we serve?

The vision process has humbled every organization that came to it with honest intentions. It casts a cold light on a company's performance and the compromises we all make to meet short-term obligations. But to those who come wanting to make their organizations matter more to the constituencies they serve, it provides a powerful Pull that can keep hope alive, over the course of many years.

> "Fool someone once and they'll be foolish for a day, but teach them to fool themselves and they'll be foolish for a lifetime."
>
> *Michael Fry*

The Character Theme

A characteristic of many change initiatives is the creation of a "second bottom line," or reason for the corporation's existence. Thus, zero defects could be asserted as a primary corporate goal, alongside net profits; or total customer satisfaction; or the provision of steady employment—whatever the chairman and board decide is as important as quarterly profits.

The second bottom line of a principle-centered organization is virtue. Doing good while doing well, is the motto of the character crowd. A good company is honest and above-board in its dealings; hews to strict ethical guidelines on corporate and individual behavior; acts only in consonance with its convictions; is fair to employees and suppliers and considerate of the community it does business in.

While not usually a corporate initiative, character or organizational ethics is an important theme of New Age management. It shows up in the Baldrige Award criteria, slightly veiled, as the "Public Responsibility and

Corporate Citizenship" category. It is a modeling system that begins with the leadership, and over time, as ancient suspicions are put to rout by decency and justice, infuses the entire organization, and goes on to make the marketplace itself an incrementally more moral place.

It is the organizational equivalent of the notion of "acts of random kindness," which holds that good deeds encourage more good deeds. An ethically oriented organization cleans up its little corner of the world with right action. Other organizations do the same with their corners. Right action stimulates and models still more right action. Soon the entire world is transformed, corporate raiders start saying "Mother, may I" before they pounce, the sun comes out, and the birds sing.

Increasing the amount of decent behavior in the business world is all to the good. But making righteousness a "second bottom line" can lead to unforeseen problems. In the first place, there is really no such thing as "organizational morality." Organizations are not people and do not have free will, not even when the individuals in the organization are wholly empowered.

Leaders are necessarily political creatures, balancers of many interests. Their job is to choose what is best for the most people over the most significant time period. This is less an ethical task—choosing the binary right thing—than a Machiavellian exercise of finding the lesser of evils in a rainbow of grays. "Good" leaders still administer predictable doses of pain to people, families and communities, just as "good" generals still send soldiers to their deaths. Morally indelicate decisions come with the job of seeking the most good for the largest number.

The most authentic measure of corporate character may be the ethical conduct of the company's leaders, not as leaders but as human beings. Though there cannot really be such a thing as a "good organization," an organization where people behave ethically—where they are allowed to do the right thing, never mind being encouraged to—is the next best thing.

The Relationship Theme

The metaphor of the Industrial Age was the gear. The machines people operated were gears and so were the people operating them. Squirt a little oil on our teeth from time to time, and presumably we would remain in good working order.

In the New Age, we're not gears any more, and the machine itself is now seen as a living organism composed of many interdependent living cells, all different, needing not oil but sustenance, community, and meaning. The Relationship theme is an umbrella over a handful of initiatives that acknowledge this new insight. Their emphasis is on understanding and strengthening the membranes between these living cells.

The significance of the Relationship theme is that introducing the human factor to the managerial task greatly expands the role of managers—it means managers must be different kinds of people than they were a generation ago. The weakness of the theme is that, because it is about people and their passions, it is susceptible to passing fashions.

Theories X, Y, and Z

These were theories of the 1950s that grew out of the first realizations that there was something important missing in the existing and very successful manufacturing model. The image that comes down to us is of Charlie Chaplin being pulled through the giant gearmill in *Modern Times*, then becoming a kind of machine himself, treating every challenge he encountered as a bolt needing tightening.

> **"Management isn't about making friends, it's about getting things done."**
>
> *Dave Marquette*

Douglas McGregor, the godfather of humanistic management, fired the first volley of the New Age in a 1960 book called *The Human Side of the Enterprise*.[18] First he described what he saw as the status quo, an essentially mechanistic model combining the principles of scientific management and the metaphor of the assembly line. McGregor called this model Theory X. In Theory X:

➤ workers dislike and avoid work
➤ supervisors must threaten punishment
➤ workers avoid responsibility and seek direction

In this theory managers are the repository of all important information. They and only they know what's best for the organization. Rank and file workers are essentially children, driven only by their own concerns and oblivious to the organization's needs. Any system attempting to shift the responsibility for organizational vision from management to the total workforce is therefore doomed to failure.

In McGregor's counterproposal, Theory Y:

➤ workers want to find job satisfaction
➤ greatest results come from willing participation
➤ workers seek opportunity for involvement and self-respect

The heart of Theory Y is that workers are not children, that they often care about the organizations they are a part of, and this concern ought to be harnessed through proper motivation and a more humane workplace, for the corporate good. Treat people better, McGregor said, and you will see productivity that makes the existing order of button-pushing and results-demanding pale.

Theory Y was a warning shot, a message to the old ways that the days of Pummel were numbered. McGregor's humane ideas made him a savior to a generation of young managers. There was a great rush at better companies to show that the management had a new attitude toward workers and a new paradigm for control. There were a few showcase Theory Y companies that one could point to as examples of the new thinking—IBM, S. C. Johnson, Pan Am.

In a way, Theory Y was a blueprint for the management revolution that followed—how to redefine control, from buttons to be pushed by management, to a healthy, productive system that generated its own rewards and motivation.

It quickly became apparent to everyone trying to leverage change that while Theory Y was powerful on paper, Theory X was more powerful on the shop floor. Trying to reconcile the two visions, McGregor took another shot at Utopia with Theory Z, which embodied elements of both tight centralized and loose decentralized control—roughly analogous to our yoking together of Push (control) and Pull (autonomy).

But the world of managerial thought was picking up speed. Ken Blanchard ("One Minute Managing") and Tom Peters ("management by wandering around") were just around the corner, with simple fads that would co-opt the humane principles of McGregor, and make a sleepy publishing category, business books, a best-selling phenomenon.

The New Age gathered steam so quickly that no one mentioned to William Ouchi, who wrote a book two years later with the title *Theory Z*, an examination of Japanese organizational ideas that worked just as well in the U.S., that the name had already been taken.

The Life Cycle of a Business Fad

There is a balloon game every child has played. It is too simple to have a name. The idea is simply to keep a falling balloon in the air, no matter what, without actually holding it in your hands. You can bump it with your fingertips, fists, forehead, or nose.

It's great for young kids because the balloon moves slowly, and it takes neither speed nor muscle to keep the balloon in the air for several minutes at a time. And oh yes, the penalty for letting it touch the ground is the destruction of the universe.

That game is a lot like the life cycle of a business idea, how it comes into being and gradually infiltrates the organizational world. It usually begins with an elegant new metaphor, a new way of looking at structure, process, or strategy.

The taut new idea is then sent aloft by its creator to make its way through the atmosphere. As it descends, the first tier of clever people, mostly consultants, seize on it as if it were theirs, codify it, simplify it, rename it as something of their own. The game is now on, as the next tier of players—the managers—bump the idea up as long as they can, using heads, elbows, and heinies.

Eventually the laws of physics and of organizations intervene. Either the once-taut idea loses its surface tension and deflates by itself, or the idea comes into contact with something sharp, like an astute criticism, or worst of all, it touches the ground, the universe is not destroyed, and everyone playing realizes the idea was never magical to begin with.

When too many balloons touch the ground, the creator—the person who put the idea into play, usually the CEO—deflates, loses credibility. New ideas must then come from another source, a new leader or an outside adviser who can pump new helium into the organization. And the process begins anew.

One Minute Managing

One Minute Managing is one of the grandaddies of change fads. A good alternate name for it might be "Son of Theory Y," for it sprang from the intuition Douglas McGregor had, that great things were possible if organizations would start treating people more like human beings and less like rats in mazes.

The One Minute idea appeared in a series of very brief, very readable best-selling (7 million sold) books by Kenneth Blanchard and a series of coauthors in the early 1980s. The core idea was that managing people—the core task of managers—wasn't as hard as all the managerial systems being taught in business school suggested. What managers needed to do, Blanchard suggested, was to forget about the "systems" and start paying attention to people as individuals, at least for one minute.

The blinding insight of *The One Minute Manager* was that managers could perform the three primary tasks of management in minute-long installments.[19] Individual goals could be set, and individual persons could be praised or repri-manded, in a minute. More than a minute was more than most individuals were willing to hear; on the other hand, a minute of attention was 60 seconds more than most people were getting from their bosses.

> **"A good catchword can obscure analysis for fifty years."**
>
> *Wendell L. Wilkie*

That this idea struck people as ingenious speaks volumes about how mechanical the art of management had become at that time.

The One Minute Manager was a clarion call to organizations to start using their hearts as well as their heads, and to get involved one-on-one with the people whose lives they hold in their hands. As a sustainable innovation, the practice came up a little short. It is worth noting that Blanchard's latest book is titled *Empowerment Takes More Than a Minute*. But it changed the way many people thought about business. It was no longer about pushing buttons; it was now about relationships.

Management by Wandering Around

"Management by wandering around" was one of the first ideas Tom Peters put forth that caught the imagination of managers. The idea is simply that executives and other managers can learn more about their organizations by getting out and seeing things firsthand than by examining monthly reports.

MBWA is a prevention-based approach, because it lets managers find out what's eating employees and do something about it, before the irritations fester into full-blown pustules.[20] At its best it means coming down from the executive floor and getting involved—participating in teams, running a finger over doorsills for dust, asking people at the loading docks what's on their mind, seeing for yourself if the vision you think you've been inculcating has taken root.

Having breakfast with workers in an informal setting with small groups or individuals is a great way to deepen your understanding of employees' issues, while uncovering operational glitches that stand in the way of customer satisfaction.

An insurance executive we know sees himself as a kind of organizational mole or double agent, spending well over half of his time walking around, talking to workers, uncovering problems or perceptions of problems, and then challenging his senior managers to come up with solutions. When an employee resigns, the executive personally reads through the transcripts of the exit interview to find out what made the person want to leave.

> **"Feedback is the breakfast of champions."**
>
> *Ken Blanchard*

MBWA is a Pull initiative in that it is about doing a better job, not avoiding pain. But in a company where Pull is a new concept, MBWA will have employees running for the hills. "The boss is coming!" If a dog knows you by your club, do not expect him to greet you with wagging tail.

In multisite organizations, MBWA presents an interesting challenge: how do you walk around when the "around" is transglobal? You walk when you can walk, and you use other means when you have to. Federal Express executives are expected to visit local stations whenever they visit a city where FedEx operates.

Technology also comes in handy. Interactive intranets maintain an ongoing public, yet anonymous, Q&A session between workers and bosses. Companies like FedEx maintain global television networks to give associates around the world a chance to talk live with the head honchos.

Access is more than a ploy to make workers feel they are important; it's a vital conduit for ideas that can keep organizations competitive.

Customer Satisfaction

Like most good change ideas, customer satisfaction comes at us with all the power of something that should have been perfectly obvious, but which organizations have too long ignored.

Customer satisfaction has always merited lip service: "The customer is always right." "The customer comes first." In recent years, however, the customer has become king with a vengeance. Everyone is scurrying to learn what customers want, whip up something approximating that, and shine it back at the customer base. "See?"

Unfortunately, American business has succumbed wholesale to substituting marketing gimmicks (the manipulation of customer perceptions) for the genuine article (treating customers with respect and providing them with products and services that help them achieve their objectives). Vast, grisly books could be written about this trend, which continues today, even at companies that mouth solemn pieties about customer satisfaction.

> **"The most important skill of managers and leaders in the years to come will be conversation."**
>
> *Alan Weber*

The customer satisfaction idea saved quality control from itself. Years ago, quality was an internally defined idea. Engineers and designers prided themselves on designing high-quality items, exceeding everyday specs. At the beginning of the video revolution, 3M put great store in designing tape cases that could survive falls from a height of 30 feet. Problem was, customers weren't dropping cases from that height—30 inches was about the maximum. No wonder Fuji, which actually met and talked with customers, could sell truckloads of tape for a third of 3M's initial cost. 3M was making Cadillacs for customers who wanted Chevys.

It would be a good thing if most organizations simply reverted to the old nostrums and put the customer first. There are many easy ways to get employees who are working at a far remove from customers to think about customers. One is to select a few, take them to meet customers and talk to them, and have them inoculate other workers with the new thinking upon their return.

The Customer as God

It is important not to make customers into gods. Many companies, in the fast-food and overnight delivery industries, for instance, achieve success not through catering to individual customer requests but by providing a simple universal operational model that saves customers money. They don't ignore the customer, exactly, but they ignore the individual customer's druthers in favor of the average customer's needs.

Ford Motor made affordable automobiles, so long as you liked black. McDonald's serves cheap burgers fast, so long as you like them with the works. Southwest Airlines will get you where you want to go at the lowest cost, but please don't slow down the boarding process.

Lots of organizations get carried away (see box). They apply the external customer model to people working inside the organization as well—"internal customers"—a mistake. Or they allow customer judgment to smother the entrepreneurial spark of management and the engineering talent of designers.

We warned earlier that Pummel organizations only concern themselves with the happiness of ownership and that the imbalance threatened the long-term security of the organization. Pamper organizations cater to their employees' every need, with the same result. Customers are another constituency that can be overserved.

> "It is no use walking anywhere to preach unless our walking is our preaching."
>
> *St. Francis of Assisi*

Wise companies understand that customers cannot be relied upon for the best insights into the future. Customers generally ask for some variation on present-day products and services—a VCR that is easy to program, for instance. A truly new idea or technology, like interactive video or virtual reality television programming, is something a company can only come up with on its own—by intuiting what customers of the future may find delightful or indispensable. Intuiting means guessing, which means risking. So even in a customer-driven era, there is a place for entrepreneurial spark.

When "customer satisfaction" means you take your eyes off the distant horizon and your organization's long-term prospects, it has ceased to be a tool and has become a crutch.

Tom Peters based an entire book[20] on the good things that happen when "meeting customer requirements" is set aside, and designers head off toward their own best sense of what is great. Peters calls it the wow! factor, and it is a smart antidote for lazy "customer sat."

But wow! works best when the poetic side of design is invoked, when imagination takes hold of the process and Pulls. Companies that set customer satisfaction aside and hew to strictly mechanistic product improvement strategies are back to making Cadillacs.

Adventure Learning

Adventure learning is a group event in which a team is put through a series of challenging physical and mental tasks. The events often take place outdoors, in an idyllic setting, at a retreat in the mountains, or a dude ranch, or a park. They are facilitator-led, and they build on the psychological lessons learned years ago in seventies-ish, Carl Rogers–style encounter groups for normals.

Back then it was discovered that people could experience sensational breakthroughs in behavior if asked to do things they would not ordinarily do, with the rest of the group acting as support. The classic example is "Trust Falls." In this exercise, you stand a blindfolded person on a table, then let him fall backward, with the other group members catching the falling individual.

There are higher-risk and lower-risk levels of adventure learning. High risk involves climbing mountains, crossing rope bridges, rapidly descending on pulleys, and the like. There is some degree of actual physical danger in high-risk exercises—your teammates could decide not to belay you with their support ropes, and you could fall off the mountain. Low-risk is adventure learning on a budget, usually a series of physical outdoors exercises that can be done in a park or backyard.

These games are a lot of fun to play. Most new teams are pretty stiff and formal with one another. They have never met outside the work situation. These games help break the ice and get people physically involved with one another. We are talking group grope here, and there are moments that will strike some as risqué, a sort of company-sanctioned Twister.

The lessons people learn in these groups include overcoming fear, overcoming distrust, and the synergistic power of a group working to support the individual. People who do this rave about it. They say it enabled them to do things they could never do before. They say it changed their lives. Afterward there is much hugging, exulting, people saying, "Why didn't we do this years ago?"

Everyone is ecstatic, certain that the lessons of teamwork will naturally translate to something wonderful once they get back to the office. But . . . when the team folds up its ropes and packs away its carabiners and heads back to the city, are they a better team?

Usually they are not. People may be friendlier. They may feel that they got to know one another out of the work setting. They may have lots of good warm fuzzies toward one another—which is good. They may head back with better intentions to team with one another—also good.

But they will not be a better team because the mountaineering or web-climbing exercises were not really about teaming. These activities were not developed to improve teamwork. They were developed to explore various dimensions of personal development. They are fantastic for achieving personal breakthroughs with one's own demons and fears. And yes, they are very good at improving one's personal attitudes about being in groups and allowing oneself to trust others.

Teams are not failing because people have fears and phobias, or are unable, in a broad generic way, to "trust." Teams are failing because members are confused about what their roles are, what their missions are, whether or not they have the authority to do whatever needs to be done.

All this stuff with the carabiners and pulleys is great fun and personally exhilarating. It is also pointless. Training firms that sell adventure learning for its personal exploration benefits are giving you your money's worth. Training firms that sell adventure learning for its team-building benefits are selling you a bill of goods.

Internal Customers

The internal customer idea was first propagated in Richard Shonberger's 1989 book *Building a Chain of Customers*. Shonberger saw that the customer relationship did not exist solely between the end-customer and the company serving or selling to that customer. Instead, there was a chain of "customer" relationships at every stage and every process in the creation, design, and delivery of that product or service.

The internal customer idea swayed enough people in and out of the quality movement that for years it constituted an official item under the Quality Assurance section of Baldrige Award criteria, "Business Process and Support Service Quality."[21] In truth, the concept was a great way for organizations whose functions had traditionally been at war with one another to make peace and focus on a common adversary—the company's competitors. Books were written about ingenious programs linking intracompany teams in a necklace of vision statements, internal guarantees ("your work returned in 24 hours or we won't charge your corporate account"). It was a great consciousness-raiser.

A backlash developed when observers criticized internal customers as justifying bureaucracy and distracting workers from their true customer, the one who buys the product/service and thus pays for everyone's groceries.

The best way of using the internal-customer concept may be as a *what-if*. Rather than instituting formal programs to legitimize the parties you hand work off to and issuing guarantees and signing peace treaties and all that, why not cultivate an attitude within teams and functions that the next team and function down the hall is not the enemy. *What if* they were your customer—how differently would you deal with them? Would you withhold information and communication? Would you ignore them, or throw work over their transom and run away?

What if you began seeing the guy working at the next desk instead of as competing against you for corporate payroll resources as your customer, and thus an ally in obtaining greater company profits? Big difference there. *What if* your company began seeing you not as someone to heap stress on, but instead as someone to be kept happy and productive—as a kind of customer, who must be persuaded to keep your brain and muscle in the organization's employ?

The Culture Theme

We said earlier that the best way to change is to be new—to not have an existing infrastructure or culture that will constantly be calling you back to the way you were. Infrastructure is buildings, roads, and machines; culture is what a company is after the buildings, roads, and machines are blown up and hauled away. Culture is the more durable of the two.

Culture is tough to consciously change because it is seldom consciously put in place to begin with. Instead, it usually arises unbidden from employees' perceptions of the boss's personality. Because its purpose is to minimize the pain of nonadaptation, it focuses on avoiding negatives—wearing unpressed pants or speaking out of turn.

This culture is often at odds with the stated culture. Most places have a *de jure* culture that they claim adherence to and a *de facto* one that is the obvious object of their allegiance. The unofficial one is the more powerful of the two. It thrives on Pummel from above and cowardice from below; so long as everyone agrees to abide by these unspoken rules, they will hold sway.

There are happy-talk books out there that suggest that altering corporate culture is no more difficult than reducing product defects or speeding up cycle time. You simply assess what you are like now, describe what you would rather be like in the future, and take the necessary action steps to transform. Only three steps, but each one is a doozy—you will need carabiners and grappling hooks and long, long ropes to get to the top of them.

Of all the attributes an organization has, culture is the most human, and it will not yield quickly or easily to any mechanistic solution. The only way we know for an organization to bring disparate cultures into alignment is to behave the same way in real life as you say you will in your mission statement. And give yourselves six months before expecting to see even minor improvement. That is like giving up fatty foods; few organizations have the willpower for such a commitment.

Suggestion: if you are CEO or team leader, and you have been in that position for a significant period of time, and you perceive that the group you lead needs a life-giving jolt to the heart of its culture, go away. Chances are excellent that you are at least part of the problem and not the best person to lead to its solution.

The Boundaryless Corporation

One way organizations have tried to beat the culture problem is by pretending its walls aren't there any more. GE's Jack Welch got a lot of mileage from his idea of a "boundaryless corporation." William Davidow

Just Ask

To understand the de facto culture of a place, all you need to do is ask employees. We elicited these remarks—ranging from the quirky to the obnoxious—describing the atmosphere where they work from workers at a single site. Needless to say, none of this appeared in the mission-and-vision brochure:

> "Individual effort is encouraged, but mavericks are terminated."
> "We talk about cooperation, but build organizational firewalls."
> "We think strategically, but manage tactically."
> "We promote strong performers into do-nothing positions, the Peter Principle in reverse."
> "Our value measures are internal, our customers are external."
> "We promote quality, but reward quantity."
> "We manage the many to correct the problems of the few."
> "They put out free doughnuts in the cafeteria on the Tuesday before Thanksgiving, which is the day that all employees and retirees receive a turkey. Anyone other than a retiree who tries to take a doughnut is hunted down by one of the Nazi kitchen staff."
> "If they hear we are gossiping they post notices telling us to stop gossiping."
> "They don't really want us to have more than two company-provided writing utensils at our desk. (I have over 100.) On the other hand, they spare no expense on computer equipment."
> "They give us fruit on Tuesdays and Thursdays at lunch. If we take more than two pieces, we get scolded."
> "They don't allow professionals to work part-time or from home."
> "They throw a Men's Party and a Women's Party, on different days, each year. The Men are served brats and beer, and they all smoke big cigars and play poker. The Women are served thimblefuls of cheap champagne, receive pastel-dyed carnation corsages, and get to listen to peppy organ music. "
> "They mail us soft cheese and a depressing letter at Christmastime."

and Michael Malone wrote a best-selling book called *The Virtual Corporation*, about ad hoc organizations that form, perform, and melt away again when the task is completed.

Other wall-erasing approaches include partnering, outsourcing, supplier empowerment, core competencies, and consolidation through mergers, acquisitions, and spinoffs. In each case, the original organization loses some of its contour, and a new shape springs into existence.

And why not? It is said that an ordinary corporation is a "legal fiction." Chemical Bank and Ralston Purina are treated under the law as if they were people, but obviously they are not. Well, these corporations are even more fictional:

A *virtual corporation* is an electronic fiction. It brings people with special talents together, partners them for the duration of a project, then vanishes back into the mists. It exists only to the extent that phone lines, computers, video, and fax technology link its parts together. A virtual corporation is thus not only boundaryless, it is nearly substanceless as well. The advantages of a virtual corporation are flexibility, low cost, and the very high quality that comes from hand-picked people.

Partnering is when two or more organizations team up and pretend they are one organization. The partnership can be between two equals, as when IBM and Apple cooperated on chip development. Or it can be between a hub corporation that calls the shots and numerous subordinate partners, working essentially as suppliers to the hub. Texas Instruments, long a leader in the semiconductor business but losing market share in the 1980s, was having problems coordinating its Pacific Rim subcontractors. How to integrate seven competing vendors 5,000 miles from corporate HQ? TI devised a "virtual factory" concept that treated far-flung warring suppliers as if they were working side by side under one roof.[22] True partners must learn to behave as if they were one company, and that means getting beyond the old win/lose mentality. Partnering cannot succeed if one party is preying on the other.

Supplier empowerment is when a supplier relationship is lifted to the level of near-equal with the hub company. The suppliers are trained to make decisions on the client organization's behalf, have access to information systems, and otherwise behave as if they were one company, not two. An example would be Roadways Logistics acting as Ford Motor Company's logistics unit, managing all inbound and outbound shipments from within Ford's parts docks. In the New Age, suppliers must not be pitted against one another. One of Deming's 14 Points is to use just a few suppliers and aim for quality, not the low bid.

Outsourcing is the decision by a company to let an outside entity do work that used to be done inside the company. The conventional wisdom: only farm out tasks not central to your organization's identity: accounting, information management, printing, legal. Farm out all tasks and you have reduced your organization to being a broker.

Core competencies distinguish a visionary corporation from a confederacy of SBUs. They answer the question, "What combination of talents do we possess that no other company in the world has?" A company's core competency is whatever talent or skill or knack it has, as an organization, that it dare not abandon. In an age of outsourcing, subcontracting, and partnering, a core competency is the one thing you do not outsource, offload, subcontract, or hand off to a partner. It's the most valuable knowledge a company has, its true, essential product or service.

In the wake of all this wisdom, organizations everywhere are scratching their heads trying to determine what their core competency is. Guess what? Most of us are extremely plain vanilla. We don't have any core competency beyond being ourselves and bringing whatever unique charm we can to the business at hand. Yes, we have a challenge to distinguish ourselves from our competition, but no, core competency may not be the mechanism with which we do that.

Core competencies are an example of selling old wine in new bottles. What is there about the concept that is not recognizable in the old adage, "Stick to your knitting?" The genius of the idea, as with so many, is its ability to take the truth of this worn-out thought and reinvest it with modern meaning.

There are dozens of relationship-related initiatives that violate the traditional corporate shell. In each case they cause problems relating to culture. The fallacy is that two or more cultures can collide and simply merge together like molten glass; they tend rather to shatter, more like cold glass.

Here are the characteristic miscalculations of boundaryless organizations:

➤ **Some are more equal than others**. However much a hub partner like IBM promises to let you maintain your identity, be afraid. When another company buys all of your food, it is not a relationship between equals. Which means their culture will inevitably try to dominate yours.

➤ **Add their problem to yours.** You may be three years into an ISO 9000 registration plan, but your new hub partner wants you to do the Baldrige assessment as well. To get on the same page with your partner, you will either have to force employees through two mind-wrenching regimens, or dump one that other people were committed to.

➤ **Sell the farm.** Many companies have partnered themselves into the intellectual graveyard, spinning off competencies that lay too close to the core. Kodak lets IBM do its data processing, which is fine. But Chrysler and Toyota both farm their auto designs to design partners—how they can do that and still call themselves car companies is a puzzlement.

➤ **Strings attached.** When Control Data restructured in the 1980s it created a partner to perform human-relations tasks and charged it to market its skills to the outside world. Before letting it go, though, it crippled the new creature by saddling it with handling all of the old corporation's personnel problems, leaving it no time to attract outside clients. The partnership was just a ruse for dumping bad business.

➤ **The carnivorous collaborator.** Most outsourcing is done to cut costs. By retaining high-value competencies while farming out lower-value competencies, an organization signals that the partner is little more than a sweatshop, working its people to the bone while the hub partner buys another ten years of the good life.

➤ **How convenient.** Many partnerships move accountability outside the hub organization's control. "You say our offshore partner uses prison slave labor or makes kids work 12-hour days? News to us." File this tactic under either "plausible deniability" or "Gifford, Kathie Lee."

"Boundarylessness" is not a bad idea, and in the years ahead it will contribute greatly to the flexibility that success in the information age will demand of organizations. But it will be very hard on the rank and file as they carry the water and feel the pain for these evanescent entities.

In dealing with new partners, always seek equity with them. To be on the spoke end of a hub-and-spoke relationship is never pleasant. At its worst, you will have old-line Pamper organizations feathering their nests by exporting Pummel to yours.

Teams

The subject of teams could go under several other themes—Relationship, Improvement, or Democracy. It involves all those ideas to a strong degree. We choose to place it under Culture, because team failure can usually be traced to problems in moving from a non-team culture to one encouraging cooperation.

Teams are an old concept, dating back at least to the cave era, to the notion that people who collaborate together perform better than people who compete against one another. In a few short years since importing the notion from Japan, teams have become as American as apple pie, hot dogs, and Chevrolet combined. It is the biggest of all change initiatives, implemented in more organizations than TQM and reengineering combined.

The apex of the team movement is the self-directed work team, an amalgam of empowerment, cross-functional participation, and "leaderless leadership." The core idea is that people with different skills and talents can be exceptionally productive and creative working together without conventional supervision.

> **"If one synchronized swimmer drowns, do the rest have to drown too?"**
>
> *Internet graffito*

In all this implementation, there have been lots of successes. Companies have saved billions by moving people out of purely supervisory positions and into flatter work groups. Teams have improved quality and productivity nearly everywhere they have been tried. Teams do work—eventually.

But few of these team successes were achieved without misdirection, false starts, demoralization, and unwanted turnover, as valuable people decided they could not adapt to the new regime.

There are a dozen different reasons for team failure, chief among them:

➤ **Inexperienced or ineffective team leadership.** The designated team leader either doesn't know what he or she is doing, or is not up to the task.
➤ **Lousy communication.** Team members are unsure what their tasks are, what their roles are, how they make decisions, and whether they are on the right track.

➤ **One size fits all.** Teams are not the answer to all of life's problems, and no one kind of team is better in all circumstances than other kinds. Teams should be trained and equipped for the mission they must accomplish. How they decide things, who's in charge, who gets rewarded how, and who does what job are matters that must be tailored to each individual team.

➤ **Doing today's work with yesterday's tools, policies, and structures.** When you switch to teams, you have to change just about everything about the way your business operates—measurement, compensation, reporting, job classifications, the works.

Other, lesser problems:

➤ **Unled teams.** In the rush to create self-directed work teams, organizations either neglect to assign leadership roles, or they allow leadership vacuums to develop and grow. Not every group will intuitively find its natural leaders.

➤ **Ungainly teams.** Teams peak in efficiency at three or four people; in many cases they peak at two. Calling a department of twenty people a team is a figure of speech. What you more likely have is a necklace of teams and teams-within-teams. What's nice for departmental morale is not nice for team functionality. Figure out where the team begins and ends. Everyone else is an adjunct.

➤ **Unready teams.** Teaming takes time. A new team must pass through many ritual stages before it has the trust and will to move forward as a unit.

These are the nuts-and-bolts problems teams have. The core problem is more pernicious, and it is that, all too often, the happy talk about team productivity is a smoke screen for downsizing, the stripping of middle management from the bureaucratic grid.

The rationale for this downsizing is often good: why have trained professionals working between levels in an organization when we can apply all our muscle to customer solutions? Companies thinking this way move their middle managers out to the edge of the circle, where the customers supposedly are, and all that formerly "wasted" corporate genius is applied directly to giving value to customers.

At most organizations, however, a different dynamic is at work. The company only changes because it is in trouble. It identifies teaming as a way to get more bang for the payroll buck. It keeps some middle managers, but lays off many more, who are never to return. Hurray for the morale of stockholders; boo for the morale of surviving workers and for the careers of those who have been given the team axe.

Teams provide a textbook example of how all change initiatives fail. Management presents the idea as a gift to employees, and wheels its Trojan horse inside the corporate walls. But employees can hear the gang of downsizers already sharpening the axe inside the horse's gut. When employees sense betrayal, the negatives flow to the fore and the change is crippled at the worst possible moment. Just when an organization is trying to cultivate a new atmosphere of sharing and trusting among its fledgling teams, it hurts its efforts by withholding key information about who lives and who dies, violating the very trust it is trying to inculcate.

Our last collaboration, *Why Teams Don't Work*, was about the problems inherent in team theory. Our conclusion was that teams were failing because the theory didn't go far enough. Team theory represents a giant leap in our time from a view of organizations that was anchored in a traditional philosophy of management to a new view, in which groups are capable, with a little leadership and a little encouragement, of managing themselves.

Teams ask organizations to alter their entire way of thinking, away from pitting people against one another in the old grid and toward allowing them to work together. Away from intracompany competition and toward intracompany collaboration. It is a big step, and most companies slip up because their culture is too competitive to allow the change to take hold.

Teams are not going to go away. They draw on a very important wellspring in nearly every human being—the fascination and allure of group activity. But teams have natural limits. And they will never perform up to expectations until organizations learn to look one layer deeper than teams, beyond small groups to the individual's heart and mind, where the three circles of change overlap and where change succeeds or fails.

The Democracy Theme

As we travel further to the left side of ChangeLand, we come to the Democracy theme, which has many points in common with a theme way

Boundary Management

To make empowerment work, throw out the word empowerment and replace it with boundary management.

Boundary management sets strict parameters to empowerment. So instead of telling employees: "Do whatever you think seems right and we'll probably back you up on it"—a prescription for dread—you inform workers what their decision-making limits are:

- You have the power to adjust bills up to $100 on your own, on the spot, to make amends for customer dissatisfaction. Over $100, you ask permission.
- You have the power to delay delivery of a product for one week on your own, to make sure it is done right. Longer than that, you ask permission.
- You have the power to allocate purchasing costs 5 percent of the total to improve the order (enlarging type size on a print order, for instance) on your own. Above 5 percent, you get permission.

The range removes the guesswork and allows the worker to exercise judgment without being second-guessed.

Ironic downside: If you're on a use-it-or-lose-it budget, ranges can have a low as well as a high end. If your employer won't allocate your department an equal share next year unless it spends all of this year's money (and what a fine policy that is) you may be empowered to spend only amounts that bring you close to your allocation ceiling. Below that, don't bother.

---

back on the right side—the Reform theme. The two themes tend to seek the same ends, but for very different reasons. Reform initiatives like reengineering, flattening, and downsizing seek to create new organizational shapes that Push people to better results. Democracy initiatives seek changes that Pull people to a higher level of interactivity and accountability, with the pleasant side effect of improved results. Though the spirits are very different, the net results are often the same. To flatten an organization is to liberate those who once toiled at the base, and vice versa.

Empowerment

The most celebrated of the democratic initiatives is empowerment. It is the magical ingredient of Pull. In its simplest form, it is the boss saying to employees, "You no longer have to ask me for permission to do the right thing for customers. You are empowered to do it yourselves."

Nordstrom, the Seattle-based department store, is the archetypal empowerer. Their entire policies and procedures rule book fits on a matchbook:

➤ Don't steal.
➤ Don't chew gum.
➤ Use your best judgment at all times to guarantee customer satisfaction.

Nordstrom rode this philosophy to unheard-of heights in the 1980s. It was perfect for a high-end, customer-oriented retail outfit, where mistakes could be absorbed into high profit margins. But it isn't perfect for companies working closer to the bone. And it isn't right for every employee, not even at Nordstrom.

Done right, empowerment, the transmission of decision-making power down from management to ordinary workers, is the most powerful change element at work in organizations today. But it is also the most paradoxical.

One paradox concerns the transferability of power. If I have all the power and I give you half, with the expectation that you will use it precisely the way that I would, are we then equally powerful? Or have I retained all but a ghost of the power I "transferred" to you? Will you exercise power confidently if you know I can snatch it back from you at the first sign of trouble?

Nordstrom, for instance, is an empowerer with an asterisk, for its brand of empowerment does not include worker organization. Nordstrom is copying the Japanese empowerment model of weak unions and patriarchal employers. Workers who have been burned in the past—and retail sales is one of the most flammable industries—may think twice about empowerment that does not include the elemental power of collective bargaining.

The other paradox is the plight of the puppet master. So long as workers perform your will, they make the decision you know is right. Once you free them and they follow their own intuition, they will be

Empowerment: Three Views

In the typical organization, battered silly by decades of untrustworthy behavior, an empowerment program may be launched with no side subscribing to it except the consultant selling the package. It is a case of trying to make a leap in one day from the dark age of Pummel to the New Age of Pull, and it is preposterous.

> **Consultant's optimism:** "Empowerment frees workers up to use their heads, do their best, be on the lookout for opportunities to improve, identify and prevent quality failures before they occur, and transmit information about failures back through the company in order that others can learn from it. Key point: always get paid in advance."
>
> **Management's nostalgia:** "In the old days of Horatio Alger and spunky entrepreneurialism we were not empowered by patrons—we secured power on an individual basis by acting intelligently and responsibly. We'll give this empowerment thing a run but our hearts still yearn for the way things were. If they transmit information about too many failures, we go to the mattresses. Key point: pass out the guns but hold on to the ammo."
>
> **Employees' cynicism:** "Horatio Alger's plucky youths would have as much of a shot in this organization as the Energizer Bunny would have in a den of lions. We'll nod our heads and pretend to swallow this garbage, but be on the lookout for the inevitable switchback. And continue to sweep those foul-ups under the carpet. Key point: no sense volunteering to give blood."

right one day and very wrong, in your view, the next. The question is: If you still define right and wrong, did you really empower them? Like toothpaste out of the tube, they will never be quite under your control again, and tons of peppermint-flavored frustration will pile up on both sides.

Sometimes empowerment fails because it is never taken seriously. Workers know from the get go that the initiative is hypocritical, because, well, they know management. So these people never blossom into the empowered angels of the literature, going to uncalled-for lengths to ensure customer satisfaction, and damn the cost. They know it is just a developmental phase management is going through, which will soon loop back into the customary mode of Pummel or Push.

And that's the optimal empowerment failure. Worse is the betrayal that workers did not see coming. They believed they were being treated like adults, for the first time ever, and were making efforts to behave like adults—and then were set back in the playpen. Empowerment failures are the most emotionally devastating of any change initiative.

Empowerment goes wrong two ways:

> Employees can be encouraged to make managerial decisions, but not given a clue as to how these are made. This is the extreme of Pamper. Giving decision making authority to someone without training or equipping them with some sense of the parameters of decision-making isn't empowering them; it's abdicating your own authority. It is both cruel and crazy, like giving a child a gun.

> **"Now let's all repeat the non-conformist oath."**
>
> *Steve Martin*

> Employees are told they are empowered and trained and equipped to make managerial decisions, but they don't believe it and are thus loath to use the power. This is the borderland between Pummel and Push, where people have been bullied too long to believe you're suddenly a nice guy. These not-quite empowered people are sadder cases than the kids with guns; they may be burning inside to do the right thing, but they are just too scared.

Even when you empower people the right way, providing them with actual authority, and teaching them exactly how to use it, there can be problems.

The biggest problem is stress. Scads of people prefer being unempowered. It is peaceful and relatively undemanding. You can work through an entire day, doing your job well, stacking crates, without once worrying about your executive judgment.

When you have the power to make decisions that may help or hurt your company and that may or may not bring down the ire of the Powers

That Be, you start to sweat a little. So the most important challenge of any organization bent on pushing power down to the trenches is to provide stress-reduction mechanisms, training wheels to help keep your empowerment efforts upright.

Examples of training wheels are mentoring systems, printed guidelines, panic buttons, hotlines, anything that allows the individual to seek assistance when unsure of a situation, or until he or she becomes more confident.

The latest findings are that empowerment, with managed boundaries, works in the few organizations that are serious about it. A 1996 University of Southern California study showed that only 10 percent of employees in Fortune 1000 companies are engaged in participative management practices. It was the first study to find a clear link between employee involvement and profitability.[23]

If your organization wants to join the ranks of the profitable, you will have to outlaw punishment for empowered people who screw up. This is a great challenge for the benign managerial mind-set—staying your hand when you are just aching to let someone have it.

Think proactive. Think prevention. Model good judgment. Provide assistance.

And when an omelet burns, as it will even in New Age utopia, eat it and pretend you like it.

Diversity

Diversity is the most mishandled of all change ideas. It grew out of the desire to comply with federal equal opportunity and affirmative action requirements, calling upon businesses to hire and promote without respect to race, gender, creed, or national origin. These measures were adopted to redress grievances of groups that had been locked out of organizations or, if allowed in, restricted to menial jobs.

These laws were passed in the wake of 1968's Kerner Commission, which found that racist hiring practices were keeping minorities, especially African Americans, from their fair share of the employment pie. Their purpose was to punish companies with unfair or exclusionary hiring practices and to award companies that complied with a badge of pride. "We are an equal opportunity employer" was a sign that a company would choose its employees from the largest possible pool of qualified applicants. It was a smart management tool, using the regulatory clout of the federal government to guarantee that the right thing would be done. It typifies the Push urgency that drives successful organizations.

In the eyes of many, however, it was not enough for a company to stop discriminating against applicants from any group. A company must proactively go out and find qualified candidates from other groups, lure them into the organization, and then train the existing workforce to acknowledge and honor all the workers' different backgrounds and use these differences to benefit the company. That's a lot of change.

In the hands of the diversity movement, companies had to go beyond what was legally and morally indicated and make a virtue out of diversity for its own sake. A backlash against diversity began.

> "The grand dogma of our times, that groups would be evenly represented in institutions and activities in the absence of discrimination, would collapse like a house of cards from a study of societies around the world."
>
> *Thomas Sowell*

Though diversity aims at creating a single diverse entity, it can have the effect of maintaining divisions between groups. To the conservative-minded, diversity signals social engineering, reverse discrimination, white-male bashing, and liberal, paternalistic racism. To the liberal-minded, diversity is a way of ushering in people who have been banished from the feast and reminding the unenlightened that the American dream is still a lot easier if you are a white male.

Diversity training is a source of bitter resentment to those who feel that multiculturalism is a stalking horse for lowered standards and "special treatment." But it is equally easy to defend, because no company wants to appear indifferent to such an important issue.

Doing diversity right requires a strong combination of Push and Pull. The Pull must be more than self-righteousness, though. It must be the understanding that cooperation and sharing the wealth is in everyone's interest, no matter what their ideology or ethnicity. The Push must be equally strong, management's unmistakable message to employees: "Integrate or emigrate."

Of course, organizations could overcome racism a lot more directly and a lot more effectively if the "right attitude" were modeled and not just

The Real Diversity

Diversity proponents claim that diversity is a secret weapon for eliciting opinions and opening markets that are unknown to the white-bread managing class.

But is it true? Is "diversity" a tactical business advantage? Yes, provided you define diversity in its broadest sense, beyond the narrow, group-based, politically correct version making the rounds.

For instance, hiring an African American with the idea of exploiting that person's African American insights for future product and market development implies that there is a monolithic African-American "wisdom" that all African-Americans have in equal amounts—a dubious supposition.

Eventually the company will find it didn't hire an African American; it hired George. Companies that hired George hoping George would present the African-American point of view found out that George could better present George's point of view. His wisdom might be terrific or it might be lousy. Its degree of "African-American-ness" is unquantifiable.

Strategic thinker Gary Hamel talks about the need to inoculate organizations with "genetic diversity"—ideas generated outside the organization's native culture. He describes the four corners of a single intersection in Toronto, each of which houses one of Canada's largest banks. All the nation's banking brains are clustered in one spot. They hire from one another, imitate one another, and breathe the same air as one another. What are the odds, Hamel asked, of a startling new idea occurring within any one of those four banks?[24]

Forget color and religion and go after difference in thought. It's a lot more effective, and it takes a load off George.

---

taught and equal opportunity were given its due, not just lip service. Fewer than forty African Americans hold any of the top three offices in Fortune 500 corporations. If boards and search committees chose more qualified black candidates for the positions of CEO, COO, and CFO, the burden of demonstrating fair-mindedness would shift from the rank and file to leadership—where the power is and where the burden rightfully belongs.

Side note: Companies experiencing stresses and strains from infighting might look to an unlikely source for leadership—the Amiables who are usually happy just to be along for the ride. The Amiable temperament is a model the rest of us can learn from, to better appreciate difference and overcome disagreements. It is slow to resentment and reluctant to blame—valuable traits in a time when everyone blames everyone else for everything.

Open-Book Management

If employees are valuable, they have the right to information bearing on their futures.

Open-book management is a Push/Pull initiative in which the Pull comes first, as the organization opens its financial books for employees to see. The Pull is the notion that employees are important, that their minds matter as much as their muscle, and that their destiny can be put squarely in their hands. The Push is linking that destiny to performance goals that must be met.

For many employees, open-book management is the first time they have ever dealt with concepts like cash flow and balance sheets. It is also the first time they have confronted head-on the business realities their jobs depend on.

Advocates of a strong Push approach are often leery of open-book management because it does not allow them to exercise the full range of Machiavellian "book-cooking" and fact-focusing. They prefer the flexibility of describing the platform as fully aflame, instead of the slow smoldering most P&L sheets show.

With the right training, employees respond well to the open-book approach. Now that they have the raw data, all that remains is to provide employees with the challenge and the tools to make the numbers better. Open-book initiatives that succeed often require that an employee's total earnings be linked to preestablished profit targets for the business they are in.

Suggestions: base compensation not on quarterly or semiannual reports but on a continuous measurement of successes occurring in important areas—customers retained, inventory turns, number of complaints received, percentage of new products to old, percentage of new customers to old. Do not contrive results by squeezing assets. A six-month report comes too late to do anything about.

And base rewards not just on companywide results, over which they have little control, but on the results of the unit or division or team that they can directly contribute to.

The Otherness Theme

The Otherness theme is the ultimate New Age realm. It is a revolutionary one, for it goes against the key aspect of human nature we have been discussing—our inherent human disinclination to view new ideas positively.

In the Otherness theme, unknowns are not painted in with negatives; they are greeted as positives. Otherness holds that whatever we currently know is inadequate to the tasks before us. In order to become adequate, we have to look outside the conventional knowledge passed painstakingly down to us by the preceding generation.

The corporation is literally housed inside one or more boxes. Our offices are boxes. Our desks and computers are boxes. Our heads, in some curious way, are boxes of business, only slightly beveled around the edges by rain, wind, and worry.

Thinking/Learning

In the unempowered machine age, people were not expected to do a lot of thinking. Or their thinking was of a regulated, mechanical kind. IBM's famous "THINK" sign was not an invitation to open-ended woolgathering, but a reminder to keep working and making widgets. *Mad Magazine* parodied this mechanistic pathway to performance in the 1950s by respelling it "THIMK."

In the New Age, that's changed. Many organizations feel they are no longer in the widget business, that widgets are just the transient fluff that arises from knowledge. Brain power, not raw materials, is what creates wealth. Software, not hardware, rules. The world is a thinking place, and we work in *learning organizations*. Closed minds win no races.

Tom Peters went so far as to suggest that managers should stop reading books about management and start reading Shakespeare, Dickens, and Dickinson. That is where surprising insights are likely to occur, not in the centennial edition of *The Practice of Management*.

The Out-of-Box Experience

The art and practice of management is largely predicated upon "the box." It is a metaphor worth exploring. Every organization is a box, an enclosure keeping the world out, except through controlled channels, and keeping resources (people, inventory, cash) inside and under control until it is time for each to be expended.

The box seems natural to us. Never mind that it is hard enough to find a single straight line in nature, never mind twelve straight lines arranged in meticulous perpendicular/parallel relation to one another. Boxes probably seem pretty natural to guinea pigs and hamsters.

We use the metaphor in our organizational charts, in our job descriptions, and our strategic plans. Whatever is in a box, as behaviorist philosopher B. F. Skinner claimed in the 1950s, is under control.

We are not guinea pigs and hamsters. But like them we dwell in a world of our own making based on the belief that a stable environment of powerful controls will yield the best outcomes for us—food, employment, and 401(k) plans.

Only when it is clear that we have exhausted the possibilities of our current box, either because we have gnawed through its walls or because it's been tipped over by a strong gust from Wall Street, are we able to breathe the real air of the world. This is what the learning organization is always doing.

The counterpoint to this open-gate philosophy is still valid. It is *systems thinking,* the theory that individual acts and processes cannot be coherent unless they are seen as elements of the entire system they are part of. The system is the big box we do our work in. Understand it, eliminate its contradictions, and it will work as it was designed to work.

The system is important; Deming in his discussions of profound knowledge says the system is everything. But even he knew the wisdom of getting out of it, composing oratorios and masses for organ in his spare hours.

Accomplished organizations succeeded by stepping outside their box or mental map. Land's End began as a sailmaker and store. Hewlett-Packard originally set out to make automatic urinal flushers and bowling alley sensors, among other things. The fabulous Frisbee began as a pie plate. IBM, the "THINK" company in the fifties and considered by many to be the best-run system of the eighties, never thought its little computers could give its big computers a run, because the company was too snug in its box.

Every visionary and every vision-driven organization spends some time out of the box, arriving at fresh perspectives on what the box contains, or just wandering freely in the larger world.

Push operations lock in on systems thinking; Pull operations focus on knowledge creation. Push wants to make a map of its paradigm; Pull wants to wad the map up, throw it away, spit in the wind, and follow where it leads.

Xenophilia

Globalization has brought us out of our Yankee burrow and got us blinking at the world of ideas outside our cozy comfort zone.

> **"Knock. Don't ring bell."**
>
> *Sign on Pavlov's door*

Not long ago Americans maintained a universal attitude of smug superiority toward other countries' efforts. Our engineers, inventors, managers, and workers made the rest of the world's look sick. But we've been out-competed, out-strategized, out-qualitied, and out-marketed so many times, in so many places, in the past two decades. Many Americans have flip-flopped completely and reverted to an inferiority complex.

We've come a long way. From xenophobia (remember when it was a joke when a product was marked "Made in Japan"?) to xenophilia, the admiration of all things foreign because they are foreign. Xenophilia is a variant on the New Age theme that all good things happen outside the sphere we are most familiar with. It's illogical, but it has had the happy consequence of bringing a world of new ideas to our attention.

The clearest instance of American xenophilia is our Japanotropism, our automatic regard for anything coming out of Japan. Our business attitudes toward Japan are analogous to our cultural affiliation with Great Britain and our political solidarity with Israel. We obviously have a soft spot for island nations. It makes it easier that they needed our help to do well. Japan emerged under our protection and with the help of American advisers like Deming and Juran. Companies like Nissan, Mitsubishi, and Sony refashioned American management and marketing practices and then clobbered us at our own game. "They copied us, then improved on us, so they must be good."

The ultimate change initiative may be one that attempts to turn a sow's ear into a silk purse—i.e., go against one thing's entire nature by transforming it utterly into something else. Thus one of the most interesting success stories of our age has been that American manufacturers adapting Japanese business practices for our use. "They copied us and beat us, and we copied them right back."

Under this theme we have combined a variety of ideas, most of them Japanese, that could easily have fit under themes such as Improvement and Reform. What unites them all is their origin in quite a different culture—and the remarkable degree of acceptance they have found in our own historically closed culture. That receptivity—a feat of imagination and "metaphilia"—is itself a sign of a strong recent shift in American business toward Pull strategies.

> **"Whenever a system becomes completely defined, someone discovers something which either abolishes the system or expands it beyond recognition."**
>
> *Brooke's Law*

➤ **Kaizen** means "continuous improvement," and it is the most conspicuous addition Japanese businesses made to Deming's platform of statistical process control. When it bounced back to the U.S. as continuous improvement, it provided an intuitive alternative to the heavy machinery of total quality management.

➤ **Knowledge-creating** denotes what many of the best Japanese companies, like Kao (the Japanese Procter & Gamble), take to be their reason for being. Not selling products, not expanding markets, not beating the opposition to a pulp—but the creation of knowledge that will sustain competitive life.

➤ **Poka-yoke** ("poka-yokay"). A poka-yoke device is any mechanism that either prevents a mistake from being made or makes the mistake obvious at a glance. As Shigeo Shingo writes, "The causes of defects lie in worker errors, and defects are the results of neglecting those errors. It follows that mistakes will not turn into defects if worker errors are discovered and eliminated beforehand."[25]

➤ **Kanban**. Kanban is the system of card-flagging, first implemented at Toyota, that was the basis for the concept of Just-In-Time. It was originally conceived by Taicho Ohno as a flow control system, involving paper cards kept with small on-hand supplies of parts. As bins were emptied, the cards (kanban means card) alerted workers to the need to replenish the supply. This system revolutionized inventory management, first at Toyota and eventually around the world.

Like many other change initiatives, Just-In-Time was rapidly transformed from a tactic into a philosophy, from an inventory management methodology to a mind-set of minimum waste and delay. Americanized, the system had nothing to do with cards, and more to do with information technologies like MPR II that kept track of lot amounts and ordered a continuous stream of small shipments of parts so they arrived "just in time" and did not have to be stockpiled (and often lost) in expensive warehouses.

Japanotropia is only one aspect of our new xenophilia. We honor other countries for contributions their companies have made:

> **"We don't know a millionth of one percent about anything."**
>
> *Thomas Edison*

➤ the Swiss for their skills in dealmaking (Nestlé) and radical decentralizing (ABB)
➤ the Germans for their historic commitment to product quality and customer satisfaction (Daimler-Benz)
➤ the British for their innovations in quality improvement and service excellence (British Airways)
➤ the Swedish for their breakthroughs in core competencies and partnering (Volvo)

As the leading edge of the New Age, it is easy to make too much too soon of American xenophilia. Our management is still a formidable force, and we are still very proud of that fact. Xenophobia should be seen not as a major theme but as a counter-theme, a crosscut against the historic theme of isolation and jingoism.

The clearest sign that ours is still an In-Between Age and not a bona fide New Age is reflected in the marketplace: no management book written solely by a Japanese writer has ever sold more than 50,000 copies here.

Chaos

Want to make a hit at your next board meeting? Announce a major change initiative with the words, "Let's take this organization down the path of total chaos."

And say it like you mean it. Your colleagues will spew coffee across the table at the words. People who have known you for years and have every reason to trust you for your experience and usually sage counsel will bolt from their chairs and demand your resignation.

Everyone present will shake their heads, close their eyes, and picture an orderly organization pushed off the cliff of all that is reasonable, plummeting, all hands screaming, down, down into the abyss of the unknown.

People balk at the notion of chaos, but organizational scholars like Meg Wheatley insist it may be our best friend as we reconfigure ourselves for modern times. The chaos movement springs from the insight that organizations are based on Newtonian notions of linear thinking that have been made obsolete by the findings of physicists and astronomers and biologists in our own time.[26]

Wheatley believes that the way we've been thinking about organizations (indeed, about everything) for the last 300 years is simply wrong. The modern view of the world is predicated upon the geometric symmetries of the ancient Greeks—pure circles, perfect squares, and absolutely straight lines. When better boxes are built, they will be along Euclidean lines.

But nowhere in nature can these pure shapes be found. Instead, we have complex, swirling fractal patterns, from the geography of a cell to the landscape of the entire cosmos.

To organizational chaos fans, it is incumbent upon management to model their organizations not after Euclidean shapes—the boxes, circles, and right angles of the organizational flowchart—but from the naturally occurring, sometimes breathtakingly beautiful structures of living things.

Instead of centralized command-and-control, Wheatley suggests, a chaos company will find its own rhythms and patterns and allow decisions to arise from the collective unconscious of all workers, regardless of "rank" (a Newtonian notion to be dispensed with ASAP). Chaos is the ultimate out-of-the-box thinking.

One shortcoming of chaos theory that we have noticed is that its view of nature relies mostly on astrophysical observations and overlooks animal behavior. Animal species tend to organize around a strong theme of hierarchical Pummel—top dog, lead bull, king lion. As it is presented, chaos seems to ask that we heed only the bizarre and beautiful New Age lessons of nature, and ignore the familiar brutalities.

> "Madness exacts its toll of us all. Please have exact change ready."
>
> *Found on the Internet*

A few, edge-of-the-edge organizations may profit from heading down this exotic path. We worry about going so far off the left side of the ChangeLand map that the resulting organization becomes ultra-Pamper.

The best use of the insights of Wheatley, David Bohm, and others is as cautionary tools for critiquing your current system: Are we too tight, too rational, too narrow, too pleased with the way we are, too predictable in the ways we design work, define customers, and manage markets?

The future belongs to organizations that learn to reach out and bring this otherness in—the foreign, the unfamiliar, the not-invented-here. These impulses and ideas remind us that the thinking we were taught is the prisoner of its own limited (and sometimes wrong) knowledge.

epilog

The in-between age

Throughout this book we have used big company examples to highlight successful change efforts. But the best example we know of a company that looked to the future and took decisive steps to meet it halfway is a humble gas station.

Tracy One-Stop is a service station located on a busy corner in a not very promising neighborhood in Saint Paul. The station has been there for thirty years, having carved out a niche in the early days as a supplier of fuels besides gasoline—liquid propane, lube, kerosene, etc.

As the station aged, and as the neighborhood became tougher, the station could have pulled the plug, let its local employees go, and relocated further out of the urban ring. Instead, it built a fabulous new service center, with four oil-change docks, a full kitchen, a car wash, and a convenience grocery. On sunny days an outdoor grill sells hot dogs and bratwurst for a few quarters apiece. The bakery is stocked with better sweets than the best grocery stores.

But it's the people who make Tracy One-Stop special. You can pull up on the coldest day of winter, and a customer courtesy man, usually a gangly, outgoing man named Bob, will be out there with you in the snow, helping with your pumping, oil, or windshield wiper fluid. These are self-serve pumps, mind you.

Over the years, we have witnessed the customer courtesy guys doing everything for customers—helping them call road service, playing wiffle ball with a child while his parents' car is lubed. If you forget your credit card, they don't stash it in a dark drawer and leave you wondering what became of it. They track you down, call you, and tell you they are holding it for you. Always with an arresting, unfakable air of sincerity.

One day we asked one of the courtesy workers, with the name Ben over his pocket, what gives. Was the head of Tracy a service quality freak? Did some four-star consultant sell them this overhaul as a package?

No, it was just a Push/Pull effort that managers and workers together patched together. This isn't the greatest neighborhood, Ben said, and the place was pretty run-down. "People decided that, if they were going to make it here, they would have to try something different. We decided we were going to be the best service station anywhere."

Just deciding that was no guarantee of success. But they had the right mix of personalities to pull it off. Everyone had family, everyone wanted to make the place a success, and there wasn't a sullen grease-monkey in the group. People like Bob at the pump island modeled for less outgoing workers what cheerful, helpful service looked like. Sure, there was visionary leadership at the top—the new center was a remarkable investment. But it was the willingness of the workers to try something new that put the effort over the top.

How successful has the effort been? People go a mile out of their way to refuel at Tracy One-Stop. Think about that. And the neighborhood itself is transforming. A new warehouse food store, a new Montgomery Ward, and expanded college campus facilities nearby are a tribute to what a positive spirit can accomplish.

> **"Decay is inherent in all compounded things. Strive on, with diligence."**
>
> *Buddha's last words*

The message in this little homily is that the most successful change initiatives are those that originate in the hearts of the people who will benefit from them. Set aside the bound volumes of procedural changes, video training courses, team-building exercises in the Rockies, and giant data systems that tell everyone everything with a single keystroke.

These things may or may not come into play as your change effort at your organization rolls out. Before any of it can work, you have to have people whose hearts can be touched, and then you have to touch them.

Tracy One-Stop may seem like an unfair example because the people there seem unaccountably terrific. They are like walking billboards for logotherapy. They have chosen to have change-positive attitudes, and that makes change easier. And it is a lot easier to mold a small family business than a big, impersonal one.

If you had a ready supply of angels to work for you, as Tracy One-Stop appears to, improving product or service quality, or business processes, or the culture of our organization would be a snap. Everyone would be fabulously great. They would be incapable of anything but excellence.

In some of the New Age managerial ideas, that's how it works. You trust in people's better natures, and their better natures take over and perform. Empowerment vanquishes sloppiness and indifference. Talented people share knowledge and create a better world for customers.

But Tracy One-Stop is not a New Age business. It's a filling station, the most conventional "Old Age" business you could imagine. The people who work there are semiskilled. They didn't undergo any expensive training, hold touchie-feelie seances, or fall blindfolded into one another's arms.

They changed because the owners and managers took what they knew from the past, made an educated guess about the future, staked out a vision of an In-Between Age way of doing business that would make use of both business philosophies—the hard edge of the old and the psychological insights of the new.

The truth is, we will always be doing business in the In-Between Age, because we will always be sorting out which past tools to hold onto, and which future visions we are not yet ready for. This picking and choosing, and then acting, is the heart and soul of management.

Though unresolved, the In-Between Age isn't such a bad place to be. It's a place:

> "Remember, we all stumble, every one of us. That's why it's a comfort to go hand-in-hand."
>
> *Unknown*

➤ where thinking is permitted. Not a place where people try to make mistakes, but where people are given a chance to outlive them. Where risks are carefully weighed and considered. Where every opinion may have value.

➤ that is learning not to treat people as fuel to be flared. That allows its reputation for fair play to grow over time until it attracts people capable of making the same kind of commitment, to the organization and to each other.

➤ where people are aware as never before that their work is important. (As distinct from the so-called "Hawthorne Effect," in which people perform better in the short term because they are being fussed over—change for change's sake.)

➤ that is looking for an honest balance of survival and fulfillment. Pummel and Pamper are on the wane, leaving most of us in the more rational middle categories of Push and Pull.

These aren't New Age or Old Age ideas. They are ideas for today, for the curious crosswalk of history we find ourselves on, caught between the blinking lights of two different eras, between the need to learn and the need to stay alive.

We began this thinkathon about change by recalling the insights of Viktor Frankl at Auschwitz. His view was a dark Pull: that life is less a place for finding happiness than for finding meaning.

The fatalism of this philosophy is not easily combined with the feel-good philosophies of the New Age. These philosophies are great if we can make them real, but if we can't make them real, they are a danger to us. The In-Between Age is where we combine New Age visions with the skepticism and competence of the age before it.

We need to remember, too, that just because an initiative fails is no reason to give up. The spirit of continuous improvement—a lovely spirit, once you get to know it—urges us not to give up hope, even as we concede the difficulty of quick success. In a world driven to achieve higher quality and higher efficiency, we're never quite there. We must content ourselves sometimes with the satisfaction of knowing that we are giving it our best effort and that tomorrow is another day.

> **"Failure is only the opportunity to begin again more intelligently."**
>
> *Henry Ford*

endnotes

Part 1

1. Michael Hammer and Steven A. Stanton, *The Reengineering Revolution*, HarperBusiness, 1995.
2. National Safe Workplace Institute, cited in a brochure for a conference, "Assessing and Preventing Workplace Violence," April 19, 1996, Sheraton Palace Hotel, San Francisco, California.
3. Richard Tanner Pascale, "The Reinvention Roller Coaster," *Harvard Business Review*, April-May 1995.
4. Eileen C. Shapiro, *Fad Surfing in the Boardroom*, Addison-Wesley, 1995.
5. Judith M. Bardwick, *Danger in the Comfort Zone*, Amacom, 1991.
6. Example from a talk given by James Collins at the Masters Forum, February 1996, Minneapolis.
7. Quote taken from James C. Collins' and Jerry I. Porras' *Built to Last*, HarperBusiness, 1994.
8. Jack Stack, *The Great Game of Business*, Doubleday Currency, 1992. Thanks to John Kotter for bringing this example to our attention.
9. Viktor E. Frankl, *Man's Search for Meaning*, Washington Square, 1963.
10. Michael Finley, "The Reengineer Who Could," Masters Forum Application Kit, June 1995. Based on remarks made by James Champy in Minneapolis, June 6, 1995.

Part 2

1. Ira Chaleff, "Overload Can Be Overcome," *Industry Week*, June 7, 1993, p. 44.
2. We came upon this story in a book by historian Garry Wills, *Certain Trumpets* (S&S Childrens, 1995). Wills uses the story to describe the challenge of leadership. It illustrates the dilemma of group change equally well.
3. For another fascinating spoof on personality tests, visit "Kingdomality" on the World Wide Web. It is a questionnaire that asks you about your likes and dislikes, and then tells you what job you would be most qualified for in the task-intensive Medieval Period. http://www.cmi-lmi.com/kingdom.html.
4. This model is drawn from the behavioral typology ideas of David Merrill at Tracom, in Denver, Colorado.

Part 3
1. Albert Ellis and Robert Harper, *A Guide to Rational Living,* Prentice-Hall, 1961.

Part 4
1. Martin Seligman, *What You Can Change and What You Can't*, Alfred A. Knopf, 1993.
2. Remarks made by Richard Pascale October 19, 1993, at the Executive Roundtable, Dallas.
3. Martin Seligman, *Learned Optimism*, Pocket Books, 1990.
4. Peter Senge, *The Fifth Discipline*, Currency Doubleday, 1990
5. Remarks by John Kotter, the Masters Forum, June 7, 1994.
6. Remarks by James Kouzes, the Masters Forum, Minneapolis, August 16, 1994.
7. Max H. Bazerman and Margaret A. Neale, *Negotiating Rationally,* Free Press, 1992; we owe much of the general sense of this subsection to this work.
8. Peter Lazes and Marty Falkenberg, "Workgroups in America Today," *Journal for Quality and Participation*, June 1, 1991.
9. Michael Hammer and Steven A. Stanton, *The Reengineering Revolution*, HarperCollins, 1995.
10. M. M. Stuckey, *Demass*, Productivity Press, 1991.
11. Tony Ecles, "The Deceptive Allure of Empowerment," *Long Range Planning*, December 1993.

Part 5
1. Tracy Goss, Richard Pascale, and Anthony Athos, "The Reinvention Roller Coaster: Risking the Present for a Powerful Future," *Harvard Business Review*, November–December 1993.
2. The best recent evidence appears in a study by Jack Mogab and William Cole, *The Economics of Total Quality Management* (Blackwell, 1995). They create a formula for comparing the relative inputs and outputs of a TQM company versus a non-TQM company, and conclude that, properly implemented, TQM will yield positive financial results.
3. Tom Peters, *Thriving on Chaos*, Alfred A. Knopf, 1987.
4. Peter Drucker, *The Practice of Management*, Harper, 1986.
5. Tom Peters, *Thriving on Chaos,* Alfred A. Knopf, 1987.
6. The outline of these criticisms is borrowed from Christopher W. L. Hart and Christopher E. Bogan's *The Baldrige* (McGraw-Hill, 1992), a project on which Mike provided editorial assistance.
7. Alvin Toffler, *Future Shock*, Random House, 1970.
8. M. M. Stuckey, *Demass*, Productivity Press, 1991.

9. Many commentators have noted the irony that the "right size" for a thing is always smaller.

10. Robert Flater, *The New GE,* Business One Irwin, 1993.

11. Michael Hammer and James Champy, *Reengineering the Corporation,* HarperBusiness, 1993.

12. Introduction by Peter Senge to Christopher Meyer's *Fast Cycle Time,* The Free Press, 1993.

13. Michael Treacy and Fred Weirsema, *The Discipline of Market Leaders,* Addison-Wesley, 1995.

14. Richard Pascale, *Managing on the Edge,* Simon & Schuster, 1988.

15. From e-mail exchange with Robert W. Rominger, Ph.D.

16. Edwards Deming, *Out of the Crisis,* MIT Press, 1985.

17. James C. Collins, from an address to the Masters Forum, Minneapolis, February 21, 1995.

18. D. M. McGregor, *The Human Side of the Enterprise,* McGraw-Hill, 1960; "The Human Side of the Enterprise," Proceedings of the 5th Anniversary Convocation of the School of Industrial Management, 1957.

19. Kenneth Blanchard and Spencer Johnson, *The One Minute Manager,* Morrow, 1982.

20. Tom Peters, *The Pursuit of Wow!,* Vintage Books, 1994.

21. The Wallace Company, one of the first small businesses to win a Baldrige, put great store in the internal customer idea. They were also the first Baldrige winner to declare bankruptcy.

22. Finley, "The Reengineer Who Could," Masters Forum Application Kit, June 1995. Based on remarks made by James Champy in Minneapolis, June 6, 1995.

23. "Managers Slow to Share Power Hurt Bottom Line," *HR News,* February 1996.

24. Gregory Hamel, remarks to the Masters Forum, Minneapolis, December 1994.

25. Shigeo Shingo, *Non-Stock Production: The Shingo System for Continuous Improvement,* Productivity Press, 1988.

26. Meg Wheatley, *Leadership and the New Science,* Berrett-Kohler, 1992.

a reading list for the age of change

Change Management
Peter Drucker, *Post-Capitalist Society,* HarperBusiness, 1993.
D. Gwinlivan, *In Search of Solutions,* Hall & Peter Renner, 1987.
Rosabeth Moss Kanter, *When Giants Learn to Dance,* Simon & Schuster, 1989.
Francis Gouillart and James Kelly, *Transforming the Organization,* McGraw-Hill, 1995.
Peter Drucker, *The Age of Discontinuity,* Heineman, 1969.
Jack Stack, *The Great Game of Business,* Doubleday Currency, 1992.

The Results Theme

"Excellence"
James Collins, *Built to Last,* HarperBusiness, 1994.
Tom Peters, *In Search of Excellence,* Alfred Knopf, 1982.

Zero Defects
Philip Crosby, *Quality Is Free,* McGraw-Hill, 1979.

Management by Objectives
Peter Drucker, *The Practice of Management*, Harper, 1986.

The Measurement Theme

Benchmarking
G. H. Watson, *Benchmarking Workbook: Adapting Best Practices for Performance Management*, Productivity Press, 1992.
Michael Brassard. *Memory Jogger Plus,* GOAL/QPC, 1989.

The Malcolm Baldrige Award
Christopher W. L. Hart and Christopher Bogan, *The Baldrige,* McGraw-Hill, 1989.

ISO 9000
David Hoyle, *ISO 9000 Quality Systems Handbook,* Butterworth Heineman, 1994.

The Reform Theme

Downsizing
Robert M. Tomasko, *Downsizing,* AMACOM, 1990.
Robert Johansen and Rob Swigart, *Upsizing the Individual in the Downsized Organization,* Addison-Wesley, 1994.

Demassification
M. M. Stuckey, *Demass,* Productivity Press, 1991.

The Integration Theme

Reengineering
Michael Hammer and James Champy. *Reengineering the Corporation: A Manifesto for Business Revolution,* HarperBusiness, 1993.

Speedup
Christopher Meyer, *Fast Cycle Time,* The Free Press, 1993.

Value Disciplines
Michael Treacy and Fred Weirsma, *The Discipline of Market Leaders,* Addison-Wesley, 1995.

The Improvement Theme

Quality
W. Edwards Deming, *Out of the Crisis,* MIT Center for Advanced Engineering Study, 1986.
Robert E. Cole, ed., *The Death and Life of the American Quality Movement,* Oxford University Press, 1995.
Harry V. Roberts and B. Sergesketter, *Quality is Personal: A Foundation for Total Quality Management,* The Free Press, 1993.

TQM
J. Gilbert. *How To Eat an Elephant: A Slice By Slice Guide to Total Quality Management,* Tudor Business Pub. Ltd., 1992.
Kaoru Ishikawa, *What Is Total Quality Control? The Japanese Way,* Prentice-Hall, 1985.
Jack Mogab and William Cole, *The Economics of Total Quality Management,* Blackwell, 1995.

The Direction Theme

Leadership
James M. Kouzes and Barry Z. Posner. *Credibility: How Leaders Gain and Lose It, Why People Demand It,* Jossey-Bass, 1993.
Alan Weiss, *Our Emperors Have No Clothes,* Career Press, 1995.
Max DePree, *Leadership Is an Art,* Currency Doubleday, 1989.
Howard Gardner, *Leading Minds: An Anatomy of Leadership,* Basic Books, 1995.
James Champy, *Reengineering Management,* HarperBusiness, 1995.
Robert Greenleaf, *Servant Leadership,* Paulist Press, 1977.

Mission and Vision
Gary Hamel & C. K. Prahalad, *Competing for the Future,* Harvard Business School Press, 1994.
Bob Wall, *The Visionary Leader,* Prima, 1992.

The Character Theme

Organizational Morality
Stephen R. Covey, 7 *Habits of Highly Effective People,* Simon & Schuster, 1989.
Tom Morris, *True Success,* G. P. Putnam's Sons, 1994.
David Bohm, *Unfolding Meaning,* Arc, 1987.

The Relationship Theme

Theories X, Y, and Z
Douglas McGregor, *The Human Side of the Enterprise,* McGraw-Hill, 1960.
William Ouchi, *Theory Z,* Addison-Wesley, 1981.

One Minute Managing
Kenneth Blanchard and Spencer Johnson, *The One Minute Manager,* Morrow, 1982.

Management by Wandering Around
Tom Peters, *Thriving on Chaos,* Harper & Row, 1987.

Customer Satisfaction
Thomas K. Connellan and Ron Zemke. *Sustaining Knock Your Socks Off Service,* AMACOM, 1993.
D. Keith Denton, *Horizontal Management,* Lexington Books, 1991.

The Culture Theme

The Boundaryless Corporation

William H. Davidow and Michael S. Malone, *The Virtual Corporation,* HarperBusiness, 1992.

James Brian Quinn, *The Intelligent Corporation,* The Free Press, 1992.

Sarita Chawla and John Renesch, *Learning Organizations: Developing Cultures for Tomorrow's Workplace,* Productivity Press, 1995.

Tom Peters, *Liberation Management,* Alfred Knopf, 1994.

Teams

Harvey Robbins and Michael Finley, *Why Teams Don't Work: What Went Wrong and How to Make it Right*, Peterson's/Pacesetter Books, 1995.

The Democracy Theme

Empowerment

Edward E. Lawler III, *The Ultimate Advantage,* Jossey-Bass, 1992.

J. F. Vogt, *Empowerment in Organizations.* University Associates, 1990.

Diversity

Alan Bloom, *The Closing of the American Mind,* Houghton Mifflin, 1990.

George F. Simons, Bob Abramms, and L. Ann Hopkins, eds., *Cultural Diversity,* Peterson's, 1996.

Open-Book Management

John Case, *Open-Book Management,* HarperBusiness, 1995.

The Otherness Theme

Thinking

Peter Senge, *The Fifth Discipline,* Currency Doubleday, 1990.

Don Tapscott, *Paradigm Shift,* McGraw-Hill, 1993.

Xenophilia

Richard Turner Pascale and Tony Athos, *The Art of Japanese Management,* Harper, 1981.

Ikujiro Nonaka and Hirotaka Takeuchi, *The Knowledge Creating Company,* Oxford University Press, 1995.

Kanban

Japan Management Association, *Kanban: Just-In-Time at Toyota,* Productivity Press, 1986.

Kaizen

Y. Yasuda, *40 Years, 20 Million Ideas: The Toyota Suggestion System,* Productivity Press, 1991.

Eliyahu M. Goldratt and Jeff Cox, *The Goal: A Process of Ongoing Improvement,* North River Press, 1992.

Chaos

Meg Wheatley, *Leadership and the New Science,* Berrett-Koehler, 1992.

David Bohm and J. Krishnamurti, *The Ending of Time,* Harper and Row, 1985.

David Bohm and F. David Peat, *Science, Order, and Creativity,* Bantam, 1987.

index